JSP™
Weekend Crash Course™

Geremy Kawaller and William Massie
with Andrew Utter

Hungry Minds™

Best-Selling Books • Digital Downloads • e-Books • Answer Networks • e-Newsletters • Branded Web Sites • e-Learning

New York, NY ◆ Cleveland, OH ◆ Indianapolis, IN

JSP™ Weekend Crash Course™
Published by
Hungry Minds, Inc.
909 Third Avenue
New York, NY 10022
www.hungryminds.com

Library of Congress Control Number: 2001091951

ISBN: 0-7645-4796-8

Printed in the United States of America

10 9 8 7 6 5 4 3 2 1

1B/SQ/QW/QR/IN

Distributed in the United States by Hungry Minds, Inc.

Distributed by CDG Books Canada Inc. for Canada; by Transworld Publishers Limited in the United Kingdom; by IDG Norge Books for Norway; by IDG Sweden Books for Sweden; by IDG Books Australia Publishing Corporation Pty. Ltd. for Australia and New Zealand; by TransQuest Publishers Pte Ltd. for Singapore, Malaysia, Thailand, Indonesia, and Hong Kong; by Gotop Information Inc. for Taiwan; by ICG Muse, Inc. for Japan; by Intersoft for South Africa; by Eyrolles for France; by International Thomson Publishing for Germany, Austria, and Switzerland; by Distribuidora Cuspide for Argentina; by LR International for Brazil; by Galileo Libros for Chile; by Ediciones ZETA S.C.R. Ltda. for Peru; by WS Computer Publishing Corporation, Inc., for the Philippines; by Contemporanea de Ediciones for Venezuela; by Express Computer Distributors for the Caribbean and West Indies; by Micronesia Media Distributor, Inc. for Micronesia; by Chips Computadoras S.A. de C.V. for Mexico; by Editorial Norma de Panama S.A. for Panama; by American Bookshops for Finland.

For general information on Hungry Minds' products and services please contact our Customer Care department within the U.S. at 800-762-2974, outside the U.S. at 317-572-3993 or fax 317-572-4002.

For sales inquiries and reseller information, including discounts, premium and bulk quantity sales, and foreign-language translations, please contact our Customer Care department at 800-434-3422, fax 317-572-4002 or write to Hungry Minds, Inc., Attn: Customer Care Department, 10475 Crosspoint Boulevard, Indianapolis, IN 46256.

For information on licensing foreign or domestic rights, please contact our Sub-Rights Customer Care department at 212-884-5000.

For information on using Hungry Minds' products and services in the classroom or for ordering examination copies, please contact our Educational Sales department at 800-434-2086 or fax 317-572-4005.

For press review copies, author interviews, or other publicity information, please contact our Public Relations department at 317-572-3168 or fax 317-572-4168.

For authorization to photocopy items for corporate, personal, or educational use, please contact Copyright Clearance Center, 222 Rosewood Drive, Danvers, MA 01923, or fax 978-750-4470.

is a trademark of
Hungry Minds, Inc.

About the Authors

Geremy Kawaller is a software developer with IBM who lives and works in New York City. His most significant work experience to date was being part of the team that established the first Internet presence of a major global bank in Tokyo, Japan. In his spare time, Geremy enjoys traveling, theater, and answering email sent to geremyk@yahoo.com.

William Massie is a consultant with SilverStream Software and has been a developer for eight years. He's taught Java programming at Columbia University and worked on JSP-based Web sites for Coca-Cola and Lucent Technologies.

Credits

Acquisitions Editor
Debra Williams Cauley

Technical Editor
William Massie

Copy Editor
Luann Rouff

Proof Editor
Eric Newman

Editorial Manager
Colleen Totz

Project Coordinator
Nancee Reeves

Graphics and Production Specialists
Kelly Hardesty
Joyce Haughey
Adam Mancilla
Gabriele McCann
Brian Torwelle

Quality Control Technicians
Laura Albert
John Greenough
Andrew Hollandbeck
Carl Pierce
Marianne Santy

Permissions Editor
Laura Moss

Media Development Specialist
Gregory Stephens

Media Development Coordinator
Marisa Pearman

Proofreading and Indexing
TECHBOOKS Production Services

To Steven and Ripley

Preface

Welcome to *JSP™ Weekend Crash Course™*. What makes this book stand out among other books about JavaServer Pages available today? This book is set up in a way that will put the subject areas most pertinent to you right at your fingertips. This is not a reference book. Instead, it is a how-to book where the information is presented with the goal of getting you started with JSP as quickly as possible.

This book will initiate you into the mysteries of using the dynamic new programming language Java to bring dynamic, exciting, relevant, timely content to users of the Internet. The age of static Web pages is already behind us.

Who Should Read This Book

This crash course is designed to present information in a readily graspable manner — so that you can learn what you need to know in one weekend. There are two categories of users for this book:

- Those who want to get going with JSP quickly. Maybe your company is moving to JSP, and you need to get up to speed quickly to keep up. Or maybe you want your personal Web site to offer more powerful features. This is the book for you. However, this book does assume some familiarity with Java syntax and with the essentials of object-oriented programming. If you haven't had any exposure to these, then you may want to look at *Java 2 Weekend Crash Course*, also published by Hungry Minds.

- Those who have some knowledge of JSP or other server-side programming paradigms. Perhaps you've worked with one of the earlier versions of JSP, or you have done server-side programming in another language. This book will help you get up to speed on the newer features of JSP that differentiate it from other approaches, and also to reinforce your command of the basics.

Specifically, to benefit from this book, you should be familiar with the following aspects of Java:

- Basic scripting syntax, including if branching and the various type of loops
- Object-oriented essentials, such as inheritance and method overriding
- Basic comfort with arrays and vectors
- Understanding of how the Java API works, and how to interpret the javadoc documentation

What You Need to Have

To best use this book, you need the following:

- A text editor, such as Windows Notepad
- Motivation to learn JSP

Any computer on which you can install a JSP-enabled Web server will work (more on that shortly). We have generated our examples in a Windows environment, but if you are working in UNIX and can get around on your own, this should all work fine.

What Results Can You Expect?

Can you learn JSP in one weekend? Yes, you can. JSP is a programming language that was designed to streamline the insertion of dynamic Web content into templates and make use of the overall power and elegance of the Java programming language. As such, it can be comprehended quickly, and you can be off to the races in no time.

This book was not intended as a reference book, or as an exhaustive treatment of JSP. It saves you time by focusing on the aspects of JSP most important to getting up and running quickly. It does this by omitting some secondary or tertiary information on a given command or expression in order to give you a sense of the whole JSP landscape as quickly as possible.

Finally, this book goes beyond a simple presentation of JSP syntax, although this is the heart of it. It familiarizes you with related languages like SQL and XML and discusses some of the practicalities of JSP development, such as development environment and Web application architecture. Both the information and its real context are presented.

Weekend Crash Course's Layout and Features

This book makes use of the standard Weekend Crash Course layout and includes the standard features of the series so that you can be confident that you can grasp the essentials of JSP in one weekend. Taking breaks throughout is important, to let the mind clear and to digest the new information a little before proceeding to the next topic.

We've divided the subject matter into thirty half-hour sessions. These sessions are assembled into parts that take two or three hours to complete. Each session ends with "Quiz Yourself" questions and each part with part review questions. These questions help you make sure that you have taken in the aspects of the session need to move further. (The answers to the part review questions can be found in Appendix A.) Between sessions, take a little time, grab some chow, rest your brain, and then dive into the next session!

Layout

As noted, the book consists of thirty half-hour sessions organized within six parts. The parts correspond with a time during the weekend, as outlined in the following sections.

Part I: Friday Evening

This part introduces JSP, placing it within the context of the development of the Internet. It provides a foundation in Java servlets, the technology that underlies JSP. Finally, it introduces the basics of JSP syntax.

Part II: Saturday Morning

This part continues to explore JSP syntax, and it discusses the handling of errors and exceptions in JSP. It also explores the use of HTML forms in Web applications and demonstrates the use of an editor for JSP development.

Part III: Saturday Afternoon

This part introduces JavaBeans and discusses how they integrate with JSP and how they can be used to organize JSP code effectively. It also introduces cookies and shows how to work with them from JSP.

Part IV: Saturday Evening

This part looks at tracking users with the session object and demonstrates how to create shopping cart functionality using sessions. It also presents HTTP request and response headers and their use in JSP.

Part V: Sunday Morning

In this part, an architecture for JSP applications is proposed. Also, we explore database access using JSP. The SQL language is introduced, and an actual access database is integrated into a JSP application.

Part VI: Sunday Afternoon

In Part VI, XML is introduced, and we show how data in XML can be transformed. Finally, the topic of creating custom tag libraries using JSP is introduced. Basic tags are demonstrated, as well as more sophisticated ones that interact with the content that constitutes their bodies.

Features

Each session is subdivivided into parts that are demarcated using the following four icons:

**30 Min.
To Go**   **20 Min.
To Go**   **10 Min.
To Go**   **Done!**

These icons let you know how much progress you've made as you work through each session. Other icons in this book are used as follows:

 This is an indicator of an important point that will be useful when developing your application.

 This illuminates the best ways to accomplish particular tasks, or small tricks that help you overcome obstacles.

 These items are important "gotchas" that you need to be careful to avoid.

 These point to other sessions that contain material related to the current topic.

Other Conventions

This book also uses the following additional conventions.

Java code or other kinds of code are separated from the body of the text with the following typeface:

```
out.println("Weekend Crash Course starting shortly");
```

Accompanying CD-ROM

In the back of this book is a CD-ROM. The CD-ROM includes a skills- assessment test, source code for the examples in the book, a driver for the database examples, the server software needed, JDataConnect Professional Evaluation v2.19.3, test packages for the Weekend Crash Course series, HomeSite 4.5 for Windows evaluation, and Tomcat JavaServer Pages Implementation Server.

Reach Out

Both the publisher and the authors want your feedback. After you have had a chance to use this book, send any feedback to my2cents@hungryminds.com. (Please include the book's ISBN and/or title in the subject line so that your comments reach the right people.) There you'll have an opportunity to provide any feedback you'd like, including any problems with any of the examples that may arise.

You're all set to go. Pick a weekend, gather provisions, get yourself something good to drink, find a comfortable chair, and away we go!

Acknowledgments

I'm grateful to Bill Massie, my technical editor, who was invaluable in helping with all aspects of the book. I started my technical career with Bill at "The Mill," and I've never looked back. Bill is a friend and mentor, and I often called on him to help me puzzle through the examples and structure of this book. His imprint can be felt in every chapter.

Valerie Perry, my editor at Hungry Minds, was indispensable in this process. Valerie, thank you for helping me structure the work and for the many helpful suggestions you made about the chapters. I could not have completed this book without you. Also, thanks to Debra Williams Cauley for giving me the opportunity to write for Hungry Minds. It was a great experience. To the rest of the editors at Hungry Minds, including Mildred Sanchez, Chris Jones, and Luann Rouff, I appreciate your contributions to the final product.

Finally, thanks to Steven and Ripley, who endured my many hours staring at the computer on beautiful days that might have been spent outside. To my father and mother, thanks for your interest and support.

Contents

JSP™
Weekend Crash Course™

 Friday

☐ Saturday

☐ Sunday

Part I — Friday Evening

PART

I

Friday Evening

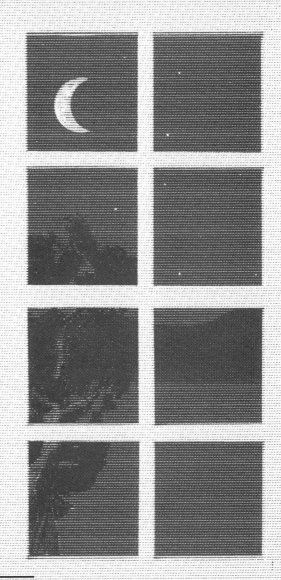

SESSION

JSP Overview/Web Architecture Explained

Session Checklist

✔ Understand the evolution of Web architecture

✔ Learn about CGI and ASP

✔ Explore servlets

**30 Min.
To Go**

Java Server Pages (JSP) enable the separation of presentation logic from business logic. They also utilize the power of the Java language, increasingly a standard in the software development environment. In addition, unlike ASP, JSP compiles its code, instead of repeatedly interpreting it, thus reducing performance demands on the server.

Before you learn just how JSP accomplishes all of these things, let's look at how software runs on the Internet. If you are embarking on software development for the Web, you should understand the principles that enable computers to speak to one another over the huge network we call the Internet.

Understanding the Evolution of Web Architecture

With the current sophistication of Web sites and the nearly ubiquitous access to the Internet that people around the world are enjoying, one might think that browsers and the Internet have been around for decades. Of course, that's not the case. The Internet became possible as the sophistication of software applications has evolved.

N-tier architecture, which is evangelized by most technologists today, refers to a system configuration in which there are multiple tiers, or processing components, all of which make up a functioning program. N-tier architecture inserts a business logic layer in between the client and the server, which leads to a thin data server/thick middle tier/thin client architecture.

The beauty of the n-tier paradigm is that as application requirements grow, as they inevitably do, additional tiers may be added without unnecessary interference with the existing system. Moreover, in the tiered approach, because each tier is responsible for a discrete piece of functionality within the larger system, it is easy to isolate the cause when a problem arises, or to add specific functionality to a single software component when necessary.

While n-tier architecture is an extension of client/server architecture, it is interesting to note that n-tier architecture is like mainframe architecture, with the application server and Web server acting as the mainframe, and the browser acting as the equivalent of the dumb terminal. The advantage of this architecture, then and now, is that the bulk of the application is installed in one place, and anyone with a browser can instantly run an application or see the upgrade. With mainframes, users accessed the mainframe through dumb terminals, or clients that did not have any substantial processing ability. In the client/server model, the application harnessed heretofore-wasted processing power available in the personal computers, or "not-so-dumb" clients, accessing the server. Instead of existing on one machine, the processing load was shared between the two corresponding pieces, the client and the server. However, with the client/server model, maintenance was tedious and difficult when users across an enterprise needed to upgrade the software that resided on their PCs.

Client/Server Architecture

When the Internet was in its infancy, connected users could view limited information in the form of text. The "Web," as it was coined, referred to a group of computers on a network that, in effect, spoke the same language to one another. That language was *Hypertext Transfer Protocol* (*HTTP*), which describes the method computers use to communicate with one another. Using the HTTP protocol, computers could request to view documents located on other connected machines. HTML, or HyperText Markup Language, is the language that is used to tell Web browsers how the requested document should be formatted and displayed. There was no standard for the display of images, and the distribution of binary files over the Internet (such as Word documents) was time-consuming and unreliable.

HTTP has evolved into an efficient way to transfer text-based documents, images, and other binary files over the Web. Because of the explosive growth of the Web in recent years, the demands of the protocol have increased. Consumers and businesses want more information transferred over the Web, and they want the transfer to be faster and more secure.

The HTTP protocol transfers chunks of information, called *packets,* between a client and a server in the form of requests and responses.

 Refer to Session 19 for more on requests and responses.

Although the basic nature of the protocol remains unchanged, it continues to evolve as Internet traffic increases. The major recent improvements to the protocol, according to the World Wide Web Consortium (W3C) Web site (`http://www.w3.org/Protocols/HTTP/Performance/Pipeline.html`), include the following:

- The capability to transfer multiple objects over one connection instead of one object per connection. An *object* is defined as a text document (HTML) and any of its associated embedded objects (images, PDFs, and so on).
- The introduction of persistent connections that leave a Transmission Control Protocol (TCP) connection open among multiple consecutive operations. The 1.0 version opened and closed a TCP connection between the server and browser for each inefficient and slow transfer operation.

For more information about the HTTP protocol, refer to the W3C site listed above.

Just as the demands of the Web have necessitated modifications to HTTP, Web developers have had to make adjustments to the method of "architecting"and developing applications on the Internet to allow for scalability. It has been necessary to mimic for the Web the same division of labor in business client/server applications.

According to the client/server paradigm, software components can run in two locations: on the user's PC and on another computer on the network. So long as the user's PC is connected to a live network, the client/server application makes two major effects possible: multiple users can access a single store or centralized file system concurrently, and different software components can be run on different machines on the network, each sharing a piece of the processing load.

The client/server system opened the door to thinking about a software application as a series of layers, with each layer accomplishing one specific task. In most cases, the two tiers consist of a relational database management system (RDBMS) for storing mission-critical data, and the rest of the application, which includes all of the code for manipulating data and the user interface.

Although this method of separation was a step forward, there was still a problem. Even though data was separate from the application code and the user interface, in a two-tier client/server system, *business logic* (the implementation of business rules in software), *application logic* (the implementation of software-specific rules, such as load balancing and failover in software), and *presentation logic* (the implementation of the user interface) were still inextricably entwined. Therefore, if the user interface changed or if business rules changed, there was no real division of labor — the whole application had to be recompiled, packaged, and installed on a user's machine for updating.

N-Tier Architecture

N-tier architecture separates each part of an application into a discrete software component that can be updated and maintained individually. The idea behind distributed application development (and, for instance, the capability to separate business logic from application logic from display and presentation of content) is that applications should not only be portable, or able to be run in different environments, but also easily broken up. Therefore, if some of the rules change in one of the components of the application, the change does not affect the rest of the application. The Java 2 Enterprise Edition (J2EE) is a framework for the implementation of n-tier architecture. JSP, along with Enterprise JavaBeans, is a part of this framework. Figure 1-1 shows how J2EE implements n-tier architecture, and where JSP pages fit into the scheme.

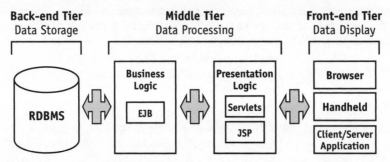

Figure 1-1 *The J2EE architecture separates business logic from presentation logic and can deliver data to a variety of different applications on different devices.*

For effective communication to take place among computers, the HTTP protocol describes the method for communication as well as the rules to which computers on the network must adhere. Each computer has a unique identification number, or an IP address. A Web server sends and receives information to and from the computer on a port; for Web servers, the port is usually 80. The Web server uses the port to "listen" for requests and to send information to the requesting computer.

Learning About CGI and ASP

20 Min.
To Go

JSP's predecessors include the Common Gateway Interface (CGI), Microsoft's Active Server Pages (ASP), and the Java language. JSP incorporates platform independence and the capability to separate program logic from presentation logic without the limitations of CGI and ASP, which you will learn about in this section.

CGI is a standard for enabling Web servers to interact with external programs. This interaction provides the platform for making static Web pages dynamic: the Web server runs in one process, and programs that generate dynamic content run in another. When a browser issues a request to the Web server, the Web server triggers another process on the same machine or on a networked machine. The triggered process, usually a call to a database or the execution of some type of program logic, generates HTML output that is sent back to the browser as a response.

Although CGI enables dynamic page creation, the multiple-process aspect of CGI is problematic: for each request received, a new process has to be started; consequently, when CGI programs receive a lot of user requests, the machine's resources can be overtaxed.

Therefore, even though a CGI program is platform-independent, there are two central problems with its implementation:

- It is difficult to separate the program logic and the presentation logic of a CGI program.
- CGI programs are interpreted each time they are invoked, taxing a server's resources.

Microsoft's ASP enables developers to embed JavaScript or Visual Basic Script (VBScript) code directly into HTML pages, a solution for separating program logic from presentation logic. The Web server interprets the ASP code and sends dynamically generated HTML to the browser. Embedding the code in the HTML page itself makes it easier to embed dynamic content in HTML, as opposed to having to write code to output *all* of an HTML response. ASP is typically confined to the Windows platform and to Microsoft's Internet Information Server (IIS).

Exploring Servlets

**10 Min.
To Go**

Like CGI programs and ASP pages, servlets can receive HTTP requests and issue HTTP responses that are readable by Web browsers. Web servers can employ add-ons to run Java servlets, allowing the programs that manage business logic to interact with the server as part of the same process. In CGI, the Web server and the CGI processor were two separate processes. Additionally, servlets are compiled code, not interpreted code, and do not require the resources needed for interpretation each time the servlet is run.

Earlier attempts to write server extensions intrinsically linked to the Web server led to problems with safety and security. If a server extension crashed, the server would likely follow. With servlets, however, Java's strong-type safety and exception handling mechanisms typically prevent such mishaps. Additionally, servlets take advantage of Java's powerful *multithreading* capabilities. Multithreading means that a single process can execute multiple tasks by alternating among the tasks at the millisecond level. It is easier to program multithreading in Java than it is to program multithreading in Java's ancestor, C++. With servlets, multithreading is built into a standards-compliant servlet engine, so as a developer, you do not have to implement multithreading yourself. Best of all, servlets share the advantage of Java's portability: they can be developed once and deployed on any platform.

Despite the strengths of Java servlets, they are Java classes and can be cumbersome to write. Unlike ASP, servlets do not follow an intuitive separation of program logic from presentation logic. For example, to output HTML to the HTTP response in a servlet, you have to add it to the output stream; in JSP pages, you can embed Java code directly into an HTML page. JSP pages enable the developer to easily separate program logic from presentation logic in the same manner as with ASP pages, while taking advantage of the platform independence and speed of servlets.

The first time a user requests a JSP page, the servlet-enabled server translates the JSP into a servlet, compiles it, runs it, and generates output that is returned to the browser. Because the JSP page is compiled into Java byte code, and because servlets are designed to persist between requests (once the servlet corresponding to a JSP page is compiled, it is kept around to be of use again by the next request), JSP achieves an advantage over its predecessors. A JSP page, transformed into a compiled, persistent servlet, is ready at an instant's notice to serve up dynamic content.

All of the JSP pages you will write in the course of reading this book take advantage of the servlet API, as well as all of the available Java APIs. The code used in JSP pages is Java, which means it is possible to develop code in one environment and run it in another. Portability is a boon to developers because it significantly reduces the amount of time it takes to deploy an application in different environments. Java is also object-oriented, it has multithreading capabilities, and it has strong-type safety. Moreover, Java is an open standard, which means developers can develop their own code to sell or distribute freely by using the class libraries Sun Microsystems has provided. The open standard has produced an extremely fertile environment for application development.

Java serves purposes as broad as control of remote devices to rendering three-dimensional graphics. Even the servlet API, which is primarily used with the Internet, is designed to function in a variety of client/server architectures, not just in the context of a Web client/server architecture. The implication of this for the developer is that while learning JSP is valuable in the immediate context of the Internet, it can be applicable as well to other development environments. Furthermore, because learning JSP means increasing familiarity with the Java language, developers who learn JSP will be better prepared to face the types of challenges inherent in the ever-shifting world of information technology.

Done!

REVIEW

- The JSP implementation enables developers to separate the layers of logic (business, application, and user interface) that compose software.
- JSP is part of an n-tier framework designed to speed software development and make code maintenance easier and more efficient.
- The Hypertext Transfer Protocol, HTTP, refers to the way information is exchanged over the Web between servers and browsers.
- The HyperText Markup Language, HTML, dictates how Web documents are displayed in a browser.
- The n-tier application framework utilizes a thick middle tier to handle application processing, and a thin processing layer for the server and the client.
- JSP code does not run in a separate process from the Web server, as CGI programs do.
- JSP utilizes the servlet and Java language APIs.

QUIZ YOURSELF

1. What is the difference between client/server and n-tier architecture? How have applications evolved according to the n-tier paradigm?
2. How do Web servers and Web browsers communicate with one another?
3. How is the Hypertext Transfer Protocol improving in response to the demands of Web consumers?
4. What does HTML stand for? What does HTML do?
5. What are some of the limitations of the Common Gateway Interface?
6. How does JSP rely on the servlet API?

Installing and Configuring the JSP Development Environment

Session Checklist

✔ Install the JDK

✔ Download and install Tomcat

✔ Troubleshoot the Web server installation

**30 Min.
To Go**

By the end of this book, you should be able to develop and deploy JSP applications with some degree of fluency. However, setting up, deploying, and administering a production-grade Web server with a JSP engine is not a simple task. You can run all of the examples in this book by using Tomcat 3.2.1, a servlet and JSP engine that supports JSP 1.1.

As JSP becomes the standard for creating dynamic Web pages, more Web servers are providing add-ons to turn their servers into JSP engines. Apache, Allaire Jrun, and iPlanet are just a few server products that support JSP and servlets in concert with a Web server. Again, setting up these environments can be tricky, and we do not attempt to cover that type of setup in this text.

The tutorials in this book assume you have a Windows installation. The Tomcat software will work with any of the following, so long as the processor is a Pentium 166 MHz or faster: Windows 95, Windows 98, Windows NT 4.0, or Windows 2000. To get started, you must install the Sun Java Development Kit (JDK) 1.1.8 or 1.3.0 (the most recent version at the time of this writing).

Sun maintains a list of all server products that have either a built-in JSP engine or downloadable plug-ins at http://java.sun.com/products/jsp/industry.html.

Installing the JDK

If you do not have a version of the JDK installed on your computer, download and install the most recent version from http://java.sun.com/j2se/. When you install the JDK, you also install the JRE by default. The JRE contains the Java Virtual Machine (JVM), which runs Java classes.

Sun packages the files into one large bundle for downloading; however, if your connection to the Internet is slow, you can download several smaller bundles that Sun packages. If you choose to download the smaller bundles, you must concatenate them using the MSDOS copy command, as in the following example:

```
C:> copy /b file-a.exe + file-b.exe + . . .  file-n.exe file-all.exe
```

The executable is self-extracting. Double-click the file to run the installation program, and follow the instructions. We recommend placing the JDK in a relatively accessible directory on your C:\ drive. Doing so makes setting the system variables simple when the time comes.

Set your computer's PATH variable to point to the location of the Java compiler and to the supporting SDK executable files. The CLASSPATH variable tells the Java Virtual Machine and other Java applications like the compiler (javac.exe) where to look for class libraries. You can find the Java compiler in the \bin subdirectory of your JDK installation.

To set the PATH and CLASSPATH variables in Windows NT, right-click the My Computer icon on your desktop. Click the Environment tab and navigate to the appropriate variable underneath the System Variables: heading, as shown in Figure 2-1.

For Windows 2000, right click on the My Computer icon, select Properties from the drop-down menu, click on the Advanced tab, and click the Environment Variables button.

 If you enter the values for the variables in the System Variables multiselect box as opposed to entering the values in the User Variables multiselect box, the values apply to all users on the machine regardless of who is logged in to NT. Enter values for user variables only in a situation in which more than one user uses the machine and each user needs a different configuration.

For the value of the PATH variable, add the path to the \bin subdirectory of the JDK installation. For example, if you have installed the JDK to your C:\ drive (which is recommended!), add the value C:\jdk1.3.0\bin to the front of the PATH variable. The PATH variable may have multiple values listed, each separated by a semicolon (;). There shouldn't be any white space in the PATH variable value, except in the event that the name of a directory, such as "Program Files," has white space. Capitalization is irrelevant also. To add the variable value permanently on Windows NT, click the Set button and then the Apply button. There is no SET button for Windows 2000. To change the variable value on Windows 2000, double-click the PATH variable listing and edit the Variable Value text box. The new value will take effect when you close the Environment Variables dialog by clicking the OK button.

From the list of system variables, locate the CLASSPATH variable on the Environment tab of the System Properties dialog box. If the CLASSPATH variable does not exist in the dialog box, its default value is set to period (.). The period means that the JVM and other Java programs look for class libraries in the present directory in which the classes are invoked at runtime. If your CLASSPATH variable does exist, make certain that at least one of the semicolon-separated values is a period.

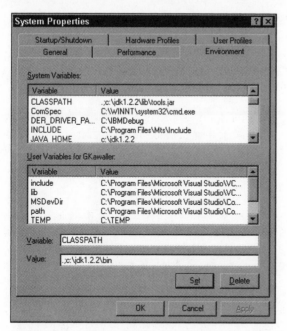

Figure 2-1 *Set the PATH and CLASSPATH variables in the Environment tab of the System Properties dialog box. This figure shows the dialog box on a Windows 2000 computer.*

For Windows 95 or Windows 98, you must modify the system variables in the `autoexec.bat` file by using the sysedit utility. The sysedit utility allows you to to modify the system configuration settings such as the PATH and other environment variables. To run sysedit, select Start ⇨ Run from the Windows taskbar and type `sysedit` in the dialog box. When the sysedit window opens, you see a series of system-configuration files inside the parent window. To set the necessary system variables, navigate to the `autoexec.bat` file and change the PATH variable to include the path to your JDK \bin directory. For example, if you have installed the JDK to your C:\ drive, you would add the value `C:\jdk1.3.0\bin` to the PATH variable, as shown in Figure 2-2. If your PATH or CLASSPATH variables already have values assigned to them, add the new values separated by semicolons (;).

 Always be careful when running sysedit, as you could change important computer settings.

Installing the JDK on either Windows NT or Windows 98 should be a relatively painless process, and the Sun site does a good job of documenting installation instructions. For complete instructions on installing the Java 2 SDK on Windows, refer to http://java.sun.com/j2se/1.3/install-windows.html.

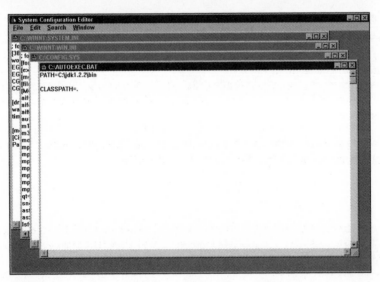

Figure 2-2 *Set the PATH and CLASSPATH variables by using the sysedit utility for Windows 98 installations of the JDK.*

Downloading and Installing Tomcat

**20 Min.
To Go**

Tomcat is the servlet and JSP engine, provided by Apache, that you will use to run the examples in this book. Tomcat is an implementation of the Java Servlet 2.2 and JavaServer Pages 1.1 specifications. At the time this is written, the most recent version of Tomcat is version 3.2.1, and it is available for download at http://jakarta.apache.org/builds/ jakarta-tomcat/release/v3.2.1/bin/jakarta-tomcat-3.2.1.zip.

Download the zip file to your hard drive and extract it using Winzip (or another zip utility) directly under one of your disk drives. The files will extract by default to a directory called \jakarta-tomcat-3.2.1. You may change the name of the root directory to whatever you like.

Configuring Tomcat

Just as in setting up the JDK, you must set additional system variables for Tomcat to run:

1. Add the variable JAVA_HOME to your list of system variables, and set the value to the location of the installation of your \jdk directory. For example, if you have installed the jdk to your C:\ drive, add the value C:\jdk1.2.2 to the JAVA_HOME variable.

2. Add the variable TOMCAT_HOME to your list of system variables, and set the value to the root directory of Tomcat's installation. For example, if Tomcat was installed in C:\jakarta-tomcat, that is the value of the TOMCAT_HOME environment variable.

Starting and Stopping Tomcat

Tomcat is now configured and ready to go. To launch Tomcat, navigate to the <tomcat-install>\bin directory and double-click on the startup.bat file. When it is time to shut down Tomcat, navigate to the same directory and double-click on the shutdown.bat file. Open up a browser and navigate to http://localhost:8080. The two main configuration files, server.xml and web.xml, located in the <tomcat-install>\conf directory, can be used to further configure Tomcat.

 Whenever you make changes to the configuration files, you must stop and restart Tomcat in order for the changes to take effect.

Site Directories

The default root directory of your Web site is <tomcat-install>\webapps\ROOT. To add additional directories that you want to be accessible from your Web site, first create the directory underneath the <tomcat-install>\webapps directory. Then stop and restart Tomcat. The directory will immediately be available from your Web site. To illustrate the point, create a directory called myWork underneath <tomcat-install>\webapps that you will use to store the work you do. Add a file called index.html that contains a Hello World! message, as shown here:

index.html

```
<html>
<body>
Hello World!
</body>
</html>
```

Then stop and restart Tomcat. The index.html file you just created will load when you navigate to http://localhost:8080/myWork.

Tomcat has already set up three subdirectories, test, admin, and examples, which are all accessible underneath the root directory. To get to them, navigate to http://localhost:8080/test, http://localhost:8080/admin, and http://localhost:8080/examples, respectively.

Modifying server.xml and web.xml

The server.xml file, located in the <tomcat-install>\conf directory, is the main configuration file for Tomcat. There may be times when you will want to allow users of your site to access files that do not exist in the <tomcat-install>\webapps directory. To grant access to files that exist elsewhere in the system, you must modify server.xml. Locate the following code in the server.xml file:

```
<Context path="/examples"
         docBase="webapps/examples"
         crossContext="false"
         debug="0"
         reloadable="true" >
</Context>
```

To add a new context, or subdirectory, to your Web site, add the following xml to the server.xml file:

```
<Context path="/mypics"
         docBase="C:\My Pictures"
         crossContext="false"
         debug="0"
         reloadable="true" >
</Context>
```

In the example, we are sharing the directory C:\My Pictures on our Web site and we are calling that directory mypics. So, the contents of the C:\My Pictures directory will be accessible on the site from http://localhost:8080/mypics.

The server.xml file controls the port over which Tomcat will communicate with the browser. The default port for the Tomcat installation is 8080. The default port for http communication, however, is 80. Whenever communication between the browser and server occurs on *any port other than 80*, it is necessary to specify that port in the URL when requesting information from the site. The syntax for the request is

```
http://someserver.com:<port-number>/somedirectory/somefile.htm
```

To modify the port number on which Tomcat is running, modify the Connector xml element in the server.xml file. Locate the following code in the server.xml file:

```
<Connector className="org.apache.tomcat.service.PoolTcpConnector">
    <Parameter name="handler"

value="org.apache.tomcat.service.http.HttpConnectionHandler"/>
    <Parameter name="port"
        value="8080" />
</Connector>
```

Change the value of the port from 8080 to 80 (or whatever number you wish):

```
<Connector className="org.apache.tomcat.service.PoolTcpConnector">
    <Parameter name="handler"

value="org.apache.tomcat.service.http.HttpConnectionHandler"/>
    <Parameter name="port"
        value="80" />
</Connector>
```

If you've set the value of the port to 80, once you've stopped and restarted Tomcat (see Figure 2-3), you will be able to navigate to your site by typing in http://localhost in your browser. The reason you don't have to type in a port number when you go to popular sites on the Internet, like Yahoo! or Amazon is that they are running on the default port for http communication, port 80.

Only one Web server may be running on any given port at any one time. So, if you have IIS or any other Web server installed on the machine you are using to run the examples, make certain that none is running on the same port. As long as you follow the rule of one Web server to one port, you may have as many Web servers as possible running concurrently on your machine at once.

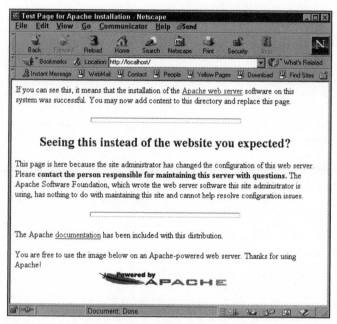

Figure 2-3 *Default view for the home page of the Tomcat server*

The web.xml file also holds important configuration information for your Tomcat installation. Tomcat uses this file, for example, to determine the length of a default session, mime types for different types of media being transferred, and the default file that will display in the browser when a directory is accessed. For a complete explanation of the configuration settings, refer to the comments in the web.dtd file, located in the <tomcat-install>\conf directory.

Running the examples

Tomcat comes with a series of servlet and JSP examples that should be fully functional before you proceed with the examples in this book. From the home page of the server installation, follow the JSP Examples link and click the Execute link for the first example, titled "Numberguess." The screen shown in Figure 2-4 appears.

10 Min. To Go

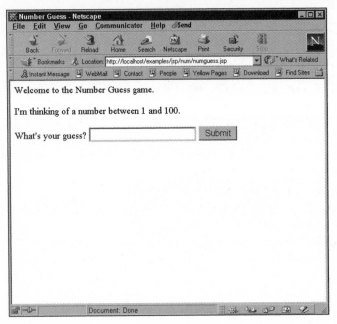

Figure 2-4   *The Number Guess Game is a JSP example that ships with Tomcat.*

Go ahead and take a guess. It's not the most interesting program (or the most fun game), but if you can play it, you have successfully installed your JavaServer Pages engine and your Web server. If the page shown in Figure 2-4 does not load or if you cannot complete the game, refer to the next section, "Troubleshooting the Web Server Installation."

Troubleshooting the Web Server Installation

If you can't view the Web page (shown in Figure 2-4) when navigating to `http://localhost`, check to make sure each of the following conditions is true:

- Your `CLASSPATH` variable has the value of "." somewhere in its string of values.
- Your `PATH` variable has both of the following somewhere in its string of values: `<jdk_install_dir>\bin\tools.jar` and `<jdk_install_dir>\bin`.
- You have set the `JAVA_HOME` system variable to the directory in which you have installed your jdk.
- You have set the `TOMCAT_HOME` system variable to the directory in which you have installed Tomcat.
- No other Web server is running on port 80 of your computer. To be certain of this, stop any other Web server running on your machine.

Done!

REVIEW

- To run JSP pages, your Web server must have a JSP engine.
- By now, you should have the Tomcat Web server up and running, and it should be able able to execute the code you will be writing in the coming sessions.

QUIZ YOURSELF

1. What is the purpose of the CLASSPATH system variable? What is the purpose of the PATH system variable?
2. Does the Tomcat software support the JSP 1.1 specification?
3. What is the default port that Web servers run on? In the Apache software environment, how do you change the port number?
4. Take a look at the configuration files for Apache (httpd.conf). Where is the setting for the root directory of the Web server? Try changing the value.

SESSION

Servlets: An Introduction

Session Checklist

✔ Understand what a servlet does

✔ Create a basic servlet

✔ Learn how JSPs work with servlets

**30 Min.
To Go**

Before you jump in and start looking at JSP syntax, it's valuable to have an understanding of servlets, the building blocks of JSP. Servlets are Java programs that handle HTTP requests and responses, just as Common Gateway Interface (CGI) programs handle them. Unlike CGI, servlets avail themselves of Java features such as multithreading where a single process can execute multiple tasks concurrently, and sessions, which track a user's state throughout an application. Each JSP page that you code eventually generates a Java servlet, which is specially designed to receive HTTP requests from a browser and to transmit HTTP responses in return.

Understanding What Servlets Do

Servlets, like applets, are Java programs. An *applet* is a client-side program, downloaded to a user's machine, and executed by a Java Virtual Machine (JVM) inside the browser. Although applets don't necessarily have a visual component, many do. Applets may be any size, but it is pragmatic to restrict the size to reduce the amount of download time. Instead of being downloaded to a user's browser, servlets are executed on the server. Servlets can be thought of as the foundation for Web-based applications that utilize Java. They have access to all of the Java APIs; therefore, they are platform-independent, and can extend the capabilities of most Web servers.

Servlets differ from generic Java applications in their ability to handle HTTP requests. An HTTP request is issued from a browser when a hyperlink is clicked, when a form is submitted, or when a user enters an address into the URL field.

For more information about HTTP, see Session 19.

When a Web server receives an HTTP request, it looks at the URL to see what type of page the browser is requesting. If the browser requests a servlet, the Web server passes the request to the servlet container. A servlet container manages the creation, utilization, and destruction of servlets, or the servlet life cycle. The servlet container that you will use throughout this book is Tomcat, whose installation was covered in Session 2.

For any given servlet that is requested via an HTTP request, the servlet container loads the servlet into memory and instantiates an object instance of the Servlet class. The container then places the servlet into service, or initializes the servlet, by calling the init() method of the Servlet interface and passing a ServletConfig object as a parameter to the method. The ServletConfig object contains servlet configuration information in name/value pairs that are passed to the calling servlet.

Once the servlet is successfully initialized, meaning the init() method has completed its work without error, the servlet can begin handling HTTP requests and sending HTTP responses. The service() method passes the ServletRequest and ServletResponse objects to the servlet. Unless specifically instructed to not utilize multithreading, the servlet container can handle multiple requests at a single time, passing requests back and forth to the servlet as separate threads, as illustrated in Figure 3-1.

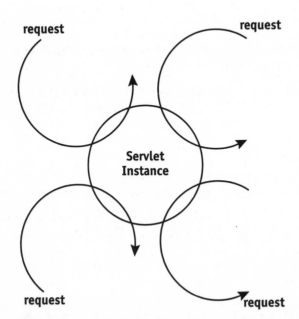

Figure 3-1 *A single servlet instance can handle multiple requests.*

The alternative to multithreading is for the servlet to implement the SingleThreadModel interface, which queues each successive request for execution one at a time, as shown in Figure 3-2.

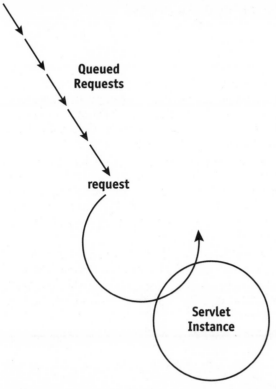

Queued
Requests

request

Servlet
Instance

Figure 3-2 *A servlet can implement the SingleThreadModel interface to handle one request at a time.*

Once the servlet has executed each request, the servlet container calls the destroy() method to remove the servlet instance from memory. The process begins again when another request is made for the same servlet.

Creating a Basic Servlet

Listing 3-1 creates a basic servlet that prints out a simple message to the browser.

20 Min.
To Go

Listing 3-1 *HelloWorld.java is a servlet that prints a message to the screen.*

HelloWorld.java

```
import java.io.*;
import javax.servlet.*;
import javax.servlet.http.*;

public class HelloWorld extends HttpServlet {
    public void doGet (HttpServletRequest request, HttpServletResponse
response) throws ServletException, IOException
```

Continued

Listing 3-1 *Continued*

```
    {
        PrintWriter out = response.getWriter();
        out.println("<HTML>");
        out.println("<HEAD>");
        out.println("<TITLE>");
        out.println("An HTML Hello World");
        out.println("</TITLE>");
        out.println("</HEAD>");
        out.println("<BODY>");
        out.println("<H1>Hello World</H1>");
        out.println("</BODY>");
        out.println("</HTML>");
    }
}
```

Follow the instructions below to execute the HelloWorld.java program.

1. Type the HelloWorld.java code into a text editor and save the file to the <tomcat-install>\webapps\ROOT\WEB-INF\classes directory, where <tomcat-install> is the directory where you installed Apache Tomcat. The .java file will serve as the source for what will ultimately be a compiled servlet.

2. Compile the .java file into a .class file. Make certain that the CLASSPATH variable points to the servlet.jar file that came with Tomcat. This servlet.jar file is necessary for compiling servlets. If you installed Apache in the C:\jakarta-tomcat directory, you would add C:\jakarta-tomcat\lib\servlet.jar to your CLASSPATH environment variable. Refer to Session 2 for more instructions on setting environment variables.

3. Once your CLASSPATH environment variable has been set correctly, open a command window and navigate to the <tomcat-install>\webapps\ROOT\WEB-INF\ classes directory. Once inside the classes directory, type the following to compile the .java file:

   ```
   javac HelloWorld.java
   ```

   If the file compiles successfully, you will not see any error messages. If the compiler returns error messages, you may have mistyped the HelloWorld.java file, or you may not have correctly set your CLASSPATH variable. Check both. After you successfully compile the program, take a look in the directory; there should be a file named HelloWorld.class. This file is the compiled servlet.

4. Stop and start Tomcat. To stop Tomcat, double-click the shutdown.bat file in the <tomcat-install>\bin directory. To restart Tomcat, double-click the startup.bat file in the <tomcat-install>\bin directory.

5. Typing the word "servlet" after our root domain tells Tomcat that we want it to pass along our request to the servlet container. Therefore, to access our newly created servlet, and assuming Tomcat is running on port 8080, navigate to http://localhost:8080/servlet/HelloWorld. It is important that you do not append the .class extension to the servlet name. The output should look like what is displayed in Figure 3-3.

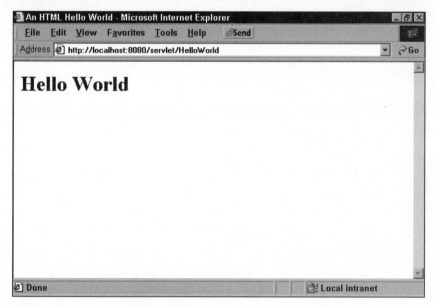

Figure 3-3 *A simple Hello World program*

The first part of the HelloWorld.java file is the import statements. The java.io package contains the `PrintWriter` object, which is called later in the program. The other two packages, `javax.servlet.*` and `javax.servlet.http.*`, provide support for the servlet API. Notice that the `javax.servlet.http.*` package resides inside the `javax.servlet.*` servlet package, hierarchically speaking. It requires its own `import` statement because the servlet API supports servlets other than `HTTP` servlets on the Internet.

The servlet package statements begin with "javax," not "java." Servlets are not a part of the core Java class libraries that make up the Java language; they are a specialized enhancement of the Java programming language. The servlet classes are extension classes.

The second part of the program is the class declaration. The HelloWorld servlet extends the `HttpServlet` **class, which means that it inherits the methods and properties of the class. Most servlets extend the** `HttpServlet` **class that exists in the** `javax.servlet.http` **package.**

Inside of the class declaration is the `doGet()` method, which processes the GET request issued from a Web browser. The `doGet()` method exists in the `HttpServlet` superclass; it accepts two parameters and throws two exceptions. The two parameters, `HttpServletRequest` and `HttpServletResponse`, are generated by the servlet engine upon receiving an HTTP request. Once invoked, the objects are available to the servlet. The `HttpServletRequest` object contains information for the servlet about the HTTP request sent from the browser, and the `HttpServletResponse` object facilitates an HTTP response.

The `HelloWorld` subclass overrides the superclass's `doGet()` method and injects whatever functionality is desired. In the HelloWorld example, the method obtains a handle to the response's `PrintWriter` object and uses it to write out a full HTML document to the output stream. With each line of code that starts `out.println(`, the HTML content specified is added to the output stream. The servlet forwards the data from this output stream to the browser, and the Web page renders the HTML.

Learning How JSP Pages Work with Servlets

A JSP page is actually a servlet waiting to happen. When a browser makes a request to an existing servlet, as in the HelloWorld.java example, the servlet container takes over and passes the request to the already compiled servlet. With a JSP page, all the developer has to do to compile her code is request the page from a browser. When the page is requested, a servlet is generated on the fly by the JSP container, Tomcat. In the next example, you will see how Tomcat handles the process of compiling a JSP page into a servlet.

Type the HelloWorld.jsp page listed below into a text editor, and save the file to your <tomcat-install>\webapps\ROOT directory. The page is simply placing a text string — Hello World — inside of an expression to be printed to the screen.

```
HelloWorld.jsp
<html>
<head>
  <title>Hello World</title>
</head>
<body>
<%= "Hello World" %>
</body>
</html>
```

Navigate to the page in your browser. After a brief delay, the page should load successfully and you should see the output of this very modest page. What actually happened when you requested the page was that Tomcat, realizing that you had requested an uncompiled JSP page, generated a servlet from your JSP page and compiled it. That compiled servlet is what generated the HTML sent to your browser. The delay is caused by the JSP container's creating and compiling the servlet. On subsequent visits, there won't be a delay as long as the underlying JSP page remains the same.

Tomcat stores the uncompiled source code in the <tomcat-install>\work directory. To locate the servlet that was generated from the HelloWorld.jsp page, navigate to the work directory. Inside that directory, there should be a directory named localhost_8080 that corresponds to the root directory of your Web server. Inside the localhost_8080 directory, there should be two files with long names, each of which contains the word HelloWorld somewhere in the name. These two files, one with a .java extension, one with a .class extension, are the uncompiled servlet of HelloWorld.jsp and the compiled servlet, respectively. Listing 3-2 shows the contents of the .java file. The portion of the servlet in bold is where the servlet publishes our HTML content to the output stream.

Listing 3-2   *The HelloWorld.jsp example generates this code.*

_0002fHelloWorld_0002ejspHelloWorld_jsp_0.java

```
import javax.servlet.*;
import javax.servlet.http.*;
```

```
import javax.servlet.jsp.*;
import javax.servlet.jsp.tagext.*;
import java.io.PrintWriter;
import java.io.IOException;
import java.io.FileInputStream;
import java.io.ObjectInputStream;
import java.util.Vector;
import org.apache.jasper.runtime.*;
import java.beans.*;
import org.apache.jasper.JasperException;


public class _0002fHelloWorld_0002ejspHelloWorld_jsp_0 extends
HttpJspBase {


    static {
    }
    public _0002fHelloWorld_0002ejspHelloWorld_jsp_0( ) {
    }

    private static boolean _jspx_inited = false;

    public final void _jspx_init() throws JasperException {
    }

    public void _jspService(HttpServletRequest request,
    HttpServletResponse  response)
        throws IOException, ServletException {

        JspFactory _jspxFactory = null;
        PageContext pageContext = null;
        HttpSession session = null;
        ServletContext application = null;
        ServletConfig config = null;
        JspWriter out = null;
        Object page = this;
        String  _value = null;
        try {

            if (_jspx_inited == false) {
                _jspx_init();
                _jspx_inited = true;
            }
            _jspxFactory = JspFactory.getDefaultFactory();
            response.setContentType("text/html;charset=8859_1");
            pageContext = _jspxFactory.getPageContext(this,
            request, response,
            "", true, 8192, true);
```

Continued

Listing 3-2 *Continued*

```
application = pageContext.getServletContext();
config = pageContext.getServletConfig();
session = pageContext.getSession();
out = pageContext.getOut();

// HTML // begin [file="C:\\jakarta-
tomcat\\webapps\\ROOT\\HelloWorld.jsp";
from=(0,0);to=(6,0)] out.write("<html>
\r\n<head>\r\n\t<title>Hello
World</title>\r\n</head>\r\n\r\n<body>\r\n");
// end
// begin [file="C:\\jakarta-
tomcat\\webapps\\ROOT\\
HelloWorld.jsp";from=(6,3);to=(6,18)]
out.print( "Hello World" );
// end
// HTML // begin [file="C:\\jakarta-
tomcat\\webapps\\ROOT
\\HelloWorld.jsp";from=(6,20);to=(9,0)]
    out.write("\r\n</body>\r\n</html>\r\n");
// end

} catch (Exception ex) {
    if (out.getBufferSize() != 0)
        out.clearBuffer();
    pageContext.handlePageException(ex);
} finally {
    out.flush();
    _jspxFactory.releasePageContext(pageContext);
}
    }
}
```

The real value of JSP is illustrated in this example. Tomcat generates the code for the servlet, over 70 lines, from a JSP file with less than ten lines of code.

Done!

REVIEW

- Servlet technology is the backbone of JSP technology.
- A servlet container manages the servlet life cycle.
- Multithreaded servlets can handle multiple requests at a single time.
- Servlets that implement the `SingleThreadModel` interface queue requests for execution one at a time.
- The servlet's `doGet()` method handles HTTP requests and sends HTTP responses.
- The JSP container compiles JSP pages into servlets.

QUIZ YOURSELF

1. What is an HTTP request?
2. What packages must be imported to support servlets?
3. What does the `SingleThreadModel` interface do?
4. Which objects are passed as parameters to the servlet's `init()` method?
5. Which method removes a servlet from memory?

SESSION

4

JSP and HTML Combined

Session Checklist

✔ Separate JSP from HTML

✔ Understand expressions

✔ Write scriptlets

**30 Min.
To Go**

Before you delve into the nuances of creating advanced JSP applications, you must first learn the basic structure and syntax of a JSP page. This session provides you with an overview of the general syntax you use when composing JSP pages and integrating JSP code and HTML.

Separating JSP from HTML

The main benefit of using JSP is the ability to embed logic in HTML pages. This obviates the need for CGI scripting, which is often slow and cannot maintain session state. JSP pages have a .jsp extension instead of an .html or .htm extension and are made up of *elements* and *template data*. JSP elements are defined as anything that is part of the Java Server Pages 1.1 specification, and template data is everything in the page that is not JSP code. More specifically, template data is the HTML markup part of the page.

The JSP engine knows to compile the JSP elements because they are enclosed in start tags (<%) and end tags (%>). The four types of JSP elements that you will see enclosed in the start and end tags are expressions, scriptlets, declarations, and directives.

- `<%= expressions %>`
- `<% scriptlets %>`
- `<%! declarations %>`
- `<%@ directives %>`

Remember that white space does not matter when it appears before or after the initial opening and closing tags. However, you may not separate any elements of the tags by using white space. The <, %, and =,!, or @ must always be contiguous.

Because element data is evaluated and can return different results every time the page is accessed, JSP pages, which are created as a result of a combination of elements and template data, are, by definition, more dynamic than static HTML.

To deploy the examples that follow in this session, and the rest of the book, follow these instructions:

1. Type the example code from the book into your text editor. You can use a sophisticated editor, like Homesite, but you may also use Notepad, which comes with the Windows operating system.

2. Save the file you just created underneath the <tomcat-install>\webapps\ROOT directory, or in the myWork directory you created in Session 3. The figures shown in this book are stored in the ROOT directory, and the URLs in the figures reflect that.

3. Make sure that Tomcat has been started. If it hasn't, navigate to your <tomcat-install>\bin directory and double-click on the startup.bat file to launch Tomcat.

4. Open your browser and navigate to the file. If you saved a file, foo.jsp, in the <tomcat-install>\webapps\ROOT directory, you would access it by navigating to http://localhost:8080/foo.jsp. If you saved the same file in the <tomcat-install>\webapps\myWork directory, you would access it by navigating to http://localhost:8080/myWork/foo.jsp. The first time you try to access the JSP page, it might be slow to open because the JSP engine is compiling the page into a servlet. Once it has been compiled, subsequent requests will be very fast.

Understanding Expressions

An *expression* is any bit of code that, when compiled, returns a value. When the JSP page is compiled; the expression is evaluated and converted to a data type of String; and the code is replaced where the expression appeared in the .jsp file. Typically, you will use an expression to return a value of a variable in your JSP page.

Listing 4-1 uses expressions to get some basic information about the server in which the page is being run.

Listing 4-1 *The serverInfo.jsp page returns information about the server.*

serverInfo.jsp
```
<html>
<head>
  <title>Server Information</title>
</head>
```

```
<body>

This page gets some basic information about the server.
<p>
<b>Server Name:</b> <%= request.getServerName() %>
<p>
<b>Server Port:</b> <%= request.getServerPort() %>
<p>

</body>
</html>
```

Figure 4-1 shows the output of the page.

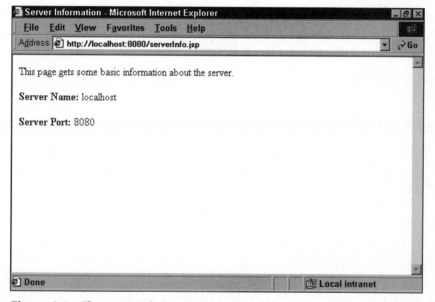

Figure 4-1 *The serverInfo.jsp page in a browser. Use expressions to return a String value to the screen.*

The = sign after the first <% tag signifies that the information inside the start and end tags is an expression to be evaluated. In the preceding example, we are using simple functions, getServerName(), and getServerPort(), to obtain the server's name and port from the server. These functions are part of the request object, an implicit object for all JSP pages.

Just as in the Java programming language, case is important when compiling the code within the JSP page. The function getservername() **is not the same function as** getServerName(), **and if you make a capitalization error, your JSP page fails to compile.**

**20 Min.
To Go**

Writing Scriptlets

When JSP code appears inside a start and end tag and does not have an additional designator, it is called a *scriptlet*. Scriptlets can contain any combination of Java code, including function and variable declarations and expressions. Take a look at Session 5 for a better picture of how scriptlets work and what you can do with them.

In Listing 4-2, the scriptlet contains a for loop that iterates through the code 10 times and displays the number of the iteration on the screen. Although the code in the example is nicely formatted with indentation and appears on separate lines for readability, the code neither needs to be formatted nor must it appear on separate lines for compilation and proper running.

Listing 4-2　　*The counter.jsp shows a scriptlet in action.*

counter.jsp

```
<html>
<head>
  <title>Scriptlet</title>
</head>

<body>

This page iterates through a counter and writes the results to the screen.
<table border="1" width="100%">
<% for (int count = 0; count < 10; count++) { %>
  <tr>
      <td align="center"><b>Count = <%= count %></b></td>
  </tr>
<% } %>
</table>

</body>
</html>
```

Figure 4-2 shows the output of this page.

Notice that it is possible to combine HTML template data with JSP elements by separating them with the appropriate tags. A new table row is generated each time the loop iterates, for a total of 10 rows.

In the preceding code, we are simply creating a table that contains multiple rows — you can add as many rows as you wish. This procedure becomes especially useful when you want to display the results of a call to the database. You can use the for loop to iterate through the rows returned in a SQL call and to display them in a table in the browser.

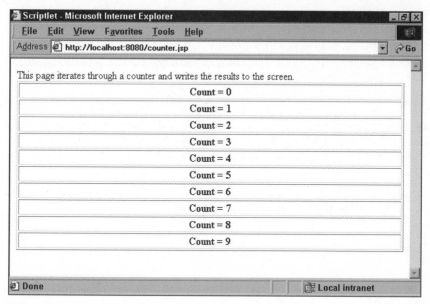

Figure 4-2 *The counter.jsp page employs a scriptlet that iterates through a for loop.*

Declarations

Declarations are included inside start and end tags that contain an ! after the opening tag. The variables and methods declared in a declaration may be used in scriptlets and expressions within the same .jsp. When declaring multiple variables or methods within a single declaration block, separate them with a semicolon.

In Listing 4-3, we take the previous scriptlet example and add a function declaration that generates a random, hexadecimal color. The code in bold between the <%! and %> tags is the function declaration.

Listing 4-3 *The colors.jsp utilizes a method declaration.*

colors.jsp

```
<html>
<head>
  <title>Scriptlet</title>
</head>

<body>

<%!
  /**getRandom Color function returns a hexadecimal color**/
String getRandomColor () {
  int red, green , blue;
  red = (int)(Math.random() * 255);
```

```
  green = (int)(Math.random() * 255);
  blue = (int)(Math.random() * 255);
String ret = Integer.toHexString(red) + Integer.toHexString(green) +
Integer.toHexString(blue);
  return ret.toUpperCase();
}
%>

This page iterates through a counter and writes the results to the screen.
<table border="1" width="100%">
<% for (int count = 0; count < 10; count++) { %>
  <tr>
        <td align="center" bgcolor="#<%= getRandomColor()
%>"><b>Count = <%= count %></b></td>
  </tr>
<% } %>
</table>

</body>
</html>
```

The function generates an RGB (red, green, blue) value for a color and converts that value to a hexadecimal value that can serve as a value for the background of a table cell.

This code is the first place we've seen comments, and there are two types of comments. The type of JSP comment in the preceding code sample is denoted by the format /** place any comments here **/. **Any information between the** /** **and** **/ **tags within a start and end tag will not be compiled. The second type of JSP comment is denoted by the format** <%-- place any comments here --%>. **You may also use HTML comments enclosed in** <!-- **and** --> **tags to comment your HTML code.**

The result might look a little like what is shown in Figure 4-3, but because a random color is generated each time the page loads, it will look a bit different each time.

Directives

Page *directives* are used to send specific information to the JSP container. The JSP container uses this information when evaluating the rest of the JSP page. For a complete list of the page directives available to the JSP container, refer to Session 6.

**10 Min.
To Go**

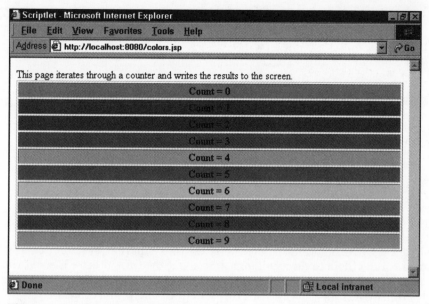

Figure 4-3 *The colors.jsp page in a browser. A random color is generated for each row each time the page is reloaded.*

Listing 4-4 uses the JSP container's `import` attribute to import a set of Java packages for use within the page.

Listing 4-4 *The calendar.jsp page imports the java.util.* package.*

---

calendar.jsp

```
<%@ page import="java.util.*" %>
<html>
<head>
  <title>Decalarations</title>
</head>

<body>
This page displays Information about the current Day.
<p>
<%! Date date = new Date(); %>
<%! Calendar calendar = Calendar.getInstance();  %>

Today is <b><%= date %></b>
<p>
Curent Era:
<b> <%= calendar.get(calendar.ERA) %>.</b>
<br>
Current Day of the Month:
<b><%= calendar.get(calendar.DAY_OF_MONTH) %>.</b>
<br>
```

Continued

Listing 4-4 *Continued*

```
Current Day of the Week:
<b><%= calendar.get(calendar.DAY_OF_WEEK) %>.</b>
<br>
Current Day of the Year:
<b><%= calendar.get(calendar.DAY_OF_YEAR) %>.</b>
<br>
Current Hour of the Day:
<b><%= calendar.get(calendar.HOUR_OF_DAY) %>.</b>
<br>

</body>
</html>
```

The directive is the bit of code at the beginning of the JSP page: `<%@ page import="java.util.*" %>`. This directive gives you access to all the classes in the `java.util` package. Date and Calendar are two of the classes in the `java.util` package, and here we are using those to display information about the current date. Without the directive, imports are not possible, and we cannot have access to the classes available in JDK. To import multiple classes or packages, separate each one with a comma.

Figure 4-4 shows what the result looks like.

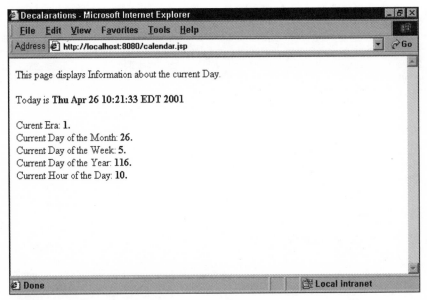

Figure 4-4 *The page directive allows you to import Java packages or classes for use within the JSP page.*

Done!

REVIEW

- Pages with a .jsp extension have two types of data. An element is Java code in the page, and template data is HTML markup.
- An expression has a <%= as its opening tag. Expressions return a value that is displayed on the screen.
- A scriptlet has a <% as its opening tag. Scriptlets can contain any valid Java code.
- A declaration has a <%! as its opening tag. Use a declaration to declare a function or a variable outside of a scriptlet.
- A directive has a <%@ as its opening tag. A common use for a directive is including classes or packages that are to be accessed within the JSP page.

QUIZ YOURSELF

1. What are the two types of information contained in a JSP page?
2. What is an expression? A directive? A declaration? A scriptlet?
3. How can you reference Java classes or packages in a JSP page?
4. What are the different ways to comment your code? What is the syntax for those comments?

PART

I

Friday Evening

1. What does HTTP stand for?

2. What does HTML stand for?

3. What is the name for the software architecture that has two processing tiers?

4. What is the name for the software architecture that has multiple processing tiers?

5. When a Web browser and a Web server exchange information, what are the two terms used to describe the back-and-forth communication?

6. What is the name of the system variable that tells the Java compiler where to look for class libraries?

7. What is the default port for HTTP communication between browsers and servers?

8. What is the term used to describe a zipped version of a webapp?

9. The opening tag <%! is used for what type of JSP element?

10. What is the data type of an expression, once it has been evaluated?

11. How does a JSP page differ from a servlet?

12. What is the difference between an applet and a servlet?

13. What are some of the advantages that Java technology brings to client/server architecture?

14. Which implicit object is associated with the getServerName() and getServerPort() methods?

15. True or false: JSP Declarations can be used only to declare variables.

16. What symbol is used to denote a directive?

17. What is a scriptlet?

18. Which implicit object is used to send output to the HTML page?

19. How do you import Java packages for use in your JSP pages?

20. What method of the underlying servlet is scriptlet code incorporated into?

☑ Friday

☑ **Saturday**

☐ Sunday

P A R T

II

Saturday
Morning

Using JSP Scriptlets

Session Checklist

✔ Write a scriptlet

✔ Code Java blocks

**30 Min.
To Go**

I n Session 4 you learned the four different types of JSP code that can be embedded in a JSP page. In this session, we will spend some more time on scriptlets. Although the features of JSP go far beyond scriptlets, and often other JSP techniques provide more elegant solutions, scriptlets are the best tool for beginning to investigate JSP capabilities.

Writing a Scriptlet

To review, a *scriptlet* is Java code enclosed in opening and closing code tags (<%) and (%>). A scriptlet can be inserted in a JSP page at any point in the document, even prior to the <HTML> tag. Typically, though, since a scriptlet generates HTML output, it often falls inside the <BODY></BODY> tags of the HTML page. According to HTML specification, all markup tags should be enclosed in greater than (<) and less than (>) symbols. If a process does not know how to handle a particular tag, it is supposed to ignore it. So, when the Web server sees the opening and closing scriptlet tags, it knows to leave the contents of the scriptlet alone and to pass it to another process, the JSP container, to execute the code.

The JspWriter Object

In Java, in order to call an object's method, that object must be instantiated. Many objects that are available to you in your JSP page are called implicit objects, meaning that their methods are available to you without explicitly instantiating the objects. The reason for this is that the objects are explicitly instantiated by the JSP container when the JSP page is translated into a servlet. The four most commonly used implicit objects are out, request, response, and session. The out object is actually the JspWriter object, a descendant of the java.io.Writer class. The JspWriter object enables you to send text data to the browser.

When you want to send information back to the client, usually in the form of HTML, use an expression like the one below, where *var* has some value that is set in the program prior to the expression:

```
<%= var %>
```

When you use an expression, the JSP engine automatically wraps the return value of the expression in an out.print() method. For instance, the above would be translated to:

```
out.print( var );
```

While the JSP engine doesn't do any automatic outputting with your scriptlet code, there will be times when you wish to send information back to the client output within a scriptlet. For example, to print the string "Hello World" to the screen, you could execute the following line of code, which functions exactly as a JSP expression:

```
out.println("Hello World");
```

While the out.println() method is useful, the real power of JSP stems from its ability to combine the kind of scripting activities that JavaScript can handle on the client side, with access to external server-side resources such as databases and mail servers. These resources provide the opportunity to generate dynamic data that can then be sent to the client through the JspWriter object.

20 Min.
To Go

The scriptletCalendar.jsp Example

You know that the first time a JSP page is requested, the JSP engine actually builds, compiles, and executes a servlet that produces the output specified in the JSP page. What this means is that the HTML part of the JSP page is wrapped in out.write()method calls that are placed in the service method of the servlet. For example, an <HTML> tag in a JSP page becomes out.write("<HTML>"); in the servlet. When the servlet engine encounters a scriptlet, it simply includes the code contained therein in the servlet.

In Listing 5-1, we do a test to see what time of day it is when the page is requested and display an appropriate message.

Listing 5-1 *The scriptletCalendar.jsp uses a scriptlet to display a dynamic message to the user.*

scriptletCalendar.jsp
```
<%@ page import="java.util.Calendar" %>
<HTML>
<BODY>
<h1>Scriptlet Example</h1>
<%
    // Calendar.getInstance will return an instance
    // of the Calendar class initialized to the
    // current date/time
    Calendar now = Calendar.getInstance();
```

```
      // See if it is morning or afternoon.
   if ( now.get(Calendar.AM_PM) == Calendar.AM ) {
      %>
          Good Morning
      <%
      }
      else
      {
      %>
          Good Afternoon
      <%
      }
   %>
   </BODY>
   </HTML>
```

The same effect could have been achieved without just a single scriptlet by wrapping the Good morning and Good Afternoon in out.write()s. This technique becomes very useful when you combine it with JSP tags and JavaBeans, as we will do in Session 12. For instance, you might have a JSP tag that displays a row of data contained in a Bean. By using a scriptlet that looped through each element in an array of Beans, you could use that JSP tag to display all the rows in a database table.

Coding Java Blocks

A Java *block* is a series of statements wrapped by opening and closing curly brackets ({}). For example, the series of statements making up the main() method of a standalone application is a block; the body of a while loop is a block. Blocks can contain other blocks and are very important in assigning and assessing the scope of variables. In Listing 5-1, the if (now.get(Calendar.AM_PM) == Calendar.AM) { statement appears as if it is not appropriately terminated: the opening curly bracket ({) is not closed. The implication of this is that the opening and closing of scriptlets has no impact on the delimiting of blocks of Java code. You can open a Java block in one scriptlet block and close it in another.

Scriptlets and HTML exist within the same block when the JSP page is compiled into a servlet at translation time. Scriptlets and static HTML content are both integrated into the service() method of the servlet. If a scriptlet is closed with an unterminated block, as in Listing 5-1, the subsequent lines of code are integrated into the block begun by the unterminated curly brace. To illustrate, take a look at the servlet that is generated as a result of the scriptletCalendar.jsp page in the following section.

Refer to Session 3 for more information on how servlets are compiled and where the JSP engine stores the generated servlet. The servlet generated from Listing 5-1 can be found in the <tomcat-install>\work\localhost-8080 directory. Tomcat will generate a unique name for the servlet, but it will contain the name of the JSP file, scriptletCalendar.

Servlet Code for scriptletCalendar.jsp

The code in Listing 5-2 is the servlet that is generated the first time you request the
scriptletCalendar.jsp page in your browser.

Listing 5-2   *The servlet that is generated from the scriptletCalendar.jsp page.*

```
import javax.servlet.*;
import javax.servlet.http.*;
import javax.servlet.jsp.*;
import javax.servlet.jsp.tagext.*;
import java.io.PrintWriter;
import java.io.IOException;
import java.io.FileInputStream;
import java.io.ObjectInputStream;
import java.util.Vector;
import org.apache.jasper.runtime.*;
import java.beans.*;
import org.apache.jasper.JasperException;
import java.util.Calendar;


public class _0002fscriptletCalendar_0002ejspscriptletCalendar_jsp_0
extends HttpJspBase {


    static {
    }
    public _0002fscriptletCalendar_0002ejspscriptletCalendar_jsp_0( ) {
    }

    private static boolean _jspx_inited = false;

    public final void _jspx_init() throws JasperException {
    }

    public void _jspService(HttpServletRequest request,
HttpServletResponse  response)
        throws IOException, ServletException {

        JspFactory _jspxFactory = null;
        PageContext pageContext = null;
        HttpSession session = null;
        ServletContext application = null;
        ServletConfig config = null;
        JspWriter out = null;
        Object page = this;
        String  _value = null;
        try {
```

```
            if (_jspx_inited == false) {
                _jspx_init();
                _jspx_inited = true;
            }
            _jspxFactory = JspFactory.getDefaultFactory();
            response.setContentType("text/html;charset=8859_1");
            pageContext = _jspxFactory.getPageContext(this, request,
response,
             "", true, 8192, true);

            application = pageContext.getServletContext();
            config = pageContext.getServletConfig();
            session = pageContext.getSession();
            out = pageContext.getOut();

            // HTML // begin [file="C:\\jakarta-
tomcat\\webapps\\ROOT\\scriptletCalendar.jsp";from=(0,39);to=(4,0)]
                out.write("\r\n<HTML>\r\n<BODY>\r\n<h1>Scriptlet
Example</h1>\r\n");
            // end
            // begin [file="C:\\jakarta-
tomcat\\webapps\\ROOT\\scriptletCalendar.jsp";from=(4,2);to=(12,3)]

                    // Calendar.getInstance will return an instance
                    // of the Calendar class initialized to the
                    // current date/time
                    Calendar now = Calendar.getInstance();

                    // See if it is morning or afternoon.
                    if ( now.get(Calendar.AM_PM) == Calendar.AM ) {

            // end
            // HTML // begin [file="C:\\jakarta-
tomcat\\webapps\\ROOT\\scriptletCalendar.jsp";from=(12,5);to=(14,3)]
                out.write("\r\n      Good Morning\r\n   ");
            // end
            // begin [file="C:\\jakarta-
tomcat\\webapps\\ROOT\\scriptletCalendar.jsp";from=(14,5);to=(18,3)]

                    }
                    else
                    {

            // end
            // HTML // begin [file="C:\\jakarta-
tomcat\\webapps\\ROOT\\scriptletCalendar.jsp";from=(18,5);to=(20,3)]
                out.write("\r\n      Good Afternoon\r\n   ");
            // end
            // begin [file="C:\\jakarta-
tomcat\\webapps\\ROOT\\scriptletCalendar.jsp";from=(20,5);to=(22,0)]
```

Continued

Listing 5-2

Continued

```
                }
            // end
            // HTML // begin [file="C:\\jakarta-
    tomcat\\webapps\\ROOT\\scriptletCalendar.jsp";from=(22,2);to=(26,0)]
                out.write("\r\n</BODY>\r\n</HTML>\r\n\r\n");
            // end

        } catch (Exception ex) {
            if (out.getBufferSize() != 0)
                out.clearBuffer();
            pageContext.handlePageException(ex);
        } finally {
            out.flush();
            _jspxFactory.releasePageContext(pageContext);
        }
    }
}
```

Notice the `out` declaration and subsequent instantiation at the beginning of the service method:

```
JspWriter out = null;
out = pageContext.getOut();
```

These two lines of code are what make the `out` object automatically available to scriptlets. The JSP specification specifies that JSP containers must make the `out` object available to JSP pages, and Listing 5-2 shows Tomcat's particular way of fulfilling the specification's requirement. Other JSP containers may do it slightly differently, but the end result will be the same.

If you look in the body of the `service` method, you should be able to find the Java code you embedded inside of your scriptlet in the `scriptletCalendar.jsp` page. The text outside the scriptlet, but inside of the `if-else` blocks in Listing 5-1, gets wrapped in `out.write()` calls in Listing 5-2.

Done!

REVIEW

- Scriptlets are Java code enclosed in opening and closing tags (<% %>).
- The `out` object is used in scriptlets to send text to the HTML page.
- All HTML content in your JSP pages is wrapped in an `out.write()` method in the servlet that is generated at translation time.
- It is not required that Java blocks be opened and closed in the same scriptlet. Java blocks can be opened in one scriptlet and closed in the next.

QUIZ YOURSELF

1. Scriptlets are opened and closed using what symbols?
2. What method of the `out` object is used to send lines of text to the HTML page?
3. True or false: JSP can be used to define the method that is called when a form element of type `Button` is pressed on an HTML form.
4. True or false: A scriptlet can be opened or closed inside the block following an `if` condition.

The JSP Page Directive

Session Checklist

✔ Learn to use page directive attributes

✔ Store information about a page

✔ Set up error pages

✔ Change MIME content types

**30 Min.
To Go**

In JSP, a directive defines attributes that apply to the servlet that is generated when the JSP page is compiled. There are three JSP directives: the page directive, the include directive, and the taglib directive. This session outlines the attributes you may define within the page directive, along with the possible values for those attributes. Session 18 covers the include directive, and Sessions 27 through 29 cover the taglib directive.

```
<%@ page
language="java"
extends="package.class"
import= "package.*"
session="true "
buffer="8kb "
autoFlush="true"
isThreadSafe="true"
info="Some Information Here"
errorPage="/errors.jsp"
contentType="text/html"
isErrorPage="false"
%>
```

The page directive may appear anywhere within the .jsp page, but because it applies to the entire page, it is a good idea to place it near the top. Although you may have more than one instance of the page directive on a single page, you may specify a value for each attribute only once, except for the import attribute.

Learning About the Page Directive Attributes

Table 6-1 lists all of the attributes available to be defined within a page directive. The attributes of the page directive further define how the directive is to be applied to the servlet that is generated from the JSP page.

Table 6-1 *Page Directive Attributes*

Attribute	Description
language	The default value for this page is java, meaning you use Java to code your pages. For the JSP specification version 1.1, the only legal language available is Java.
extends	The value of this attribute is the name of the ancestor Java class name you want to use as a superclass for the JSP page.
import	The import attribute enables you to import Java packages or classes into your JSP page. The imported classes can be accessed from the code. You do not have to import java.lang.*, javax.servlet.*, javax.servlet.jsp.*, or the javax.servlet.http.* packages. These packages are imported by default. To import more than one package or class, separate the packages or classes by a comma. The import must occur in the page before any code that calls the imported class appears.
session	The session value, true or false, indicates whether the page is to participate in sessions. The default value for session is "true," which means that the page may access the implicit session variable from the javax.servlet.http.HttpSession package.
buffer	Use this attribute to define the size of the buffer to which page content is written before outputting to the actual page. The default value of this variable is 8kb, which means that page data is sent to a buffer of 8 kilobytes. When the value of this attribute is none, there is no buffering of content.
autoflush	Use this value in conjunction with the buffer attribute. The default value of "true" flushes the buffered content automatically. A value of "false" raises an exception when more content than is allowed to be stored in the buffer is sent to the buffer. You may not define the autoflush attribute as "false" if the value of the buffer is "none."
isThreadSafe	The default value of this attribute is "true," which means that the page can handle multiple requests at the same time. If the value is set as "false," the JSP container processes requests one at a time. When you set isThreadSafe to "false," the servlet that is generated by the JSP container will implement the SingleThreadModel interface. See Session 4 for a discussion of the SingleThreadModel interface.

Attribute	Description
info	The value of this attribute can be accessed within a .jsp page by calling the function getServletInfo(). The value of this attribute can be any string.
errorPage	This is the relative URL that is designed to handle errors that occur in yourJSP page. The page must be a JSP page, and it handles the exception that is thrown from the page that contains the directive.
isErrorPage	The default value for this attribute is false, which indicates that the current page is not designed to handle errors. If the value is set to true, the page has access to the implicit exception object, which is the exception thrown by the page that declared this page as its error page.
contentType	The contentType attribute enables you to specify the type of content, such as HTML, text, pdf, and so on, that is to be returned to the user when the user has made a request to the Web server. This attribute actually sets the value for the Content-Type response environment variable. The default is "text/html;charset=ISO-8859-1"

Importing classes for use in your JSP page is one of the more important functions of the page directive. Through the page directive, you can use any of the packages available in the JDK, or other Java APIs.

Now that you've been introduced to the values for the attributes of the page directive, let's take a look at some real-world examples.

Storing Information About a Page

In Listing 6-1, the getServletInfo() method returns the value of the info attribute of the page directive. Typically, the data stored in the info attribute is about the servlet, such as author, version, or copyright information. The output on your screen should resemble Figure 6-1.

Listing 6-1   *The servletInfo.jsp uses the* getServletInfo() *method.*

servletInfo.jsp

```
<%@ page info="Fruit of the Month Club Welcome Page." %>

<html>
<head>
   <title>Page Info example</title>
</head>
```

Continued

Listing 6-1   *Continued*

```
<body>

The value of the info attribute is:
<b><%= getServletInfo() %></b>

</body>
</html>
```

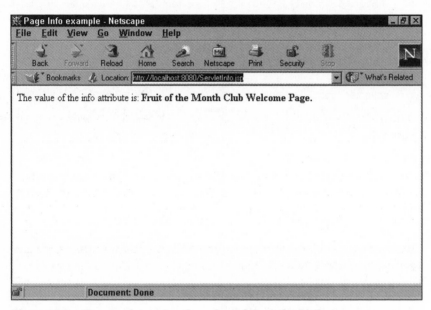

The value of the info attribute is: **Fruit of the Month Club Welcome Page.**

Figure 6-1 *You can determine the value of the info attribute.*

Setting Up Error Pages

20 Min.
To Go

The page directive enables you to handle Java exceptions in your JSPs. Consider the example shown in Listing 6-2, in which you want to perform a simple mathematical operation: dividing one number by another. Create the page in a text editor and add it to the <tomcat-install>\webapps\ROOT directory. Call the page divide.jsp.

Listing 6-2   *The divide.jsp page divides one integer by another and outputs the result.*

divide.jsp

```
<html>
<head>
  <title>Division Example</title>
</head>
```

```
<body>
This page will deliberately throw an error if you try and divide
by zero (0):
<%
    int num1 = 10;
    int num2 = 2;
    int ans = num1/num2;
%>

When you divide <b><%= num1 %></b> by <b><%= num2 %></b>, you get
<b><%= ans %></b>.

</body>
</html>
```

The result of dividing 10 by 2 is 5, and the page runs successfully. You can change the values of num1 and num2 to any number except zero, and the page will run without error.

Because the result of the division operation in the divide.jsp page is an ~~int~~ data type, it will not display the remainder if there is one.

To force an error, change the value of num2 to zero (0), and run the page. Division by zero is an illegal mathematical operation; if you attempt to divide by zero at runtime, you will get a runtime error and the page will not be displayed correctly.

For a more complete discussion of exception handling, another error handling example, and information on debugging your JSP pages, refer to Session 10.

In order to avoid displaying to the user the default Tomcat error page, create a page that handles the error created when you divide by zero. First, add the page directive to the first line of the divide.jsp page that tells the page where the error page is. Listing 6-3 shows the divide.jsp page that will trigger an error.

Listing 6-3 *The divide.jsp page will trigger an error when attempting to divide one number by zero.*

divide.jsp
```
<%@ page errorPage="error.jsp" %>
<html>
<head>
   <title>Division Example</title>
</head>
```

Continued

Listing 6-3 *Continued*

```
<body>
This page will deliberately throw an error if you try and divide
by zero (0):
<%
    int num1 = 10;
    int num2 = 0;
    int ans = num1/num2;
%>

When you divide <b><%= num1 %></b> by <b><%= num2 %></b>, you get
<b><%= ans %></b>.

</body>
</html>
```

Now code the error page to display the message contained in the exception variable. Listing 6-4 shows the code for error.jsp.

Listing 6-4 *The error.jsp page an example of an error handling page.*

error.jsp

```
<%@ page isErrorPage="true" info="This is an Error Page."
import="java.io.*" %>

<html>
<head>
    <title>Error Page</title>
</head>

<body>
You got to this page because you threw an error in the page
divide.jsp.<p>
The error was <b><%= exception.getMessage() %>.</b>

</body>
</html>
```

In this example, you are using the getMessage() method of the Exception object. Because the isErrorPage attribute of the page directive is "true," the exception variable is implied in this page, and you can access its methods and properties without an explicit declaration.

Changing MIME Content Types

Each document that is transmitted over the Internet has an associated MIME type, also referred to as content type or media type. The contentType attribute tells your browser what type of content the server is sending to the client when a request is made. The default value for the contentType attribute is text/html.

Depending on the MIME type of the document being sent to the browser, the browser renders it in the most appropriate application. In your experience surfing the Web, you may have noticed that when downloading a .pdf file, for example, both Netscape and Internet Explorer automatically launch Adobe Acrobat to render the file. When downloading an Excel spreadsheet or a Microsoft Word document, the browser will launch the appropriate application to render those files as well.

Two pieces of information inform a browser how to handle the content being transferred: the extension of the file and the value of the Content-Type response header. When a browser requests a file with an .html or .htm extension, it knows that it contains hypertext markup, and it assumes the capability to render it. If, however, the requested file has a different extension, the browser searches for the associated program to launch that file. The browser also looks at the Content-Type response value to determine how to render the Web document.

In the next example, you are setting the contentType attribute of a JSP page directive to application/msword. Doing this tells the generated servlet to set the Content-Type response header to application/msword, which notifies the browser to launch Microsoft Word in order to display the page. To run the example, you must have Microsoft Word (any version) installed on your machine. Create a new JSP page called format.jsp and store it in your <tomcat-install>\webapps\ROOT directory. Listing 6-5 shows the code your page should contain.

Listing 6-5   *The format.jsp page sends a Microsoft Word document to the browser, instead of an HTML page.*

---

format.jsp

```
<%@ page contentType="application/msword" %>
<html>
<head>
   <title>Changing the contentType Attribute</title>
</head>

<body>

Microsoft Word can display HTML as well as any browser.

It can understand:
<ul>
   <li><strong>Bold text</strong></li>
   <li><i>Italicized text</i></li>
   <li><u>Underlined text</u></li>
</ul>

It can also understand:
<ol>
   <li><h1>Heading 1</h1></li>
   <li><h2>Heading 2</h2></li>
   <li><h3>Heading 3</h3></li>
</ol>

</body>
</html>
```

Run the page by navigating to it. Notice that instead of displaying the content in the browser window, you are prompted to save or open the file. Choose Open. Your browser should launch Microsoft Word, and the page should be displayed. The extension of the file is still .jsp, so we know that the browser is using the value of the Content-Type response header to launch the external application. Figure 6-2 shows the format.jsp page.

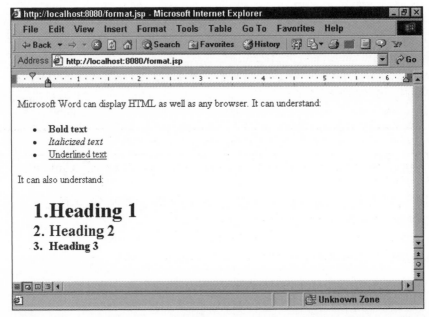

Figure 6-2 *Changing the contentType attribute to application/msword loads the document in Microsoft Word. Word can understand HTML and display it appropriately.*

More recent versions of Microsoft Word (this example was run on Word 2000) have the capability to recognize HTML markup and render it just as it would be rendered in the browser. In addition to text formatting, it can also render tables and forms.

Because of the integration of the Microsoft suite of applications, Internet Explore 5.x will launch the document within the browser, but as a Word document. Netscape 4.x will launch the document outside the browser.

Done!

REVIEW

- The page directive defines attributes that apply to the servlet that is generated from the JSP page.

- Use the `import` attribute to import Java classes that you want to access within the JSP page.

- Access the `info` attribute of the page directive with the `getServletInfo()` method.

- The `errorPage` and `isErrorPage` attributes work in concert to enable user-friendly error handling within a Web application.

- The `contentType` attribute sets the Content-Type response header that notifies the browser how to render a document.

QUIZ YOURSELF

1. Which attribute value of the page directive can be accessed through calling the `getServletInfo()` function?

2. What two attributes control error handling? How do they work together?

3. Can you set error pages through the page directive?

4. What types of content can be transmitted via http over the Web?

5. How do you tell the browser what types of content to expect?

SESSION

7

HTML Forms: A Walkthrough

Session Checklist

✔ Get acquainted with HTML forms

✔ Examine types of form input

30 Min. To Go

Much of the communication between the user and the server is mediated through HTML forms. That is, users submit information to the server through the convention of the form, and there is an HTML framework to support that. In essence, JSP "plugs into" HTML forms in the same way CGI or ASP does. In this session, you will examine form conventions and all of the different types of inputs and their possible variations. In the next session, you will see just how JSP handles the form inputs when they are sent back to the server.

Getting Acquainted with HTML Forms

All elements located in between <form></form> tags are part of a form. Listing 7-1 shows an HTML form with three elements, a text input, a password input, and a submit button.

Listing 7-1   *The form1.html page has a simple form.*

form1.html
```
<html>
<body>
    <form method="get" action="action.jsp">
        User Name: <input type="Text" name="userName"><br>
        Password: <input type="Password" name="password"><br>
        <input type="Submit" name="Submit" value="Submit">
    </form>
</body>
</html>
```

Notice that although the values of the attributes are enclosed in quotation marks, such as `userName` and `password`, the quotation marks do not matter as long as the values are one continuous word. However, it is a good habit to use quotation marks ("") when filling in a value for an HTML attribute. You will run into problems if you attempt to set a value for an attribute that consists of two or more words separated by a space. For example, you may want the value attribute of a checkbox to be Fruit and Vegetables. Without quotation marks around the value, as in the following example, the string value would be truncated at the first space, and the value would not be complete.

```
<input type="checkbox" name="order" value="Fruit and Vegetables">
```

While capitalization does not matter to an HTML parser, case does matter to your JSP page. All Java programs are case-sensitive. `UserName` is not the same as `userName` in Java, so be conscious of the names you give to your form elements.

Some HTML elements are irrelevant to the processing of forms, such as text or table cells. However, any HTML element can occur within forms in addition to form-specific HTML elements. You can nest a form within a table, or the other way around. Forms are relatively flexible.

In HTML, you will often nest certain elements inside of other ones. For example, each element in an HTML page is nested between opening and closing `<html></html>` tags. The elements that make up the body of the page are nested between opening and closing `<body></body>` tags. You may also nest tables within tables to achieve a structured look on your page.

Common Attributes

This section discusses the following attributes that you can safely use in both the form itself as well as each of its elements, which will be described later in this session:

- Name
- ID
- Class
- Style

These attributes produce the same results consistently and will not interfere with the proper functioning of the form itself.

This section also covers the following form-specific attributes and events:

- Action
- Method
- Enctype
- OnSubmit

Name

Name your form and your form elements with the Nameattribute. The name is necessary to access the value of the input in JSP and to manipulate the form with client-side script. If you plan to use JavaScript for form validation, it would be handy to name your form and its elements to be able to access them. In the example below, we use the name attribute to set the name of the text-input element to city.

```
<input type="text" name="city">
```

ID

The ID does not differ greatly in function from the Name attribute: It is used to uniquely identify the form element within the form. The ID attribute is more commonly used to identify a style for the given element. Remember that when using the JSP methods to retrieve a form element's value, as you will do in Session 8, pass the value of the Name attribute as the parameter, not the Id value. The ID attribute in the example below sets the ID of the checkbox to 16.

```
<input type="checkbox" name="city" value="New York" Id="16">
```

Class

The class attribute is used in conjunction with a style sheet. In a style sheet, you may define a class of content that has a particular style associated with it. In the form, you can set a class for an element and its corresponding style with the class attribute:

```
<STYLE>
    input.orange {background : orange }
</STYLE>
<input type="submit" name="submit" value="submit" class="orange">
```

Use the class attribute when you want to reuse a style for multiple elements.

Style

If you don't want to apply a templated style to a form element, you may use the style attribute, also called *inline* style, to assign one particular style to one particular form element:

```
<input type="submit" name="submit" value="submit" style="color: red">
```

Action

The Action attribute represents the resource to which the form is being submitted for processing. This can be a CGI script, an ASP page or, as will be represented in this book, a servlet or JSP page. If the value of the action attribute is not included in the form, the form will submit to itself. Usually, a form that submits to itself has some embedded code that can handle the form submission and then redirect the user to an appropriate Web resource.

Method

The Method attribute tells the HTML page how to communicate with the URL specified by the action attribute of the form. The possible values for the method attribute are get and post (capitalization does not matter). With get, all values submitted to the server via the form inputs are appended to the URL as a *querystring in* name=value pairs. The names are the names of the form inputs and the values are the values of the form inputs that the user has submitted. For example, were we to submit the form1.html page at the beginning of this session by entering john for the first user name, pass for the password, and clicking the Submit button, the following URL would appear in our browser:

```
http://localhost:8080/action.jsp?userName=john&password=doe&Submit=Submit
```

Note that since we have not coded the action.jsp **page, the page that accepts the form submission, the page will trigger an error. In Session 8 we will explore how to create action pages to process form submissions.**

Notice that the values that we entered in the fields in addition to the value of the Submit button are appended to the action page after a question mark (?) in the URL according to the name=value pattern.

If the action attribute of the form were post, the same information would be submitted to the server, but it would occur in the request header as opposed to the actual URL. This means that the user may not scrutinize the values, so it is a more private method of form submission.

Enctype

The Enctype attribute is necessary for instances in which a file is being submitted along with other form data. In this case, set the value of the enctype attribute to multipart/form-data. Otherwise, the default value of the enctype attribute is application/x-www-form-urlencoded. The code below shows the syntax for creating a file-upload form element.

```
<form method="post" action="formAction.jsp" enctype="multipart/form-data"
>
  <input type="File" name="upload">
</form>
```

OnSubmit

Forms support standard HTML events, such as onClick or onMouseOver. One commonly used form event is the onSubmit event, which is triggered when the form is submitted, usually by someone's clicking an input of type submit (this is covered in the section "Examining

Form Inputs"). Typically, the onSubmit event is used to code some type of form validation when the form is submitted.

Examining Form Inputs

Now that we've outlined the syntax for constructing the skeleton of the form, let's look at some of the inner elements. Almost every HTML form input is structured with the <input> tag. The only two exceptions are <textarea>, an element that captures large blocks of text; and <select>, an element that captures a single or multiple-option selection.

 When rendering forms, Internet Explorer 5.*x* and Netscape Navigator 4.*x* behave somewhat differently. IE will render form elements whether or not they are nested inside of opening and closing <form></form> tags. Conversely, Netscape will not render any form elements that are not correctly nested within the form tags. In either case, when the form is submitted, it will only pass along to the server those elements that are nested within the tags.

This section lists the following types of inputs, along with the relevant attributes and a visual representation of each:

- Text
- Password
- Checkbox
- Radio button
- Button
- File
- Textarea

Text Input

A text field captures relatively short text inputs. Maxlength is used to specify the maximum number of characters that can be input into the text field. Size is used to specify the width of the text input, relative to the number of characters. In Listing 7-2, because the size of the text box is 10 and the maximum length is 20, the user would scroll as he entered more than 10 characters into the text input. Also, the value of the text has been preset to Kentucky. Listing 7-2 shows a text input. If the user submitted the form as is, "Kentucky" would be sent to the server as the value for the input named state. If the user changed the value, the new value would override the preset value upon submission.

Listing 7-2 *The text input captures text data.*

```
<form>
State: <input type="text" maxlength="20" size="10" name="state"
value="Kentucky">
</form>
```

Password Input

The essential difference between an input of type password and an input of type text is that the password input shows up as asterisks (*) when the user types in the fieldAdditionally, unlike a text input, the browser will not allow a user to copy to the clipboard any text entered in a password input. This field is typically used for (you guessed it!) capturing user passwords or other sensitive information. Refer to Listing 7-1 for an example of a password input.

Checkbox Input

Checkboxes are used to collect multiple values for a given group, as shown in the example of pizza toppings in Listing 7-3. For the purposes of this book, a *group* is defined as a set of inputs with the same name.

Listing 7-3 *Checkboxes allow for uses to enter multiple values.*

```
<form>
<table>
      <tr>
              <th>toppings</th>
              <td>
                  <input type="Checkbox" name="topping"
value="peppers"checked> Peppers<br>
                  <input type="Checkbox" name="topping"
value="sausage" checked> Sausage<br>
                  <input type="Checkbox" name="topping"
value="cheese"> Cheese<br>
                  <input type="Checkbox" name="topping"
value="onions" checked> Onions<br>
                  <input type="Checkbox" name="topping"
value="mushrooms"> Mushrooms<br>
              </td>
      </tr>
</table>
</form>
```

In Listing 7-3, the table tags are used only for formatting purposes. Notice that each of the checkboxes has the same name, topping, despite the fact that each is a separate input. These checkboxes are part of a group, and the values will be submitted as part of the topping group.

In Session 8, you will learn how a JSP page processes multiple values for a form element.

Just as in the case of text inputs, you can preselect the checkbox by adding the keyword checked to the element. If a user deselects a checkbox that has been preselected via the checked keyword, it will override the checked status of the checkbox.

If you're using an IE browser version 4 or later, try running the code in Listing 7-4.

Listing 7-4 *Internet Explorer uses HTML label elements that allow a user to check a checkbox by by clicking on its associated text.*

```
<form>
<table>
    <tr>
        <th>toppings</th>
            <td>
                <label for="peppers"><input type="Checkbox" name="topping"
value="peppers" checked id="peppers"> Peppers</label><br>
                <label for="sausage"><input type="Checkbox" name="topping"
value="sausage" checked id="sausage"> Sausage</label><br>
                <label for="cheese"><input type="Checkbox" name="topping"
value="cheese" id="cheese"> Cheese</label><br>
                <label for="onions"><input type="Checkbox" name="topping"
value="onions" checked id="onions"> Onions</label><br>
                <label for="mushrooms"><input type="Checkbox" name="topping"
value="mushrooms" id="mushrooms"> Mushrooms</label><br>
            </td>
    </tr>
</table>
</form>
```

Visually, the form is drawn the same as the first snippet of code for the checkbox form element, but it behaves a little differently. By using the label element, the user can select the checkbox by clicking on the text associated with the element, instead of only on the checkbox itself. In order for the label element to function properly, you must assign an ID to each input that has a label, and then pass that ID to the label element via the for attribute. This example will work in IE browsers only.

Radio-button Input

10 Min. To Go

Listing 7-5 shows a group of radio buttons in which the first radio button is selected. You may preselect one or the other radio buttons by inserting the keyword checked into the element. If you do not preselect any of the radio buttons in a group, the input has a null value until one radio button or another is selected. Once one has been selected, there is no way to reassign the null value to the radio button group.

Listing 7-5 *Radio buttons behave like checkboxes except that if one radio button in a group is selected, another button in the same group cannot be.*

```
<form>
    <input type="radio" name="gender" value="male" checked> Male
    <input type="radio" name="gender" value="female"> Female
</form>
```

Button Input

The browser can draw three types of buttons: a Reset button, a Submit button, and a "plain old" button. The Reset button, when pressed, will reset all of the form values to their original value when the form was loaded into the browser; *it does not reset the values to null.* The Submit button, when pressed, will submit the form to the action page specified in the form element. A button that is not of type reset or submit has no action assigned to it. Instead, this element type is used when you want to specifically assign an action via script. In addition, the length and width attributes are available for buttons should you want a tall or wide button displayed on the page. Listing 7-6 shows the three types of buttons.

Listing 7-6   *There are three types of HTML buttons: submit, reset, and button.*

```
<form>
    <input type="reset" name="reset" value="Reset the form">
    <input type="submit" name="submit" value="Submit the form">
    <input type=button name=hello value=hello
onClick="javascript:alert('Hello World')">
</form>
```

The presence of the onClick attribute indicates that something will happen when the user clicks the button. The value of the onClick attribute, javascript:alert('Hello World'), signifies that the javascript alert('Hello World') method, a method that displays a message box, will appear with the assigned message.

File Input

The file input is drawn as a text input and a Browse button. When the user clicks the Browse button, a Choose File dialog box appears, enabling the user to select a file on his hard drive or network. As soon as the file is chosen, the text box displays the path to the selected file. Upon submission, the contents of this file are submitted to the server. You must instruct the form that there is a file input type in the form by setting the form's enc-type attribute to multipart/form-data. Refer to the section earlier in this session which describes the enctype attribute for an example of a file input.

Textarea Input

Unlike the previous form elements discussed in this session, the textarea is its own element and cannot be declared with the <input> tag. If you would like to preset the value of the text area, there is no value attribute for the textarea element. Instead, place text between the <textarea></textarea> tags, as in the preceding example. Nor is there any maxlength attribute, which means that if you wish to limit the number of characters that may be entered, you must apply client- or server-side validation to the field. To change the width and height of the textarea, change the values of the cols and rows attributes. See the example in Listing 7-7.

Listing 7-7   *A textarea element accepts large blocks of text.*

```
<form >
  <textarea name="textInput" cols="40" rows="10" >Any text here</textarea>
</form>
```

Select Input

The select input enables a user to select one or many options for the form element. The code in Listing 7-8 shows a single-select drop-down box.

Listing 7-8   *A select input may accept single or multiple values.*

```
<form>
  <select name="Connection" >
      <option value="T1">T1
      <option value="DSL">DSL
      <option value="cable">cable
      <option value="56K" selected>56K
      <option value="28.8">28.8
  </select>
</form>
```

Nest the option elements within the select element to create a select box. To nest the options, make certain they appear between the opening and closing `<select></select>` tags. To enable multiple selections within the select element, add the keyword `multiple` to the select element. To preselect a specific option, add the `selected` keyword to the option element. In Listing 7-8, the 56K option has been preselected; therefore, when the page loads, that is the visible choice in the form element.

Hidden

There is no visual representation of a hidden field; as its name suggests, it is hidden within the form. The following example shows a hidden form with the name `test` and the value `true`:

```
<form>
  <input type="hidden" name="test" value="true">
</form>
```

The value of the hidden field is passed to the server upon form submission.

 Typically, programmers use hidden fields to store information that they may later need. For instance, on a login page for which you want to allow a user only three chances to log in, you might store the number of attempts in a hidden field. You would write code that would increment the value of a hidden field each time the user tries and fails. When the value reached three, you might add a script on the server that redirects the user to an error page.

Additional Keywords

To make your Web pages function more like Windows applications, you may also use the `readonly` and `disabled` keywords in many of your form elements. They both accomplish the roughly the same thing. The `readonly` keyword prohibits users from changing the preset value of the form element that contains the keywords. The `disabled` keyword will also "gray out" (disable) the form element on the browser screen, which results in a more sophisticated presentation of your form.

The `readonly` and `disabled` keywords do not work in Netscape browsers; Netscape ignores the attributes.

Done!

REVIEW

- Structure forms by placing different form elements between opening and closing `<form></form>` tags.
- The `action` attribute of the form element tells the page where to send the form results.
- The `method` attribute of the form element tells the page how to send the form results to the URL specified in the `action` attribute.
- Each form input, with the exception of `selects` and `textareas`, are generated by changing the `type` attribute of the input tags. The different types are `text`, `password`, `radio`, `checkbox`, `file`, `button`, `submit`, and `reset`.

QUIZ YOURSELF

1. Which form elements allow for multiple values? Which allow for single values?
2. With radio buttons, how do you ensure that when one is selected, all others are deselected?
3. What is the key difference between the `post` and `get` methods when submitting a form?
4. Why might you choose a `textarea` over a `text` input? Are there any additional considerations for making this choice?

Working with Form Data in JSP

Session Checklist

✔ Process forms

✔ Access single select and radio button values

✔ Use multiple select boxes and checkboxes

✔ Try an alternate way to access form elements

**30 Min.
To Go**

Now that we've reviewed forms and inputs, we will explore the methods for extracting information from a form submission. Forms are a good way for a Web application to collect information from a user, whether it is login information, user preferences, or random data. In this session, you will learn the different types of form inputs and examine how JSP manipulates submitted data.

Processing Forms

Let's start by creating a simple screen that requests the user's first and last name. The code for creating the form is shown in Listing 8-1. Call the page `form.html` and place it in the <tomcat-install>\webapps\ROOT directory. You run the page by navigating to http://localhost:8080/login.html.

Listing 8-1   *The login.html page submits to the formAction.jsp page, which processes the form inputs.*

login.html
```
<html>
<title>form example</title>

<body>
```

Continued

Listing 8-1 *Continued*

```
<form method="POST" action="formAction.jsp">
<table cellpadding="1" cellspacing="1" border="1">
<tr>
      <td align="right"><b>First Name:</b></td>
      <td><input type="text" size="15" name="firstName"></td>
  </tr>
  <tr>
      <td align="right"><b>Last Name:</b></td>
      <td><input type="text" size="15" name="lastName"></td>
  </tr>
  <tr>
      <td colspan="2" align="center"><input type=submit
value="Login"></td>
  </tr>
</table>
</form>

</body>
</html>
```

Take note of several important items in the preceding form. Its attributes should be familiar to you from reading Session 7. For the form in the login.html example, the method is post, which means that the information submitted in the form is added to the body of the request sent to the Web server. Were the value of the method get, the form information would be appended to the URL of the action page. Additional characters at the end of a URL are called a querystring.

Unlike ASP, JSP does not differentiate between the post **and** get **methods when processing form data; you access form data for both methods in the same way. ASP, on the other hand, uses the** querystring **and** form **collections for form data submitted via** get **and** post**, respectively. To see the difference between** post **and** get **in action, change the** method **parameter and look at the URL of the page to which the form has been submitted. When the method is** get**, a string will be appended to the** formAction.jsp **URL. If "John" and "Smith" were input as the first and last name, the URL would look like** http://localhost/formAction.jsp?firstName=John&lastName= Smith.

The second form attribute after method is action. In Listing 8-1, once the form has been submitted, the formAction.jsp page is called to process the form.

The value of the action attribute must be a valid URL. The URL may or may not be part of the site where the form itself exists. For example, you may set the action page for the form to be http://www.yahoo.com. Yahoo!'s site probably won't be able to process the form that was submitted, however. In the login.html page previously listed, the value of the action attribute is set to formAction.jsp. Therefore, in order for the example to work, the formAction.jsp page must be saved in the same directory as the form.html page.

To the JSP page that accepts the request, it doesn't matter whether the method is `post` or `get` — the page will handle the information in the same way. The code for the `formAction.jsp` page is shown in Listing 8-2.

Listing 8-2   *The formAction.jsp page uses JSP code to access the values of the form elements that were submitted by the user.*

```
<html>
<title>Action Page</title>

<body>


<table>
  <tr>
      <td>Your first name is <b><%=
request.getParameter("firstName") %></b></td>
  </tr>
  <tr>
      <td>Your last name is <b><%=
  request.getParameter("lastName") %></b></td>
  </tr>
</table>

</body>
</html>
```

The general syntax for accessing the values of form elements is `request.getParameter ("parameterName")`. The first part, `request`, refers to the implicit `request` object that contains the form data. The second part, `getParameter("parameterName")`, is the name of the request function that extracts the value of the `parameterName` value.

In the code for the JSP page, the expression `<%= request.getParameter("firstName") %>` renders the value of the first name, and `<%= request.getParameter("lastName") %>` renders the value of the last name entered in the form on the preceding page. The `getParameter()` method accepts a parameter of type `String`. The parameter is used to pass the name of the input element in the form page, as designated by the `name` attribute. If you look at the code on the form page, you see that `firstName` and `lastName` are the values of the `name` attributes of the text input form elements.

It's fine to use the `getParameter()` method for accessing form element values when the form element has only one possible value. However, many different form values are available to you as a developer, and these elements can contain more than one value, as discussed in detail in "Using Multiple Select Boxes and Checkboxes" later in this session.

Now let's add the new form elements to the form, as shown in Listing 8-3; and take a look at how we can access the values. Through the use of a `select` box, `checkboxes`, and `radio buttons`, the new form enables us to collect more information about the user in a structured way. The bold items are the additions to the form.

Listing 8-3 *Checkboxes and multiple-select form inputs send multiple values to the server.*

form2.html

```
<html>
<title>Extended Form Example</title>

<body>

<form method="post" action="formAction.jsp">
<table cellpadding="1" cellspacing="1" border="1">
  <tr>
        <td align="right"><b>First Name:</b></td>
        <td><input type="text" size="15" name="firstName"></td>
  </tr>
  <tr>
        <td align="right"><b>Last Name:</b></td>
        <td><input type="text" size="15" name="lastName"></td>
  </tr>
  <tr>
        <td align="right"><b>Region:</b></td>
        <td>
              <select name="region">
              <option value="Northeast">Northeast</option>
              <option value="Northwest">Northwest</option>
              <option value="Southeast">Southeast</option>
              <option value="Southwest">Southwest</option>
        </select>
        </td>
  </tr>
  <tr>
        <td align="right" valign="top" nowrap><b>Favorite Colors
(check all that apply):</b></td>
        <td>
              <input name="color" type="checkbox"
value="blue">Blue<br>
              <input name="color" type="checkbox"
value="red">Red<br>
              <input name="color" type="checkbox"
value="yellow">Yellow<br>
              <input name="color" type="checkbox"
value="green">Green<br>
              <input name="color" type="checkbox" value="purple">Purple<br>
        </td>
  </tr>
  <tr>
        <td align="right" valign="top"><b>Age Group:</b></td>
        <td>
              <input type="radio" name="age" value="under 25">under
25<br>
              <input type="radio" name="age" value="25-50">
```

```
25-50<br>
            <input type="radio" name="age" value="50-75">
50-75<br>
            <input type="radio" name="age" value="75-100">
75-100<br>
            <input type="radio" name="age" value="over 100">over 100<br>
        </td>
    </tr>
    <tr>
        <td colspan="2" align="center"><input type="submit"
value="Submit" name="submit"></td>
    </tr>
</table>
</form>

</body>
</html>
```

The first addition is a single select box to collect region information. There are four mutually exclusive options, meaning that the user may select one and only one. Select boxes are typically used for storing lists of options that may be somewhat lengthy; whether there are four items in the list or 400, the form element takes up a small amount of screen real estate. However, users must click the form element on the screen to view the universe of options.

The second addition to the form is a series of checkboxes to collect favorite colors. Unlike the single select box, the options are not mutually exclusive. The user may choose any number of favorite colors, none of them, or all of them. The checkbox is a good way to give users the capability to choose multiple items under a single category. Because the checkboxes are all visible onscreen, they take up more space than the single select but do not require that a user click the screen to see all of the available options.

The third addition is a series of radio buttons to collect a user's age range. Like the single select, the options are mutually exclusive, but each one is immediately visible on the screen.

Let's examine how to access the values of each of the new form elements once the form has been submitted.

Accessing Single Select and Radio Button Values

*20 Min.
To Go*

Single select boxes and radio buttons behave the same because they are both used to get a single value. You can access the value of the item selected for a single select box or a radio button by passing the name of the input to the getParameter() method of the request object. Use this function the same way you use it for a text input. The difference is that the value of a text input is the text that the user entered into the form; the value of a single select and a radio button is the value specified in the value attribute of the selected form element. In both cases, the parameter passed to the method is the value of the name attribute of the form element. Take a look at the code for the select box:

```
<select name="region">
  <option value="Northeast">Northeast</option>
  <option value="Northwest">Northwest</option>
  <option value="Southeast">Southeast</option>
  <option value="Southwest">Southwest</option>
</select>
```

In this scenario, the values of the option elements are the same as the captions of the option elements (the caption is the text that appears on the browser screen between the <option></option> tags). Therefore, if the user selects "Northeast," the value passed is "Northeast." In the following example, the caption and the value are different:

```
<select name="region">
  <option value="1">Northeast</option>
  <option value="2">Northwest</option>
  <option value="3">Southeast</option>
  <option value="4">Southwest</option>
</select>
```

In this example, if the user selects "Northeast," the value of the region form element passed to the action page is "1"; if the user selects "Northwest," the value of the region form element passed to the action page is "2," and so on. Because the value of the selected item may be different from the value displayed on the screen, keep the distinction in mind when you use select boxes to transfer information.

Radio buttons behave the same way as single select boxes, in that the item selected by the user is mutually exclusive of all the other options. For example, in the following code, there is no way for a user to belong to more than one of the age groups listed. She can belong to one and only one.

```
<input type="radio" name="age" value="1">under 25<br>
<input type="radio" name="age" value="2">25-50<br>
<input type="radio" name="age" value="3">51-75<br>
<input type="radio" name="age" value="4">76-100<br>
<input type="radio" name="age" value="5">over 101<br>
```

Although radio buttons behave like single selects, they are syntactically different. Unlike the select box, the radio button inputs are not wrapped in a parent form element; notice, however, that each of the radio button inputs has the same value for the name parameter. This ensures that any time a single radio button is selected, no other radio button in the same group can be selected; each option is mutually exclusive of any other option.

Copy the code in the example, and look at the page in a Web browser. Try selecting different radio buttons. Notice that as soon as one is selected, another is deselected. Now change the name attribute for some of the radio input types, and reload the page. If the name attribute for all of the radio buttons is not identical, you will be able to select more than one in a group.

Using Multiple Select Boxes and Checkboxes

When you want to give the user the capability to select more than one value from a form element, you can use either multiple select boxes or a series of checkboxes. If you wanted to enable the user to select multiple regions instead of just one, the code would look like the following HTML:

```
<select name="region" multiple size="4" >
<option value="Northeast">Northeast</option>
<option value="NorthWest">NorthWest</option>
<option value="SouthEast">SouthEast</option>
<option value="SouthWest">SouthWest</option>
</select>
```

The `multiple` keyword in the `select` element makes it possible for users to select more than one item in the list by holding down the Ctrl key while making a selection. The `size` attribute tells the browser to expand the height of the select box to four rows.

Look at the code for the favorite-color checkboxes:

```
<input name="color" type="checkbox" value="blue">Blue<br>
<input name="color" type="checkbox" value="red">Red<br>
<input name="color" type="checkbox" value="yellow">Yellow<br>
<input name="color" type="checkbox" value="green">Green<br>
<input name="color" type="checkbox" value="purple">Purple<br>
```

The `name` attribute of each input element is the same, which means that once the form is submitted, the values are passed to the action page specified by the `action` attribute of the form element. The code for the action page of the new form is shown in Listing 8-4. The code in bold illustrates how to capture values when there is more than one value in the form submission.

Listing 8-4 *The getParameterValues() method returns all of the values of a form element which has more than one value associated with it.*

---

formAction.jsp

```
<html>
<title>Form Action Page</title>

<body>

<table>
  <tr>
      <td>Your first name is <b><%=
request.getParameter("firstName") %></b></td>
  </tr>
  <tr>
```

Continued

Listing 8-4 *Continued*

```
        <td>Your last name is <b><%=
request.getParameter("lastName") %></b></td>
    </tr>
    <tr>
        <td>Your region is <b><%= request.getParameter("region")
%></b></td>
    </tr>
    <tr>
        <td>Your favorite colors are
            <%
            //print out the multiple values for the color
            String colors[] =
request.getParameterValues("color");
            for (int i = 0; i < colors.length; i++) {
            %>
                <b> <%= colors[i] %> </b>
            <% } %>
        </td>
    </tr>
    <tr>
        <td>Your age group is <b><%= request.getParameter("age")
%></b></td>
    </tr>
</table>

</body>
</html>
```

Listing 8-4 shows a new method for getting the value of a parameter that has multiple values: getParameterValues(). The first step is to declare an array of strings to hold the checkbox values selected in the form. Then, use a for loop to iterate through the array and print each value to the screen. The code also works for a multiple select box.

Using the getParameter() method to access information from a form that has multiple values does not work correctly; it only returns the first element in the array and ignores the other elements. However, the getParameterValues() method works fine with form elements that have only one value. If you are ever in doubt as to how many values a form element contains, use the getParameterValues() method to avoid confusion.

Accessing Form Elements: Another Method

10 Min. To Go

To get the value of a form element by using the getParameter() and getParameterValue() functions, you need to know the name of the form element. You can use the JSP page shown in Listing 8-5 to access the values of the form elements without explicitly coding the name of the form elements.

Listing 8-5 *formAction2.jsp*

```
<%@ page import="java.util.Enumeration" %>
<html>
<title>Form Action Page, Second Version</title>

<body>


<table border="1">
  <%
  //first loop gets the name of each form element
  for (Enumeration formNames = request.getParameterNames() ;
formNames.hasMoreElements() ;) {
String elementName = (String)(formNames.nextElement());
out.print("<tr><td>" + elementName + "</td><td>");
String formValues[] = request.getParameterValues(elementName);

//second loop gets all values for the given form name
for (int i = 0; i < formValues.length; i++) {
out.print("<b> " + formValues[i] + " </b>");
}
out.print("</td></tr>");
  }
  %>
</table>

</body>
</html>
```

The first line of the JSP code declares a for loop that loops through an Enumeration of the parameter names. An *Enumeration* is a Java object that implements the Enumeration interface. You can think of it as an array, but it has specific methods that allow you to see if there are additional elements (hasMoreElements()), and to move to the next element (nextElement()). For each time the code loops through the Enumeration object, it displays the name of the form item and the value of the form item.

 Look at the first line of the JSP page, <%@ page import="java.util.*" %>. This line of code enables you to reference the Enumeration object. Were you to remove the import from the JSP page, you would get an error message that states, "Class Enumeration not found."

Once you've put the name of the element name into a String variable, in this case elementName, call a new loop to get all of the values for that form element's name. The advantage of this method is that you can access and print to the screen all of the form items, but you've written less code to do it.

REVIEW

- Use methods of the request object to retrieve form submission inputs.
- The getParameter() method retrieves the single value of a form element.
- Use the getParameterValues() method to access a form element that has multiple values.
- Use the getParameterNames() method to access the names of the form elements that have been submitted by a form.

QUIZ YOURSELF

1. Why do you use the getParameterValues() function instead of the getParameter() function to access the value of a form element?
2. With which implicit object is the getParameter() function associated?
3. With JSP, how do you access the multiple values that are inherent with check-boxes?
4. What object is returned by calling the getParameterNames() method?
5. What data type does the getParameter() method return?

Using an Editor to Develop JSP

Session Checklist

✔ Exploit the power of an editor

✔ Use Allaire's HomeSite

*30 Min.
To Go*

I n this section, you will learn how to use Allaire's HomeSite application, a tool for authoring JSP pages and other text-based programs. Tools for Java development (called IDEs or integrated development environments) such as JBuilder have JSP support, but Allaire's HomeSite combines a powerful interface for client-side development in HTML and JavaScript with support for server-side JSP. In addition, it presents JSP code visually in a way that organizes it clearly. If Java coders and HTML coders are both working with the pages, they can tell at a glance what portions of the code are relevant to them.

Exploiting the Power of an Editor

Many elements of JSP, such as scriptlets, `jsp:useBean` tags, directives, and expressions code recur. Also, each JSP element has its own syntactical rules. Some have attributes similar to HTML tags, and sometimes the same conceptual entity is referred to with different attributes in different tags. For example, the instance of a class is referred to with the `id` attribute in the `jsp:useBean` element, but in the `jsp:getProperty` element, it is referred to with the `name` attribute. In addition, no matter how much you try to keep your JSP code separate from your HTML, the two become entangled at some point, complicating the development process. A good JSP editor can automate tasks performed repeatedly, prompt you with options for recalling syntax, and visually style your code.

Using Allaire's HomeSite

Allaire's HomeSite 4.5.2 supports JSP authoring. HomeSite is a commercially available product, but a free evaluation copy is available for download at http://commerce.allaire. com/download/index.cfm.

To install HomeSite once you've downloaded the setup file, double-click on the file to launch the HomeSite setup program. Follow the instructions for installation in the wizard.

Once you've installed the program, launch it. You should see a screen that looks like Figure 9-1.

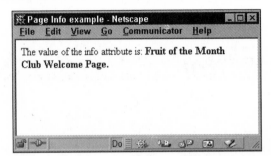

Figure 9-1   *The HomeSite Application has features to assist in authoring JSP pages.*

The interface should be familiar to anyone who has worked with Windows-based applications. Across the top of the screen are the pull-down menus and toolbar buttons. On the left is the Resource Tab, which functions like Windows Explorer. Use it to navigate to any directory structure visible to Windows. For now, navigate to your <tomcat-install>\webapps\ROOT directory. In the lower left frame, you should see the files that you have authored during the course of this book that exist in the directory. Double-clicking any one of them will open the file in the main portion of the interface, located just to the right of the Resource tab. This large area is where you compose your HTML and JSP pages. On the Tags menu, for example, are shortcuts for inserting different markup into your pages.

Create a new page by clicking File ⇨ New Document or pressing Ctrl+N on your keyboard. HomeSite will generate a blank HTML template for you, as shown in the following code:

blank.html

```
<!DOCTYPE HTML PUBLIC "-//W3C//DTD HTML 4.0 Transitional//EN">

<html>
<head>
   <title>Untitled</title>
</head>

<body>

</body>
</html>
```

To illustrate some of HomeSite's markup capabilities, add the phrase Testing HTML Markup between the opening and closing <body></body> tags. Highlight each word, one at a time, and select a different markup option from the Tags menu. HomeSite adds the HTML markup for you. HomeSite also provides a visual shortcut menu, located directly above the document window, as an alternative.

To change the editor settings of your HomeSite application, select Options ⇨ Settings ⇨ Editor from the pull-down menu. If you check the Allow undo after save checkbox, you can undo your code changes even after you have saved a document. Checking the Allow text drag-and-drop option will allow you to move code snippets in your pages with drag-and-drop, just as you can in Microsoft Word. Explore the different Settings items to customize your version of the application.

Using HomeSite to develop JSP

After you've acquainted yourself with HomeSite, create an HTML page and add a scriptlet that writes "With love from HomeSite" to the screen. The following codes shows you how to do this:

homesite.jsp

```
<!DOCTYPE HTML PUBLIC "-//W3C//DTD HTML 4.0 Transitional//EN">

<html>
<head>
    <title>Untitled</title>
</head>

<body>

<% out.println("With Love From HomeSite."); %>

</body>
</html>
```

Once you save the file to your working directory with a .jsp extension, you should notice HomeSite's color-coding feature. HomeSite will apply a default color scheme to code that it recognizes as JSP code. The default color scheme for JSP sets the background for all JSP code as gray; the HTML code is on a white background; some of the text of the JSP code is in red. With color coding, you can see at a glance whether the code on your page is server-side or client-side. On complex pages, this can be very useful.

Navigate to the <tomcat-install>\webapps\examples\jsp\cal directory and open the call.jsp file in HomeSite. Imagine you need to modify a single scriptlet amid the lengthy HTML code that surrounds it. With the help of the shaded background, the search narrows quickly. If you are collaborating with an HTML coder who knows nothing about JSP, it's easy for her to see that the gray areas are not her concern.

20 Min.
To Go

Customizing the JSP Color Code

While you have the call.jsp file open, notice how HomeSite automatically colors the various HTML tags differently depending on the tag type. HTML table tags are green, HTML comments are gray, and HTML form elements are orange. To edit a color scheme, click Options ⇨ Settings ⇨ Editor ⇨ Color Coding from the menu. A new pop-up window appears, listing every possible element that may exist on a JSP page, including elements that are not JSP, such as HTML, CSS, and JavaScript elements, as shown in Figure 9-2.

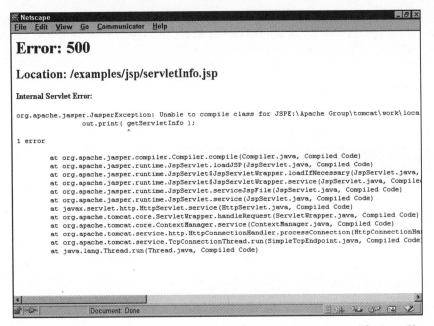

Figure 9-2   *You can customize the color scheme for JSP pages with HomeSite.*

In the list in the upper left corner of the pop-up window, select JSP Actions. In the Current Element group box next to the list on the right, you can change the color of the text, alter the background color, and change the font to bold, italic, or underline. Change the background color to yellow and check the Bold checkbox. Select OK on the current pop-up window, and then select OK on the Settings pop-up window. You should notice that the changes have taken effect and the line of code near the top of the page, `<jsp:useBean id="table" scope="session" class="cal.TableBean" />`, will have a bold font on a yellow background.

10 Min. To Go

Auto-completion, tag completion, and tag insight

Auto-completion inserts a code block into your page once the opening code fragment has been typed. To turn on Auto-Completion on, select Options ⇨ Settings ⇨ Editor ⇨ Auto Completion and check the box labeled Enable auto completion. Auto completion will end your beginning code fragments when they are typed on the page, such as appending an `%>` to end a scriptlet when you type in a `<%`.

Tag Completion completes HTML tags with their closing tags when they are typed into an editor. It also works for CSS. When tag completion is turned on, HomeSite will add a closing tag for the tags it recognizes, like `<html>`, `<body>`, and `<table>` tags.

Tag Insight displays a list of possible tags or attributes for a given element as a drop-down menu. To see how it works, open a new file and place your cursor on a blank line. Type <jsp:usebean, making sure to press the spacebar after the last letter. Notice that a short moment after you press the spacebar, HomeSite displays a drop-down list of the possible attributes for the `jsp:usebean` element. Click on one of the elements, and HomeSite

writes the attribute for you. You need only type a value for the attribute. If you'd like to add another attribute, press the spacebar after the first element, and the drop-down menu will appear again.

The JSP Toolbar

HomeSite provides a toolbar that facilitates the writing of JSP code (see Figure 9-3).

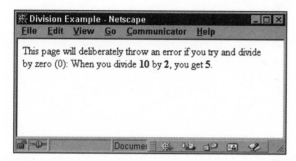

Figure 9-3 *The JSP toolbar allows you to add JSP elements quickly, without typing them.*

Some of the icons on the toolbar immediately place characters on the page: click the percentage sign, and the scriptlet symbols are placed in the active document where the cursor was positioned. Other icons, such as the page directive icon, represented by a picture of an open book, cause a pop-up window to appear, requesting additional information.

Generating a Servlet Template

In Session 3, we learned how to code a simple servlet. You can use the Servlet Wizard to create a servlet template. Select File ⇨ New... ⇨ Java ⇨ Servlet Wizard from the menu. A pop-up window appears and asks for the name of the servlet class you would like to create, the methods that are to be employed, and the destination directory to which you want to save the source code file. HomeSite creates the .java file and generates a template that has the appropriate `include` statements and the methods you chose to include.

Done!

REVIEW

- Change the color scheme of your JSP pages by selecting Options ⇨ Settings ⇨ Editor ⇨ Color Coding.
- Tag Completion completes code fragments.
- Auto-Completion completes HTML elements.
- Tag Insight presents the possible attributes for HTML tags or JSP elements.
- HomeSite will generate a servlet template for you.

Quiz Yourself

1. In what ways can an editing tool support developers?
2. What benefit does color coding provide?
3. What is Auto-Completion?
4. Which icon allows the user to compose the page directive?

SESSION

Handling Exceptions and Errors in JSP

Session Checklist

✔ Understand exception handling

✔ Debug JSP

**30 Min.
To Go**

Planning for errors is an important part of coding, whatever language you program in. In Java, there is a distinction between an Error object and an Exception object, though both are descendants of the java.lang.Throwable class. In Java lingo, a program is said to throw an exception (or an error) when an error occurs that disrupts its normal flow. An error is defined as an abnormal occurrence, such as a disk crash, that cannot be reasonably handled by the Java application. An exception is a type of error that can be reasonably handled by a Java application. There are many subclasses of exceptions, which correspond to the different types of problems that might occur during the running of a program. For a list of possible exceptions, refer to the javadoc documentation for the Exception class. This session covers basic exception handling and provides you with some tips for debugging your JSP pages.

Understanding Exception Handling

In Session 6, you learned that the two attributes of the page directive that make exception handling possible are the errorPage and isErrorPage attributes. The errorPage is the page to which the client request is forwarded once a JSP page throws an exception. If the value of the errorPage attribute begins with a forward slash (/), it is relative to the root directory of the Web site. The isErrorPage attribute should be set as true for the error page.

Listing 10-1 codes a page that intentionally throws an exception when the user chooses an incorrect option. Create the fauna.jsp page and place it in the <tomcat-install>\webapps\ROOT directory of your site. In order for the error page specified, error.jsp, to function correctly, you must also place it in the ROOT directory. Listing 10-1 uses the page directive to specify the error.jsp page as its error handling page.

Listing 10-1   *The value of errorPage attribute of the page directive specifies an error handling page.*

---

fauna.jsp

```jsp
<%@ page errorPage="/error.jsp" %>
<html>
<head>
  <title>Error Handling Example</title>
</head>
<%
String msg = "";
if (request.getParameter("Submit") != null) {
  String answer = request.getParameter("answer");
  if (answer.equals("Chrysanthemum")) {
      throw new Exception(answer + "is an example of flora.  Try
again.");
  } else {
      msg = "<tr><th>You just selected " + answer + ", an example of
fauna.</th></tr>";
  }
}
 %>
<body>
<form method="POST">
<table border="1">
<%=msg %>
<tr>
  <th>From the following list, select an example of fauna:</th>
</tr>
<tr>
  <td><input type="Radio" name="answer" value="Rabbit" checked>Rabbit</td>
</tr>
<tr>
  <td><input type="Radio" name="answer" value="Chrysanthemum"
>Chrysanthemum</td>
</tr>
<tr>
  <td><input type="Radio" name="answer" value="Deer" >Deer</td>
</tr>
<tr>
  <td><input type="Radio" name="answer" value="Border Terrier" >Border
Terrier</td>
</tr>
<tr>
  <td><input type="Radio" name="answer" value="Lynx" >Lynx</td>
</tr>
<tr>
  <td align="center"><input type="Submit" name="Submit"
value="Choose"></td>
```

```
</tr>
</table>
</form>
</body>
</html>
```

Figure 10-1 shows the results.

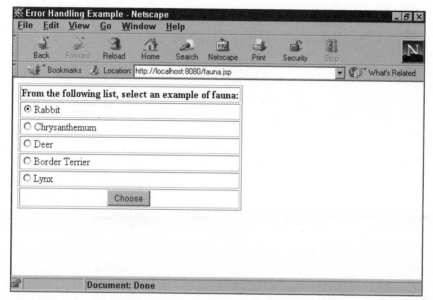

Figure 10-1   *The fauna.jsp page intentionally throws an exception when the user selects an incorrect option.*

The page sets up a test in which the user must select an item from a series of radio buttons. The user must select an example of fauna, or an entity from the animal kingdom, as opposed to the plant world. Because there is no action page specified in the form element, the page submits to itself when the user clicks the submit button.

At the top of the page, the code first tests the value of the submit button. If the Submit parameter has a value, then the user has submitted the form. Then, we test the value of the answer form element, to see if the user has selected the one example of plant life, Chrysanthemum. If not, the code generates a message to return to the user, indicating that he or she made a good choice. If the user has selected the incorrect option, the code throws an exception, or generates an Exception object, and forwards the HTTP request to the error page specified in the page directive at the top of the page. The code also passes to the Exception object a string containing a message that will ultimately be sent to the user.

Listing 10-2 contains the code for the error.jsp page, and Figure 10-2 shows the error page, rendered in a browser:

Listing 10-2   *The implicit exception object is available to error pages.*

error.jsp
```
<%@ page isErrorPage="true" %>
<html>
<head>
  <title>Error Page</title>
</head>
<body>
<h1>You have made an error.</h1>
<hr>
<h2>Description of Exception: <font
color="#FF0000"><%=exception.toString() %></font></h2>
<hr>
<h2>Message associated with Exception: <font
color="#FF0000"><%=exception.getMessage() %></font></h2>
<hr>
</body>
</html>
```

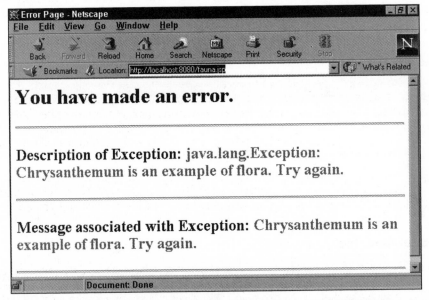

Figure 10-2   *The error.jsp page displays information about the error.*

In the `error.jsp` page, you can access the implicit `Exception` object, much in the same way you've accessed the implicit request or response objects in other JSP pages. You do not need to create an instance of the exception object; it has been created for you.

The first method in the page, `toString()`, returns a description of the `Throwable` object, including the class of the `Exception` object, `java.lang.Exception`. The second method, `getMessage()`, returns only the message associated with the exception, and not the name of the class to which the method belongs. The getMessage() method is a better method to use when displaying messages to your Web site users; the toString() method is useful for debugging.

You can use the printStackTrace() method for showing the entire stack trace that led up to the exception. This is a particularly useful method when you have pages calling other pages or other classes, because the stack trace will highlight the root cause of an error.

What is happening behind the scenes is that when the JSP engine converts a JSP page into a servlet, it places all of the JSP code and HTML into a try-catch block of code. The JSP code is placed in the try block, and the exception-handling code is placed in the catch block, as illustrated in the following example:

```
try {
  //JSP code is placed here
} catch (Exception e) {
  //exception handling code here
}
```

If you do not specify an error page as part of your page directive and the JSP page throws an exception, you will see the error page generated by Tomcat. While each JSP engine will have a different implementation of error and exception reporting, each should — at a minimum — show the page and the line number of the servlet code on which the exception occurred.

Debugging JSP

**20 Min.
To Go**

Debugging JSPs, and Web applications in general, is more difficult than debugging other types of programs. It's difficult to set breakpoints in your JSP page, and there's no effective way to step through the code you write. Moreover, because your JSP code is compiled automatically into a servlet, much of that code has not even been written by you. Some products, such as JBuilder Enterprise and IBM's Visual Age, tackle the debugging problem. These products must be purchased; they are not available free.

Errors may occur at translation time when the JSP page is compiled into a servlet or after compilation once the code is run, at runtime. In the following section, we'll look at examples of each type of error and see how information can be gathered to correct the problem.

Translation-Time Errors

To understand translation-time errors in JSP pages, think of how simple Java programs are written, not specifically for the Web. When creating a Java language program, you code the program, save the file with a .java extension, and then compile the program into a .class file, usually by invoking the javac compiler program from the command line. When coding a JSP page, you do not have to be concerned about manually compiling the program into a .class file; the JSP engine, Tomcat, does that for you the first time the JSP page is requested. A compiler error occurs when you request a JSP page that cannot be compiled because of coding errors within the page.

In the next example, we will purposely code a page with an error in it to illustrate the debugging process. Code the following debug.jsp page:

debug.jsp

```
<html>
<head>
  <title>Debugging JSP</title>
</head>

<body>
<% out.println("Hello World");
</body>
</html>
```

The close-scriptlet symbol, %>, is missing from the debug.jsp page. Save the debug.jsp page in the <tomcat-install>\webapps\ROOT directory and attempt to access the page. You will get a Tomcat-generated error page with a 500 error. A level-500 error signifies an error on the server that prevented the document you requested from being rendered.

The default Tomcat error page displays the JSP file in which the error occurred. The first line will normally pinpoint the original cause of the error and should look like the following line of code:

```
org.apache.jasper.compiler.ParseException: C:\jakarta-
tomcat\webapps\ROOT\debug.jsp(8,0) Unterminated <% tag
```

This line of code indicates that the error occurred in the debug.jsp page. The cause of the error, stated simply, was the Unterminated <% tag. Whenever possible, the error will show the line number of the generated servlet that caused the error. In the case of an unterminated <% tag, though, no servlet code is ever generated. Therefore, the error page reports the line number of the error in the JSP page, as opposed to the line number of the error in the compiled servlet.

In the debug.jsp example illlustrated earlier in this session, the unterminated <% tag makes it impossible for the JSP engine to compile the JSP page into a servlet. Fix the page by adding the closing %> tag to the end of the <% out.println("Hello World"); line.

In the next example, purposely do not initialize the counter variable that is supposed to execute a loop 10 times:

counterDebug.jsp

```
<html>
<title>Debug</title>
<%
for (int counter; counter < 10; counter++) {
  out.println(counter + "<br>");
}
%>
</body>
</html>
```

Running this page will produce an explicit error message from Tomcat:

```
org.apache.jasper.JasperException: Unable to compile class for
JSPC:\jakarta-
tomcat\work\localhost_8080\_0002fcounterDebug_0002ejspcounterDebug_jsp_0.j
ava:60: Variable counter may not have been initialized.
```

```
for (int counter; counter < 10; counter++) {
```

Unlike the error in the debug.jsp page, which prohibited the creation of a servlet, the counterDebug.jsp page generates a .java file that is the servlet version of the counterDebug.jsp page. The first part of the error message states that Tomcat was unable to compile the class, and then it lists the name and location of the .java file that was created from the counterDebug.jsp page. The .java file is located in the <tomcat-install>\work\localhost_8080 directory and has been given a long name. The name may be subtly different on your computer, but it will definitely contain the name of the JSP page, counterDebug. The number following the colon, 60, is the line number of the error in the generated servlet. Use HomeSite to navigate to the generated servlet and look at line 60. It contains the for (int counter; counter < 10; counter++) { line of code that caused the error.

The second part of the Tomcat-generated error message contains a message indicating the cause of the error; in this case, the variable counter may not have been initialized. You can correct the error by changing the line of code in the JSP page (as opposed to the servlet) to look like the following one:

```
for (int counter = 0; counter < 10; counter++) {
```

Runtime Errors

**10 Min.
To Go**

Runtime errors may occur after the JSP page has been translated. They are a result of a problem in the JSP page itself or in some code called by the JSP page, such as code in a JavaBean. Therefore, it is possible to compile a JSP page into a servlet, error free, and still leave the possibility for errors to occur.

To illustrate how Tomcat handles runtime errors without the defined error page, run the fauna.jsp example listed at the beginning of this session, but be sure to remove the page directive from the top of the page. The generated error page tells you that there was an internal servlet error; and the cause of the error, which is the same as the message we defined in the page, is displayed to the user. Underneath the first line of the error message is the *stack trace*. A stack trace is the trail of the sequential exceptions that were triggered when the servlet first threw the exception, and it is returned by the exception.printStackTrace() method. The stack trace indicates the method and object where each subsequent exception is thrown. In the debug.jsp example, the code that throws the error is actually within a method called by another method, probably in another object, which is called within another method, and so on.

When you encounter either compiler errors or runtime errors, follow these steps to troubleshoot the problem:

1. Look at the generated error page to see if it shows a traceable error in your JSP page.
2. If you cannot locate the error in the JSP page, navigate to the .java file that was generated when the JSP engine attempted to compile the page. Scan that file for errors.
3. If you cannot locate the error, compile the servlet from the command line and look at the generated error.

REVIEW

- Errors are triggered by abnormal events, such as a disk crash, and cannot be reasonably handled by a Java program.
- Exceptions are triggered by errors that occur within a Java program and can be handled by your JSP pages.
- The errorPage and isErrorPage attributes of the page directive are the most appropriate ways to manage exceptions in your JSP pages.
- Compiler errors are generated as a result of some violation of Java or JSP syntax.
- To debug your JSP pages, it is helpful to look at the servlet code that is generated from the JSP page.
- A stack trace is the trail of the sequential exceptions that were triggered when the servlet first threw the exception.

QUIZ YOURSELF

1. What might trigger a runtime error?
2. What is another name for translation-time errors?
3. What is the stack trace?
4. What is the name of the implicit object that is exposed in pages designated as error pages?

PART

II

Saturday Morning

1. Which method retrieves a single value from a request parameter?

2. What is the term for the extra characters after a page's URL?

3. If no action page is specified in a form, to which page does a form submit?

4. How do you make a series of radio buttons part of a single, mutually exclusive group?

5. Other than button and submit, what is the other type of form button?

6. Which implicit object holds the values of submitted form elements?

7. Which method retrieves the value of a form element that has multiple values?

8. Which page directive attribute allows you to specify the type of media that the page contains?

9. The getServletInfo() method returns the value of which directive attribute?

10. What is the mime type used to signify a Microsoft Word document?

11. The Error and Exception objects are descendants of which Java class?

12. What is the difference between translation-time errors and runtime errors?

13. True or false: A Java block must be opened and closed in a single scriptlet.

14. Which attributes of the @page directive have to do with error handling?

15. What is the default value of the language attribute of the @page directive?

16. True or false: JSP pages support sessions by default.

17. Name four attributes that can be used on all types of form elements.

18. What is the return value for the getParameterValues() method?

19. Which method of the exception class returns a message describing the exception?

20. Which method of the exception class is used to send the stack trace that led up to the exception to the error output stream?

PART

III

Saturday
Afternoon

SESSION

11

Introducing JavaBeans

Session Checklist

✔ Understand the rules for using JavaBeans

✔ Develop JavaBeans

**30 Min.
To Go**

J SP technology is designed to interface with JavaBeans in a way that can significantly accelerate the development of an application. You've seen that you can embed Java code directly into your JavaServer Pages. While this is a powerful feature of JSP pages, it is not always the optimal approach. Code can often be complex, and the mixture of Java code, HTML, and client-side JavaScript can make for messy pages that are difficult to understand. Using Beans promotes a strong division of labor in the development effort, which often involves client-side and server-side programmers. Hiding server code that would otherwise be present in scriptlets in a Bean results in JSPs with a cleaner appearance, and two developers can work with a greater degree of independence.

Up to this point, you have focused on the code within the JSP pages. The real power behind JSP is its ability to speak to JavaBeans, which are Java classes that adhere to a set of specific rules. In this session, you will learn what JavaBeans are and how they came to be.

Understand the Rules for Using JavaBeans

In programming, standards facilitate portability. Let's explore what this means using the metaphor of plugs and electrical sockets. If every manufacturer of electrical appliances made plugs in different widths and lengths, buying a new electrical device would be difficult: each time, you would have to make sure that the plug's dimensions matched the slots in the socket in your wall. To extend the metaphor, some devices might not be made with plugs that match certain outlets, limiting one's ability to use those appliances. Thankfully, as a result of standards in the United States, all electrical appliances plug into any electrical socket in an identical way.

In the world of information technology, the standards for application development are not as concrete as they are for electrical appliances. There are a variety of different platforms on which to program, and a variety of languages to use for the coding. As a result, application developers have found themselves coding and recoding the same functionality, just so that it will run on different platforms.

Components are standardized building blocks of software that provide specific services through an interface to clients (in this case we are talking about other pieces of code), effectively hiding the complexity of the work being done from the component's client. Using components in software programs provides for a modular approach to building large applications by creating small applications that accomplish small pieces of the overall task. Components can be thought of as objects that are designed with an eye toward reusability. Also, they typically follow some sort of standard in their construction, and this increases their ability to be quickly and easily integrated into an existing application, all in the interest of a "snap together" approach to software development.

If you've programmed in Visual Basic, Delphi, or PowerBuilder, you have seen component architecture at work. With any of these tools, the developer doesn't have to create the code to implement a drop-down list or a select button; she just drops the control onto her palette and modifies the associated properties. The pre-built components have the capability to process the entries in the property sheets and adapt the control to the specific requirements of the application. Another example of the component approach is Microsoft's Component Object Model (COM), an architecture in which components developed in C++ or Visual Basic can be plugged into an application by exposing its methods to other objects.

JavaBeans provide a standard for developing reusable, portable components in Java. The Java language is part of a solution to the problem of lack of standards in application development. Java's promise is that it can be written once and run on any platform. With the Java language also comes a standard framework for putting an application together, of which JavaServer Pages are a part. JavaBeans provide the cornerstone of what Sun refers to as the JavaBeans Component Architecture, an interlocking network of components that communicate with one another in a standardized way. The JavaBeans Component architecture, in theory, will run on any operating system and within any application environment.

JavaBeans are like standardized software building blocks that interface to other code components while hiding the internal implementation of their work. In object-oriented programming, the concept of *encapsulation* means that each object has the ability to encapsulate the logic it uses to perform its task, without informing other objects of the specifics of what is going on. Each object is a small application that can effectively work in tandem with other objects, each performing a specific task, and ultimately making up a large application.

JavaBeans Defined

**20 Min.
To Go**

Generally speaking, Beans are associated with properties, methods, and events. While there exists a lengthy specification for Beans, they are not unlike any of the other Java classes you have coded. In fact, you may have already coded a JavaBean without realizing it. A JavaBean is a software component that follows two very basic rules:

- A JavaBean must expose its properties with `get` and `set` methods. For example, if a JavaBean had a property called `color`, it would set the color by calling the `setColor()` method; it would return `color` by calling the `getColor()` method.

- A JavaBean must have a no-argument constructor, which means that it is possible to create an instance of the JavaBean without passing it any parameters.

Methods are used to get and set the values of a Bean's properties. The methods used to retrieve the values are known as *accessor methods,* and the methods used to modify the values are known as *mutators.* Accessor and mutator methods are the technical terms for what are known in the trade as "getters" and "setters," respectively. Wrapping access to instance variables in methods provides the programmer with the capability to constrain the manipulation of a variable so that, for example, a variable that is supposed to hold the age of a person could not be set to a negative number. In addition, dependencies can be enforced: If a value on which other values depend is changed, the component can take steps to ensure that the change is reflected in all necessary places.

Creating the Vegetable Bean

Let's take the example of a class called Vegetable that has a property, color. While it is possible to have a class with a single public attribute, color, the JavaBean uses getters and setters to expose the otherwise private color. The class definition shown in Listing 11-1 restricts access to the color property to the methods getColor() and setColor().

Listing 11-1   *The Vegetable.java class is a JavaBean.*

Vegetable.java

```
class Vegetable {

    private String color;

    public String getColor() {
        return this.color;
    }

        public void setColor(String newColor) {
            this.color = newColor;
        }
}
```

Any conditions appropriate to the checking or the changing of the color property can be included in the methods themselves. Using get and set methods has always been a standard practice, even before the advent of JavaBeans. The creators of the JavaBean specification, recognizing the use of getters and setters and also acknowledging that Java builder tools are common among developers, wanted these tools to be able to recognize the properties and methods of Java components in a standard way. Now, virtually all Java builder tools have the capability to recognize the getter and setter methods that expose the attributes of a Bean. For example, a builder tool would be able to change and retrieve the color property of the Vegetable Bean in Listing 11-1 by using the Bean's getter and setter methods. *Introspection* is the process by which Beans explicitly expose their methods, properties, and events to the builder tool or to the engine that is executing the Bean code. Servlet engines use introspection in order to copy values from the request stream into the appropriate Bean properties.

Developing JavaBeans

**10 Min.
To Go**

Listing 11-2, the Fruit.java class, is a JavaBean that we will be using in Sessions 12 and 13. Code the Bean and store it in your <tomcat-install>\webapps\ROOT\WEB-INF\classes directory. To compile the Bean, open up a command prompt and navigate to its directory using cd commands. Type in javac Fruit.java following command once inside the classes directory.

Listing 11-2

The Fruit class is a JavaBean.Fruit.java

```java
public class Fruit {
    private String fruitName;
    private int quantity;
    private String color;
    private boolean isCitrus;
    private float price;

    public String getFruitName(){
        return this.fruitName;
    }

    public void setFruitName(String name){
        this.fruitName=name;
    }

    public int getQuantity (){
        return this.quantity;
    }

    public void setQuantity (int quantity){
        this.quantity=quantity;
    }

    public String getColor(){
        return this.color;
    }

    public void setColor(String color){
      this.color=color;
    }

    public float getPrice(){
        return this.price;
    }

    public void setPrice(float price){
      this.price=price;
    }
```

```
public boolean isCitrus(){
    return this.citrus;
}

public void setCitrus(boolean citrus){
    this.citrus=citrus;
}

}
```

In the Fruit class, because we did not explicitly declare a constructor, the no-args constructor exists by default. Keep this in mind, because if we had written a constructor that *did* take an argument, the Java compiler wouldn't create the no-argument constructor, and thus, the class would no longer be a Bean.

A builder tool could look at the Fruit class and know that it has a fruitName property, a quantity property, a color property, a price property, and an isCitrus property, just by looking at the Bean's methods. Each property has two methods associated with it, where the method's name begins with a lowercase letter and the property name begins with an uppercase letter. The observant among you will notice a deviation from the naming convention in the case of Citrus. The accessor method is called isCitrus() instead of getCitrus(). This is because the return type is a boolean value, so it is more appropriate to use an is method because you are checking a condition rather than retrieving a value.

Done!

REVIEW

- Standards are important to promote portability and reusability.
- JavaBeans are pieces of code designed to be readily reused as parts of different applications.
- Introspection is the process by which JavaBeans use accessors and mutators, also known as getters and setters, to expose its properties.

QUIZ YOURSELF

1. Why are standards important when developing software?
2. What is a mutator method?
3. What is an accessor method?
4. Which return type uses a different naming convention for accessor methods?

JavaBeans and JSP

Session Checklist

✔ Include a Bean in a JSP page

✔ Work with Bean properties on JSPs

**30 Min.
To Go**

In the previous session we looked at the component approach to development, and we saw how this is accomplished in Java using JavaBeans. JavaBeans play an important role in JSP, as they allow the processing of data to be abstracted from the JSP pages, creating a more effective separation of presentation and logic. In this session, we look at the basic syntax for including Beans and interacting with them from the JSP page.

Including a Bean in a JSP Page

We have discussed components and the advantages of implementation hiding in application development: namely, implementation hiding provides a more organized approach to development by isolating functionality into discrete software components. By using JavaBeans with JSP, developers can effectively separate the presentation layer (the JSP pages themselves) from the logic and processing contained within the Beans. The JSP/JavaBeans relationship brings a desirable leanness to a JSP application.

Use the `jsp:useBean` element to include a Bean in a JSP page, according to the following syntax:

```
<jsp:useBean id="featuredFruit" class="Fruit" />
```

The `class` attribute names the class of object to be instantiated, and the `id` attribute is the variable name used to reference the object. Notice that the `jsp:useBean` element is case-sensitive, that it requires the use of quotation marks (") around attribute values, and that it must be closed. In the preceding example, the slash (/) at the end of the element actually closes the element with XML-compliant syntax. The following code illustrates an alternative method of closing the `jsp:useBean` element:

```
<jsp:useBean id="featuredFruit" class="Fruit" >
</jsp:useBean>
```

JSP is very rigorous about the closing of elements. Failure to comply will result in a compiler error.

By using the jsp:useBean syntax, the developer has alerted the container that this object is a Bean, which enables the additional capabilities when working with the object.

To get a sense of the code that the jsp:useBean element creates when it is compiled into a servlet, look at Listing 12-1.

Listing 12-1 *When compiled into a servlet, the jsp:useBean element generates this code.*

```
featuredFruit = (Fruit) pageContext.getAttribute
("featuredFruit",PageContext.PAGE_SCOPE);
  if ( featuredFruit == null ) {
jspx_specialfeaturedFruit = true;
  try {
featuredFruit = (Fruit)
Beans.instantiate(this.getClass().getClassLoader(), " Fruit");
} catch (Exception exc) {
  throw new ServletException (" Cannot create bean of class "+" Fruit");
  }
pageContext.setAttribute("featuredFruit", featuredFruit,
PageContext.PAGE_SCOPE);
  }
```

The jsp:useBean element will first look for an instance of the Bean in the page context before it creates a new instance of the Bean.

This syntax enables the inclusion of Bean objects into JSP pages. However, it is rarely used alone. Typically, the Bean's properties are manipulated on the JSP page. The taglet syntax supports this activity also.

Working with Bean Properties on JSPs

**20 Min.
To Go**

Beans have properties and methods that can be accessed in your JSP pages. To access the value of a Bean property, use the following syntax, where featuredFruit is the name of the Bean that has been instantiated with the jsp:useBean element, and color is the name of the property you are trying to access:

```
<jsp:getProperty name="featuredFruit" property="color" />
```

This jsp:getProperty tag causes the following code to be generated in the servlet:

```
((Fruit)pageContext.findAttribute("featuredFruit")).getColor()
```

The value of the property attribute of the element is "color," but when compiled, the JSP container changes the lowercase "c" to an uppercase "C" in the getters and setters by convention. When Tomcat tries to compile the generated JSP page, the getColor()method must exist on the Fruit class or a compiler error will result.

In the `jsp:useBean` syntax, the name of the Bean is referenced with the `id` attribute, whereas in the `jsp:getProperty` element, and similarly with the `jsp:setProperty` element, the attribute used to identify the variable name is `name`.

Setting Properties on Beans

To set the property of a Bean, use the `jsp:setProperty` element according to the following syntax, where the `name` attribute describes the name of the Bean instantiated with the `jsp:useBean` element, the `property` attribute describes the Bean property being modified, and the `value` attribute contains the new value of the Bean property:

```
<jsp:setProperty name="featuredFruit" property="color" value="red" />
```

Often, the `jsp:setProperty` element is used to set the property of a Bean in response to some user action, such as the submission of a form. You might guess that the preceding code would be executed after a user submits a form that asked for a color. In this case, `jsp:setProperty` would be found at the top of JSP pages, where it is used to make an assignment based on some user action prior to the previous request's being submitted.

The `jsp:setProperty` element has a special feature that supports the assigning of a dynamic value to a Bean's property; to assign a dynamic value to a Bean's property, use the `param` attribute instead of the value. The `param` attribute directs the JSP container to look for a request parameter with the value specified and assigns the value to the Bean that is associated with the request. If a user had selected red in a form as the color of fruit they were interested in, the request stream would contain a name=`value` pair, `color=red`, and the following code would assign the value of the `color` request parameter to the `color` property of the `featuredFruit` Bean:

```
<jsp:setProperty name="featuredFruit" property="color" param="color" />
```

This is the same as

```
<jsp:setProperty name="featuredFruit" property="color"
value='<%= request.getParameter("color") %>' />
```

In addition to the cleanness of the first approach, it has the advantage of automatically performing simple type casts. In the case of the second example, this feature is not needed because the request stream provides a string. However, if instead we were concerned with the `quantity` property of a Bean, we would need to perform an additional type cast to convert the value to a double, because the `getParameter()` method always returns a string.

A Bean Example: Creating an Order Display Page

10 Min. To Go

In the next example, we will create a screen from which users can select a fruit and specify a quantity. They can then submit their order, which takes them to a simple confirmation screen that shows them what they have ordered and what it will cost. We can use our Fruit Bean from the last chapter (see Listing 12-2).

Listing 12-2   *The Fruit.java Bean has getters and setters to access its properties.*

Fruit.java
```java
public class Fruit {
   private String fruitName;
   private int quantity;
   private String color;
   private boolean isCitrus;
   private float price;

   public String getFruitName(){
    return this.fruitName;
   }

   public void setFruitName(String name){
    this.fruitName=name;
   }

   public int getQuantityInPounds(){
    return this.quantity;
   }

   public void setQuantityInPounds(int quantity){
    this.quantity=quantity;
   }

   public String getColor(){
    return this.color;
   }

   public void setColor(String color){
     this.color=color;
   }

   public float getPrice(){
    return this.price;
   }

   public void setPrice(float price){
   this.price=price;
   }

   public boolean isCitrus(){
    return this.isCitrus;
   }

   public void setCitrus(boolean isCitrus){
   this.isCitrus=isCitrus;
   }

}
```

Refer to Session 11 for more information about installing your Beans.

Listing 12-3 shows an HTML form that asks users to select the quantity of the featuredFruit they wish to order. For the purpose of this example, assume that some data about the fruit, such as the name and the color, has been determined prior to requesting this screen.

Listing 12-3   *The action page for the FruitOrder.html is the confirm.jsp page, which sets the Bean's properties.*

FruitOrder.html
```
<HTML>
<body>
<h1>Fruit Order Form</h1>

Fruit: Mango<br>
Color: Orange<br>
Price Per Pound: $5.95 <br>
<form action="confirm.jsp" method="post">
Number of pounds: <input type="text" name="quantity"><br>
<input type="submit" value="Order Fruit" >
</form>
</body>
</html>
```

match name on page 112.

Users specify how many pounds of mangos they wish to order and submit this form (see Figure 12-1). Notice that we give the form field the same name as the corresponding Bean property, quantityInPounds.

Listing 12-4 shows confirm.jsp, which will set the properties of the Fruit Bean and display a confirmation of the order.

Listing 12-4   *The confirm.jsp page uses the jsp:setProperty method to set the properties of the Fruit Bean.*

```
<jsp:useBean id="orderedFruit" class="Fruit" />

<jsp:setProperty name="orderedFruit" property="fruitName" value="Mango" />

<jsp:setProperty name="orderedFruit" property="color" value="Orange" />

<jsp:setProperty name="orderedFruit" property="price" value="5.95" />
```

Continued

Listing 12-4   *Continued*

```
<jsp:setProperty name="orderedFruit" property="quantity" param="quantity"
/>

<HTML>
<body>
<h1>Your Fruit Order</h1>
<br><br>
Fruit: <jsp:getProperty name="orderedFruit" property="fruitName"/><br>
Color: <jsp:getProperty name="orderedFruit" property="color" /><br>
Price: $<jsp:getProperty name="orderedFruit" property="price" /><br>
Quantity: <jsp:getProperty name="orderedFruit" param="quantity" /><br>
Total: $<%=orderedFruit.getPrice()*orderedFruit.getQuantity() %>
<p></p>
<a href="FruitOrder.html">Return to order form to adjust quantity</a>
</body>
</html>
```

passed param from page 111

This code produces the output shown in Figure 12-2 when accessed from the FruitOrder. html file with a quantity of 9 placed in the form field. In Figure 12-2, the user has entered a quantity of 10. The page calculates the total price by multiplying the quantity of fruit by its unit cost.

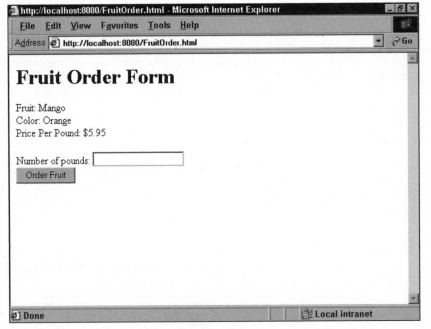

Figure 12-1   *The FruitOrder.html page collects the number of pounds from the user.*

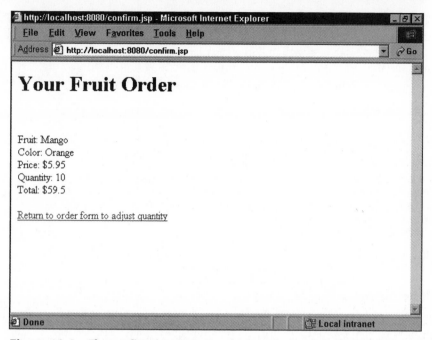

Figure 12-2 *The confirm.jsp page sets the properties of the Fruit Bean.*

In the confirm.jsp page, we used the jsp:setProperty element in two different ways. For the fruitName, color, and price properties, we used hard-coded values. In a real-world situation, these properties would probably be collected on earlier screens or retrieved from a database at an earlier point. The fourth instance of the jsp:setProperty element uses the param attribute to copy the value of the quantityInPounds form field to the quantity property of the Bean.

property="*"

The asterisk (*) will set all of the properties of a given Bean to the values that have been sent to the server as part of the request stream. For example, if you collected a series of values from form elements, the following syntax would set each of the properties in a given Bean to the values of the form fields submitted in the form, as long as the names of the form fields corresponded to Bean properties:

```
<jsp:setProperty name="Fruit" property="*" />
```

In order for the property="*" to work correctly, you must carefully ensure that your Bean properties match the form field names. In the next session, you will see an example of automatically assigning Bean properties using the property attribute.

Done!

REVIEW

- JavaBeans can be combined with JSP in ways that dramatically streamline JSP development and effectively isolate application logic from presentation logic.
- The jsp:useBean element instantiates a Bean inside of your JSP page.
- The jsp:getProperty element accesses a Bean's property.
- The jsp:setProperty element sets the value of a Bean's property.
- Substitute the param attribute for the value attribute of the jsp:setProperty element to use a request parameter instead of a hard-coded value.
- Setting the value of the property attribute to an asterisk (*) in the jsp:setProperty element enables you to copy all of the values of the request parameters to a Bean's properties, as long as the property names are identical to the names of the request parameters.

QUIZ YOURSELF

1. What are the syntax rules for coding JSP elements?
2. What does the name attribute of the jsp:getProperty element designate?
3. What does the param attribute of the jsp:setProperty cause to occur?
4. Request parameters are always strings. What happens when the jsp:setProperty element uses the param attribute to indicate that a Bean property that is a float should be set from a request parameter?

Advanced Techniques for Working with Beans

Session Checklist

✔ Share Beans

✔ Create Beans conditionally

**30 Min.
To Go**

As we've seen, Beans are useful for storing information that can be used in a single JSP page. However, Beans can be created on one JSP page and, depending on the scope assigned to the Bean, can be utilized in other JSP pages within the same application. In this session, we will explain the implications of a Bean's scope.

Sharing Beans

Beans may be used by multiple pages across a user session, or across an entire application. What determines whether or where a Bean is shared is its *scope*. A Bean's scope can be set as a attribute of the jsp:useBean element as follows:

```
<jsp:useBean id="orderedFruit" class="Fruit"  scope="session"/>
```

The scope attribute can have a value of page, session, request, or application, and we will go over the meaning of each in this session. In the example above, the Bean object bound to the reference orderedFruit will be available across a user's session.

page

The default value of a Bean's scope is page, the most limited of the scope types. The Bean with a page scope is alive only for the length of the call to that servlet's service() method. Each subsequent call to the servlet returns a completely new instance of the Bean.

When we give the Bean a page scope, the JSP container puts a copy of the Bean in an object called `PageContext` which is referenced by the implicit variable, `pageContext`; the `PageContext` is instantiated in the servlet when the JSP page is first compiled. Using the `getAttribute()` method of the `PageContext` object with the name of the Bean instance as a parameter returns a pointer to the Bean. Any changes to the underlying Bean are instantly available to any other variable that points to the Bean.

request

A Bean with a request scope means that in addition to its status as a local variable in the servlet `service()` method, the Bean is to be placed in the current `HttpServletRequest` object. In simple cases where a single JSP page is handling an entire request, the request scope is equivalent to the page scope. In more sophisticated architectures where several objects are handling a single request, a Bean with a request scope makes that Bean available to all the objects handling the request.

session

If the scope of the Bean is set to session, the Bean can be accessed from any page that the user accesses inside a single session.

20 Min.
To Go

Refer to Session 16 for a more in-depth discussion of sessions.

All JSP pages have a reference to the `HttpSession` object in an implicit object called session. To retrieve a Bean from the session object, the `getAttribute()` methods is used with the instance name of the Bean as a parameter.

By setting the value of the session attribute of the page directive to false, a page can be excluded from an `HttpSession`, which means that it won't have access to the implicit session object.

application

If the scope attribute is set to application, the Bean is available to all servlets (and JSPs) running on a given servlet engine. Some servers, such as Tomcat, allow the designation of distinct Web applications, which allow multiple applications to run in a partitioned fashion on a single servlet engine. In this case, Beans given application scope are accessible only from within the given Web application.

To retrieve a Bean with application scope, call the `getAttribute()` method of the application. The application object is another implicit object in JSP pages, similar to the session- and `pageContext` object.

**10 Min.
To Go**

Decisions about which scope to assign to a Bean must be made carefully based on the needs of various resources to make use of the Beans. In the next section we'll look at the servlet engine's ability to create new Beans when needed, or use existing ones where available.

Creating Beans Conditionally

In the previous session, we said that the `jsp:useBean` element creates a Bean of the specified type and binds it to the variable name specified by the `id` attribute. This is only partially true; the `jsp:useBean` element behaves in this way *only* if a Bean of specified type and name does not already exist in the specified scope. If such a Bean does already exist because it has been created earlier by another JSP or servlet, then the existing Bean is used. Also, if an attribute of that name already exists, but it isn't the correct type, you get a `ClassCastException`. *Conditional Bean creation* means that Beans are not always instantiated anew; we can embed within our code conditions that determine the circumstances for the creation of a new instance of a Bean.

It is possible to include initialization code for the Beans on a JSP that is executed only at the time the Bean is created. The following syntax is normally used to create a Bean, or call for an existing Bean to be used:

```
<jsp:useBean id="orderedFruit" class="Fruit"  scope="session"/>
```

However, the following is also possible:

```
<jsp:useBean id="orderedFruit" class="Fruit"  scope="session">
    . . . initialization code here
</jsp:useBean>
```

The code between the two `jsp:useBean` tags in the second case is executed only if a Bean is created. If an existing Bean is found and used, this code is ignored. Let's look at an example that uses this technique.

Listing 13-1 is the Fruit.java file we used in Session 12. In the next example, we will create a Fruit object and set its properties. This is the type of exercise that might be executed by an administrator who wanted to input a fruit into a database.

Listing 13-1   *The Fruit.java Bean has getters and setters to access its properties.*

Fruit.java
```
public class Fruit {
    private String fruitName;
    private int quantity;
    private String color;
    private boolean isCitrus;
    private float price;

    public String getFruitName(){
```

Continued

Listing 13-1

Continued

```
        return this.fruitName;
    }
    public void setFruitName(String name){
        this.fruitName=name;
    }

    public int getQuantityInPounds(){
        return this.quantity;
    }

    public void setQuantityInPounds(int quantity){
        this.quantity=quantity;
    }

    public String getColor(){
        return this.color;
    }

    public void setColor(String color){
      this.color=color;
    }

    public float getPrice(){
        return this.price;
    }

    public void setPrice(float price){
        this.price=price;
    }

    public boolean isCitrus(){
        return this.isCitrus;
    }

    public void setCitrus(boolean isCitrus){
        this.isCitrus=isCitrus;
    }

}
```

Listing 13-2 shows a form used by a site administrator to add a fruit to the database. In the page, the user sets the values for the different properties of a given item.

Listing 13-2 *The catalogForm.html page collects information that is used to set the properties of the Fruit Bean.*

catalogForm.html

```html
<html>
<head>
    <title>Add Fruit to the Catalog</title>
</head>

<body>
<h1>Add Fruit to the Catalog</h1>
<form method="post" action="addToCatalog.jsp">
<table border="1">
    <tr>
        <th bgcolor="#c0c0c0">Name</th>
        <td align="right"><input type="text" name="fruitName"
size="10"></td>
    </tr>
    <tr>
        <th bgcolor="#c0c0c0">Quantity</th>
        <td align="right"><input type="text" name="quantityInPounds"
size="10"></td>
    </tr>
    <tr>
        <th bgcolor="#c0c0c0">Color</th>
        <td align="right"><input type="text" name="color" size="10"></td>
    </tr>
    <tr>
        <th bgcolor="#c0c0c0">Citrus?</th>
        <td align="right">
            <select name="citrus" >
                <option value="true">True
                <option value="false">False
            </select>
        </td>
    </tr>
    <tr>
        <th bgcolor="#c0c0c0">Price</th>
        <td align="right"><strong>$</strong> <input type="text" name="price"
size="10"></td>
    </tr>
    <tr>
        <th bgcolor="#c0c0c0" colspan="2"><input type="submit" name="Submit"
value="Add To Inventory"></h>
    </tr>
</table>
</form>

</body>
</html>
```

The `catalogForm.html` page submits to the `addToCatalog.jsp` page in Listing 13-3.

Listing 13-3   *The addToCatalog.jsp page collects information that is used to set the properties of the Fruit Bean.*

---

addToCatalog.jsp

```
<jsp:useBean id="fruitItem" class="Fruit" scope="page">
    <jsp:setProperty name="fruitItem" property="*"/>
    <%
        //Add code here to insert Item into database
    %>
</jsp:useBean>

<html>
<head>
    <title>Add Fruit to the Catalog</title>
</head>

<body>
<h1>Add Fruit to the Catalog</h1>
<form method="post" action="catalogForm.html">
<h2>You've added the following fruit: </h2>
<table border="1">
    <tr>
        <th bgcolor="#c0c0c0">Name</th>
        <td align="right"><jsp:getProperty name="fruitItem"
property="fruitName" /></td>
    </tr>
    <tr>
        <th bgcolor="#c0c0c0">Quantity</th>
        <td align="right"><jsp:getProperty name="fruitItem"
property="quantityInPounds" /></td>
    </tr>
    <tr>
        <th bgcolor="#c0c0c0">Color</th>
        <td align="right"><jsp:getProperty name="fruitItem" property="color"
/></td>
    </tr>
    <tr>
        <th bgcolor="#c0c0c0">Citrus?</th>
        <td align="right"><jsp:getProperty name="fruitItem"
property="citrus" /></td>
    </tr>
    <tr>
        <th bgcolor="#c0c0c0">Price</th>
        <td align="right"><strong>$</strong><jsp:getProperty
name="fruitItem" property="price" /></td>
    </tr>
    <tr>
        <th bgcolor="#c0c0c0" colspan="2"><input type="submit" name="Submit"
value="Add Another Fruit"></h>
```

```
    </tr>
 </table>
 </form>

 </body>
 </html>
```

At the top of the page, we use the `jsp:useBean` element to create an instance of the Fruit Bean. Between the opening and closing tags of the `jsp:useBean` element, we use the `jsp:setProperty` element with the `property` attribute set to asterisk (*) to set each property of the Bean to the form inputs submitted in the prior form. The code between the opening and closing `jsp:useBean` tags will get executed only when the Bean class is instantiated.

Since our Bean has only a page scope, each time the user comes to the `addToCatalog.jsp` page, the Bean does not exist , and so the `jsp:setProperty` code is executed. To see the effects of conditional Bean creation, change the value of the session attribute of the `jsp:useBean` element from page to session. The first line of your page should look like this:

```
<jsp:useBean id="fruitItem" class="Fruit" scope="session">
```

When you go through the exercise of setting the properties of the fruit a second time with a session-scoped Bean, you will notice that it is impossible to change the properties of the Bean after it has been set once. The reason is that when a Bean is instantiated with session scope, it does not get instantiated again until a new session begins.

REVIEW

Done!

- The scope of Beans may be set to control the sharing of Beans across a page, request, session, or application.

- Creation of Beans with the `jsp:useBean` element is conditional. When the JSP container encounters a `jsp:useBean` element, it checks the specified scope (the page is the default) to determine if a Bean with the correct name and scope already exists. If so, it uses this Bean. If not, it creates a new Bean.

- Initialization code for a Bean can be included in the body of the `jsp:useBean` tag. This code is executed if and only if the `jsp:useBean` element causes a Bean to be created.

QUIZ YOURSELF

1. What value must the property attribute of the `setProperty` element have to cause Bean properties to be set automatically from the request stream?
2. What are the various scopes that can be assigned to a Bean?
3. Under what circumstances does the `jsp:useBean` element not cause a Bean to be created?
4. Under what circumstances is code in the body of a `jsp:useBean` element executed?

JSP and JavaScript

Session Checklist

✔ Use JSP to populate JavaScript

✔ Write complementary client-side and server-side code

**30 Min.
To Go**

JSP is only one of the tools you have at your disposal to make your Web applications interactive. With JavaScript, code that is run at the browser instead of at the server allows a user to interact with your page without having to send requests and responses back and forth to the server. While JavaServer Pages and JavaScript may sound similar, they are very different languages. In this session, we explore how JSP and JavaScript can be used together in your pages. You will examine a few examples that use JSP to populate a JavaScript and learn how JavaScript can work behind the scenes to modify a request sent to the server. This session assumes a basic knowledge of JavaScript, including familiarity with structuring your scripts, document events, and the Document Object Model (DOM).

Using JSP to Populate JavaScript

You can embed JSP code into your JavaScript code in precisely the same manner you would embed it into HTML. In this section, we will embed an expression into a simple JavaScript. Consider the example shown in Listing 14-1.

Listing 14-1 *You can embed JSP code into JavaScript, just as you would embed it in HTML.*

```
javascript.jsp
<html>
<head>
<script language ="javascript">
  <%!String msg = "Hello User!"; %>
  function sayHello() {
      alert("<%=msg%>");
  }
```

Continued

Listing 14-1   *Continued*

```
</script>
</head>
<body>
<h1>A custom JavaScript greeting</h1>
<input type="Button" onclick="sayHello();" value="Click Me!">
</body>
</html>
```

Inside the opening and closing <script></script> tags, we've created a method, sayHello(), that is executed by the browser. Inside sayHello(), we've put a JSP expression, <%=msg%>. Remember how JSP is executed: First, the servlet engine evaluates anything it recognizes as JSP, or those elements that are inside opening and closing <% %> tags and other JSP elements. It then sends a response to the browser that contains only browser-readable code — in this case, a combination of JavaScript and HTML. By the time the page reaches the browser, the JavaScript looks like the following code:

```
<script language ="javascript">

    function sayHello() {
    alert("Hello User!");
    }
</script>
```

The blank line after the first script element is where our JSP declaration was, which assigned a value to the msg variable. The parameter for the JavaScript alert() method, originally a JSP expression, has also been evaluated.

Creating the FruitMap.java Class

The next example is a more realistic scenario of how JSP can be used to populate JavaScript. The fruitPrice.jsp page reflects a situation in which a user may select a given fruit, see its price per pound, and then calculate a total price based on the number of pounds selected. The page uses a JavaBean called FruitMap, and the code is as follows:

Listing 14-2   *The FruitMap.java class extends the java.util.HashMap class and will store inventory information.*

FruitMap.java
```
public class FruitMap extends java.util.HashMap{}
```

The FruitMap class is actually HashMap object. We will use the FruitMap class to store the name and price of each fruit we are going to list on the site. Ordinarily, the names and the prices of the fruit would be stored in a database, but because you do not learn about retrieving information from a database until Session 20, we will use the HashMap to store our fruit information. In order for the fruitPrice.jsp page in Listing 14-2 to work, first code the FruitMap.java file and save it to your <tomcat-install>\webapps\ROOT\Web-Inf\classes directory. From a command prompt, navigate to the directory and compile the class by typing the following:

```
javac FruitMap.java
```

Next, stop and restart the Tomcat server so that it loads the class into memory. Code the fruitPrice.jsp page shown in Listing 14-3 and save it in your <tomcat-install>\webapps\ ROOT directory. Run the page by navigating to http://localhost:8080/fruitPrice.jsp. While both of the examples that follow may be run on either Netscape 5.*x* or Internet Explorer 5.*x* or later, each utilizes the readonly and disabled keywords for the form inputs. These keywords will function in an IE browser only.

Listing 14-3   *The fruitPrice.jsp uses JSP expressions to populate JavaScript methods.*

---

fruitPrice.jsp

```
<%@ page import="java.util.*" %>
<%
String selectedFruit = request.getParameter("selectedFruit");
if (selectedFruit == null) {
    selectedFruit = "apples";
}
%>
<jsp:useBean id="fruitList" class ="FruitMap">
<%
fruitList.put("apples","2.99");
fruitList.put("oranges","2.59");
fruitList.put("plums","3.99");
fruitList.put("pomegranites","5.99");
fruitList.put("figs","2.99");
fruitList.put("mangoes","4.99");
fruitList.put("limes","2.99");
%>
</jsp:useBean>

<html>
<head>
    <title>Fruit Price Calculation</title>
    <SCRIPT language="JavaScript">
        price = parseFloat(<%=fruitList.get(selectedFruit)%>);

        function submitForm() {
            document.fruitForm.submit();
        }

        function roundNumber(number, digits){
            return
Math.round(number*Math.pow(10,digits))/Math.pow(10,digits);
        }

        function calcTotal() {
document.fruitForm.total.value =
roundNumber(price*parseInt(document.fruitForm.quantity.value),2);
```

Continued

Listing 14-3

Continued

```
        }

    </SCRIPT>
</head>

<body onload="calcTotal()">
<h1>Fruit Price Calculation</h1>
To change the fruit, select a different fruit from the list.<br>
To calculate the total price for the fruit you select, enter the number of
pounds you would like, and hit the tab key on your keyboard.

<form method="POST" name="fruitForm">
<table border="1" cellpadding="3">
    <tr align="left" valign="top">
        <th bgcolor="#c0c0c0">Fruit Type</th>
        <td>
            <select name="selectedFruit" onchange="submitForm();">
                <%
                Iterator fruitNames = fruitList.keySet().iterator();
                while (fruitNames.hasNext()) {
                    String newFruit = (String)fruitNames.next();
                    out.print("<option value='" + newFruit + "' ");
                    if (selectedFruit.equals(newFruit)){
                        out.print(" Selected ");
                    }
                    out.print(">" + newFruit);
                }
                %>
            </select>
        </td>
    </tr>
    <tr>
        <th bgcolor="#c0c0c0"">Price($):</th>
        <td><input type="text" size="15" name="price" disabled readonly
value="<%= fruitList.get(selectedFruit) %>"</td>
    </tr>
    <tr>
        <th bgcolor="#c0c0c0">Pounds:</th>
        <td><input type="text" size="15" name="quantity" value="1"
onchange="calcTotal();"></td>
    </tr>
    <tr>
        <th bgcolor="#c0c0c0">Total($): </th>
        <td><input type="text" size="15" name="total" disabled readonly
value="" ></td>
    </tr>
</table>
</form>
</body>
</html>
```

Stepping through the code, we first look for the fruit that has been selected. If none has been selected, the default fruit is apples. Second, we add a series of fruit names and prices to the fruitList HashMap in our FruitMap class.

Inside the <SCRIPT></SCRIPT> tags, we get the price of the selected fruit using JSP, and then set the value of the price variable in the JavaScript. Next, we code three methods: submitForm(), roundNumber(), and calcTotal(). We'll call the submitForm() method from the onChange event of the selectedFruit drop-down list. Instead of having to click a Submit button, users will effectively submit the form as soon as they select a fruit from the drop-down list. The roundNumber() method rounds the final total price to a number with two decimal places. The calcTotal() method calculates the total price by multiplying the value of the price variable by the number of pounds the user enters in the quantity input. Notice that the calcTotal() method is called in two places: the onLoad event of the page, and the onChange event of the quantity input.

In the body of the page, we create a form that, because it has no action attribute, submits to itself. The first form element is the selectedFruit drop-down, built dynamically by iterating through the fruit names that exist in the fruitList HashMap. We step through the HashMap with the help of an Iterator object, and print the names to the screen as options in the select input. Once we get to the fruit that matches the one selected, we print the selected keyword to the screen.

When working with an Iterator **object, it is necessary to assign each value to a variable as it is retrieved, as it can be retrieved only once per** Iterator **instance.**

Note a potential bottleneck with this approach: Every time the user changes the value of the drop-down menu, a new request is sent to the server, and a new response is sent to the browser, causing a fair amount of server traffic. Nonetheless, using JavaScript eliminates the need for a round trip to the server to calculate the total price of a given basket of fruit. Figure 14-1 shows the fruitPrice.jsp page in a browser.

Creating Basket.jsp

10 Min. To Go

Listing 14-4 shows more of a synergy between JavaScript and JSP in that we use JSP to dynamically create a JavaScript method call. The page, basket.jsp, shows a list of items that are included a fruit basket. Beside each item in the list is an "X" button, which enables a user to delete the given item from the fruit basket. Given that each Submit button has exactly the same value (X), without the use of JavaScript it would be impossible to determine which Submit button was selected and, hence, which item should be eliminated from the basket.

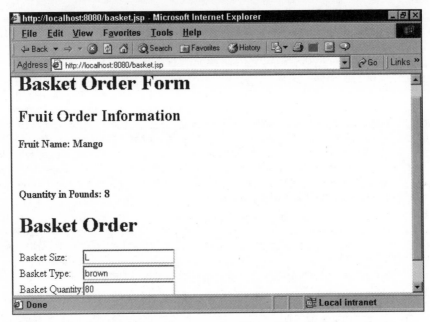

Figure 14-1   *The fruitPrice.jsp page uses JSP and JavaScript together.*

Listing 14-4   *The basket.jsp page use JavaScript to set the value of a hidden variable before the form is submitted.*

basket.jsp

```
<%@ page import="java.util.*" %>
<%
String deletedFruit = request.getParameter("Deleted");
if (deletedFruit == null) {
  deletedFruit = "";
}
%>
<jsp:useBean id="fruitList" class ="FruitMap">
<%
fruitList.put("apples","2.99");
fruitList.put("oranges","2.59");
fruitList.put("plums","3.99");
fruitList.put("pomegranites","5.99");
fruitList.put("figs","2.99");
fruitList.put("mangoes","4.99");
fruitList.put("limes","2.99");
%>
</jsp:useBean>

<html>
<head>
```

```
    <title>Fruit Basket</title>
    <SCRIPT language="JavaScript">
        function setDeletedFruit(fruit) {
            document.basketForm.Deleted.value=fruit;
        }
    </SCRIPT>
</head>

<body>
<form method="POST" name="basketForm" >
<table border="1">
    <tr>
        <td colspan="2"  bgcolor="#c0c0c0"><font size="+1">A fruit Basket
contains the items listed Below</font></td>
    </tr>
    <tr>
        <td colspan="2" >To delete an item from the basket, click the "X"
next to the item.</td>
    </tr>
    <tr>
        <td colspan="2">You have deleted: <input type="input" readonly
name="Deleted" value="<%=deletedFruit %>"></td>
    </tr>
    <%
        Iterator fruitNames = fruitList.keySet().iterator();
        while (fruitNames.hasNext()) {
            String newFruit=(String) fruitNames.next();
            out.println("<tr>");
            out.print("<th >");
            out.print("<input type=\"Submit\" name=\"Submit\" value=\" X \"")
;
            if (deletedFruit.equals(newFruit)){
                out.print(" disabled ");
            }
            out.print(" onClick=\"setDeletedFruit('" + newFruit +"')\"");
            out.print(" >");
            out.println("</th>");
            out.println("<td>" + newFruit +"</td>");
            out.println("</tr>");
        }
    %>
</table>
</form>
</body>
</html>
```

The solution to the problem is to code the onClick event of the button to call a JavaScript method, setDeletedFruit(). Just before the form is submitted, the setDeletedFruit() method sets the value of the deletedItem hidden form element to the name of the fruit being deleted.

Using JSP, we iterate through every fruit in the `FruitMap` object and print a table row to the screen. The table row contains the name of the fruit in the inventory list and a Submit button with the letter X as its value. For each Submit button, we dynamically create the `onClick` event call for each row to pass the id of the fruit in that row to the JavaScript method. Then, when the page is submitted, we just look at the value of the `deletedItem` field to determine which row the user wanted to delete. This page, like the `fruitPrice.jsp` page, uses the `FruitMap` class. Figure 14-2 shows the `basket.jsp` page in the browser.

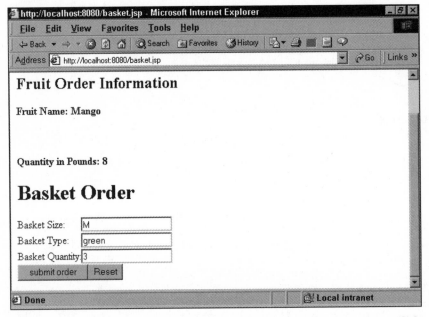

Figure 14-2   *The JSP code in basket.jsp page dynamically codes the onClick event for each of the buttons on the page.*

Done!

REVIEW

- JSP can be used to populate JavaScript scripts, and JavaScript can be used to alter the data to be submitted to the server with a form.

- Using JavaScript, rather than JSP, to accomplish certain functions eliminates the need for a round trip to the server.

- Using JSP, it is possible to dynamically code JavaScript methods.

QUIZ YOURSELF

1. Is JavaScript the same as JSP?

2. True or false? An onChange event always triggers a submit to the Web server.

3. What steps must you take in order to generate a drop-down menu dynamically from a HashMap?

4. What are the advantages and disadvantages of either client-side or server-side code?

Cookies

**30 Min.
To Go**

T he term *cookie* refers to a bit of information stored on a user's computer in a `name=value` pair as opposed to residing on the server. Cookies are beneficial when you use them to store data about your user that does not compromise the user in any way. Many have thought cookies might contain dangerous, hidden programs that can interfere with the functioning of a user's operating system. They cannot. Cookies contain discrete pieces of information, not programs, and are used for storing information on a user's machine, as opposed to the machine, or server, that's serving up the Web page.

Concerns do exist over the use of cookies with respect to a user's privacy. Cookies *can*, in fact, be used to track which sites a user visits from within a network of sites. For example, an advertiser who advertises on a series of sites has the ability to track a single user across the multiple domains that support that advertiser's banners. The advertiser cannot, however, track users in other domains. Ultimately, every user has the ability to not accept cookies if they do not wish to.

Learning the Cookie API

Cookies are an excellent way to maintain state in a Web application, or track a user from page to page. Cookies allow the Web server to send a piece of information, behind the scenes, to the browser. Each cookie is associated with the particular domain that sent it to the browser. By accepting a cookie, the browser agrees to send that exact same piece of information back to the Web server on each subsequent request it makes to that Web server. Every time a browser visits a site, it looks to see if it has a record of cookies that have been sent by that site. If it does, it will send the cookie as part of the request to the server. This simple agreement is all it takes for the Web server to recognize repeat users. The Web server might also send specific information, like the user's name, or a unique identifier for the user, and then use that to greet the user on subsequent visits. In all cases, the browser will send cookies only to the domain that originally sent them to the browser.

Depending on your browser, cookies are stored in different locations. For Netscape browsers, cookies are stored in `<Netscape root>\Users\default\cookies.txt`. You can open the file and look at the cookies that have been deposited on your operating system.

Looking at the file, you can read the name and value of the cookies and their associated domains. On a Windows system, each cookie has its own file name, with a `.txt` extension. On Windows 98, for example, your cookies directory is `C:\Windows\cookies`. On NT, cookies are stored under your personal user profile.

When executing the code examples in this session, take advantage of the feature that allows the browser to warn you with a pop-up message every time a cookie is issued. From Netscape 4.*x*, choose the Edit ⇨ Preferences... menu item. Select the Advanced category from the list on the left-hand side. Then select "Accept all cookies," and check the box that states "Warn me before accepting a cookie." For Internet Explorer 5.*x*, choose the Tools ⇨ Internet Options... menu item and select the Security tab. Click the Custom Level... button. Click the prompt radio buttons underneath both the `Allow Cookies to that are stored on your computer` **and** `Allow per-session cookies (not stored)` **headings.**

By using either browser, users can refuse to accept cookies. Therefore, as a site developer, you probably should not depend on cookies to manage your site. For example, if you intend to use cookies for your site's critical functions, some segment of the browsing population will probably be excluded from your site. It is also a good idea not to store sensitive or critical data inside a cookie that leaves a user vulnerable when someone gains access to the user's machine. You shouldn't, for example, store a user's credit card or other sensitive or compromising information in a cookie.

One good way to personalize a site with cookies is to store a unique identifier in a cookie. That identifier can exist in your site's database and can be linked to information such as the user's name, preferences, and other information. In this method, all of the user's profile information is stored securely on the host system, rather than on the user's machine, which might be more vulnerable.

To use cookies in your Web applications, you can look to the `javax.servlet.http.Cookie` class and its methods. Table 15-1 shows a summary of the methods you can use in your JSP pages.

Table 15-1 *Methods for the javax.servlet.http.Cookie class*

Method	Description
Clone()	Gets a copy of the cookie object.
getComment()	Gets the comment associated with the cookie.

Method	Description
setComment (String comment)	Sets the comment associated with the cookie.
getMaxAge()	Gets the maximum age of the cookie.
setMaxAge (int numberOfSeconds)	Sets the maximum age of the cookie in seconds. Setting the Number of Seconds to a negative number means that the cookie is not stored on the user's computer, but rather is stored in memory while the session is alive. A zero stores the cookie but deletes it as soon as the session ends. A positive number makes the cookie a persistent cookie, stored for the number of seconds specified.
getName()	Gets the cookie's name.
setName(String name)	Sets the name of the cookie.
getDomain()	Gets the domain under which the cookie is valid.
setDomain(String domain)	Sets the domain for the cookie.
getPath()	Gets the path under the domain to which the cookie applies.
setPath(String path)	Sets the path under the domain to which the cookie applies.
getSecure()	Gets the true/false value indicating whether the cookie is only to be transmitted between client/server over SSL.
setSecure(boolean flag)	Sets the true/false value indicating whether the cookie is to be transmitted only between client/server over SSL.
getValue()	Gets the value of the cookie.
setValue(String value)	Sets the value of the cookie.
getVersion()	Gets the protocol version the cookie adheres to.
setVersion(int version)	Sets the protocol version the cookie adheres to.

You can also get and set cookies by using client-side javascript. Getting and setting cookies by using server-side scripting or client-side scripting achieves the same result. Executing code on the server, however, gives you some degree of privacy from the scrutiny of curious users.

Creating Cookies on the Fruit-of-the-Month Club

Two good reasons to use cookies on our Fruit-of-the-Month Club are to recognize repeat visitors with a personalized greeting and to track the fruits users intend to purchase with their shopping carts. In the next session, we will build a cookies-based shopping cart. For now, let's take a look at executing the first of these functions.

Personalized Greeting

Often, users feel more welcome at a site, and thus use it more, when you personalize their experience. One way to make users feel more welcome is to record their names and to present it when they revisit the site.

The code in nameCookie.jsp stores a user's first name in a cookie (see Listing 15-1). When the user comes back to the site, he or she is greeted by name.

Listing 15-1　　*The nameCookie.jsp page sets a cookie with a user's first name.*

---

nameCookie.jsp

```
<html>
<head>
  <title>IDGB Fruit-Of-The-Month Club Home</title>
</head>

<%
boolean cookieExists = false;
boolean showForm = false;
Cookie nameCookie = null;
String cookieValue = "";
String welcomeText = "";

//First, check to see if the user submitted the form?
String firstName = request.getParameter("firstName");

//Create the cookies object which is an array of cookies available to this
page.
Cookie[] cookies = request.getCookies();

//Loop through the array and find the NameCookie cookie
for (int i = 0; i < cookies.length; i++) {
  nameCookie = cookies[i];
  if (nameCookie.getName().equals("NameCookie")) {
      cookieValue = nameCookie.getValue();

      //The user's been here before!
      cookieExists = true;
  }
}
```

```
//The user has been here
if(cookieExists){
  welcomeText = "Welcome back to the IDGB Fruit-Of-The-Month Club, " +
cookieValue + "!";
}else{
        //Check if they've submitted the form
        if(firstName != null){
               welcomeText = "Thanks for registering, " + firstName
 + ".  We'll remember you next time!";
               nameCookie = new Cookie("NameCookie", firstName);
               nameCookie.setMaxAge(3600);
               nameCookie.setPath("/");
               response.addCookie(nameCookie);
         } else {
               welcomeText = "Thanks for visiting the Fruit-Of-The-Month-
Club.  Please enter your first name so that we'll be able to recognize you
in the future!";
               showForm = true;
         }
}
%>

<h1><%=welcomeText%></h1>

<p>
<%
if (showForm){
%>
<form>
First Name: <input type="text" name="firstName" value="">
<br>
<input type="submit" name="submit" value="submit">
</form>
<%
}
%>

</body>
</html>
```

When users first visit the page, they see Figure 15-1.

Figure 15-1 *Ask for the user's first name.*

Upon entering their first names, users see a "Thanks for registering" message. When users visit the page after having input their name, they see Figure 15-2.

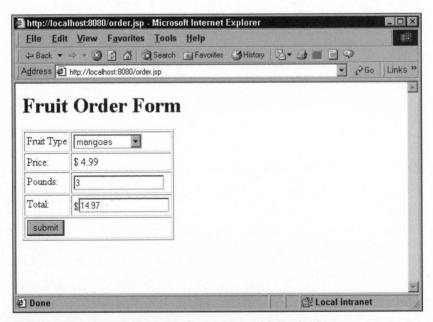

Figure 15-2 *Present the user's first name and hide the form.*

Refresh the page, or close the browser. Then open a new browser window, and navigate to the page. You will see Figure 15-3.

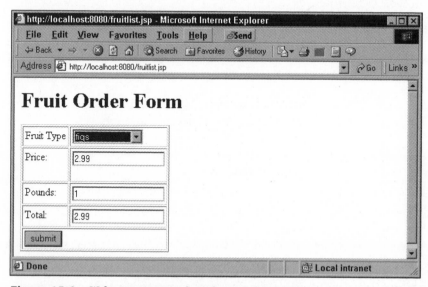

Figure 15-3 *Welcome message based on cookie value*

**10 Min.
To Go**

Let's take a look at some of the more important parts of the code.

```
Cookie[] cookies = request.getCookies();

//Loop through the array and find the NameCookie cookie
for (int i = 0; i < cookies.length; i++) {
  nameCookie = cookies[i];
  if (nameCookie.getName().equals("NameCookie")) {
      cookieValue = nameCookie.getValue();

      //The user's been here before!
      cookieExists = true;
  }
}
```

When you execute the getCookies() function of the implicit request object, the method returns an array of cookie objects that represent all cookies available to the page. No single function enables you to grab a cookie's value by name, so you need to iterate through the cookies array by using a for loop. With each iteration, you can test the cookie to see if it's the one you're looking for: if (nameCookie.getName().equals("NameCookie")) {}.

When no cookie named NameCookie exists, the value cookieExists remains false, and you check to see if the user has submitted the form. If the value of request.getParameter ("firstName") is not null, you know the user has submitted the form, and you set the cookie by using the following code:

```
nameCookie = new Cookie("NameCookie", firstName);
nameCookie.setMaxAge(3600);
nameCookie.setPath("/");
response.addCookie(nameCookie);
```

The first line sets the cookie's name and value. The setMaxAge(3600) method sets the life of the cookie as 3600 seconds (one hour); if the user returns to the site after an hour has passed, the cookie will no longer exist, and he will be asked to input his name once again. The setPath("/") method means the cookie is available to all pages of the site under the domain.

In the next session, we use cookies to store the items that a user has placed in his shopping cart. The shopping cart is integral to any e-commerce application.

Done!

REVIEW

- Use cookies to store discrete pieces of information on a user's machine.
- Cookies cannot contain harmful programs that interfere with a user's operating system.
- The getCookies() method returns an array of cookie objects that are available to a page.
- Use the get- methods to retrieve a cookie's properties, such as getMaxAge(), getDomain(), and getPath().
- Use the set- methods to set a cookie's properties, such as setMaxAge(), setDomain(), and setPath().

QUIZ YOURSELF

1. Which implicit object and which function do you use to find the cookies available to a specific page?

2. Can you call a function to get a cookie by name? If so, what is the function? If not, how do you get a cookie by name?

3. What types of information should you not store in a cookie? Why?

4. When you execute cartCookie.setMaxAge(10000);, in how many hours does the cookie expire?

Tracking Users with Sessions

Session Checklist

✔ Understand the session tracking API

✔ Work with sessions and cookies

**30 Min.
To Go**

C ommunication between a browser and a Web server is by its nature stateless. This means that, left to its own devices, the Web server would not track information about the client between requests; it opens and closes a connection each time a Web page is accessed. *Session tracking* describes the process of keeping tabs of a user across page requests. A session is the invocation HttpSession object. For a more complete list of session methods, refer to the javadoc documentation for the HttpSession class. It should be noted that by default, the session object uses cookies to store its information.

Understanding the Session Tracking API

In a JSP page, the session is treated as an implicit object, like the request object, and you do not need to declare it in order to access it. The object is implicit because the servlet that is generated when the JSP page is compiled instantiates the object explicitly, meaning that the developer does not have to be concerned with instantiating the object.

The session attribute of the @page directive controls whether a page can participate in sessions or not. By default, the value of the session attribute is set to true, meaning that the JSP page does participate in the session. If you set the value of the session attribute to false, the servlet does not instantiate the session object, and trying to access the object within your page will result in a compiler error.

You can think of the session object as though it were a Java HashMap: you can store information in sessions in key/value pairs. The getAttribute(String name) method is used to retrieve a value from the session.

The getAttribute() **method returns a** java.lang.Object **object. The examples in Listings 16-1 and 16-2 use an explicit cast for String when using the** getAttribute() **method.**

The setAttribute(String name, Object value) method is used to add a value to the session with the given name and value passed. These two methods are the most often used methods for sessions.

Canine Website Example

The next example stores information about a user's dog in a session and presents it to the user once he's announced who he is. When the user enters his user name and submits a form, the action page of the form populates the user's session with information taken from the storage class, DogTable.java. When a user logs out, the data is deleted from the session.

Java Classes Used for the Example

Listing 16-1 is the Dog class that we will use to store a dog's breed, name, and preferred food brand.

Listing 16-1   *The Dog class stores a dog's properties.*

Dog.java
```
public class Dog {
    private String dogBreed;
    private String dogName;
    private String foodBrand;
    private String ownerName;

    public Dog(String dogBreed, String dogName, String foodBrand){
        setDogBreed(dogBreed);
        setDogName(dogName);
        setFoodBrand(foodBrand);
    }

    public String getDogBreed(){
        return this.dogBreed;
    }

    public void setDogBreed(String dogBreed){
        this.dogBreed = dogBreed;
    }

    public String getDogName(){
        return this.dogName;
    }

    public void setDogName(String dogName){
        this.dogName = dogName;
    }

    public String getFoodBrand(){
        return this.foodBrand;
    }
```

```
    public void setFoodBrand(String brand){
        this.foodBrand = brand;
    }
}
```

To create a list of dogs and their owners that is accessible to our site, we will use the DogTable.java class in Listing 16-2. Under ordinary circumstances, this data would be stored in a database. For the purpose of this example, however, the data is stored in an extension of the `Hashtable` object. For each row in the hashtable, the key is the owner's name and the value is a `Dog` object.

Listing 16-2   *The DogTable class is a hashtable which links a dog to an owner.*

DogTable.java
```
public class DogTable extends java.util.Hashtable{
    public DogTable() {
        this.put("Mario", new Dog("Border Terrier", "Ripley",  "Flint River
Ranch"));
        this.put("Priya", new Dog("Beagle", "Simon", "Iams"));
        this.put("Sean", new Dog("Border Terrier", "Skipper", "Nutro Max"));
        this.put("Dvora", new Dog("Maltese", "Callie", "Eukanuba"));
        this.put("Babs", new Dog("Jack Russell Terrier", "Snacks", "Alpo"));
    }
}
```

Save the Dog.java and DogTable.java classes to your <tomcat-install>\webapps\ROOT\Web-inf\classes directory. The JSP pages in Listing 16-3 and Listing 16-4 should be saved to your <tomcat-install>\webapps\ROOT directory.

JSP Pages for the Example

**20 Min.
To Go**

Listing 16-3, dogForm.jsp, has a few instances of conditional logic. At the top of the page, the code checks the value of the signout `request` parameter. If the parameter has a value, then the user has signed out and the code removes all of the attributes from the session so that a new user may log in.

Listing 16-3   *The dogForm.jsp page displays different outputs, depending on the value of session attributes.*

dogForm.jsp
```
<%
String user = "";
String signout = request.getParameter("signout");
if (signout != null){
    session.removeAttribute("name");
    session.removeAttribute("breed");
    session.removeAttribute("food");
    session.removeAttribute("owner");
```

Continued

Listing 16-3 *Continued*

```
    }
%>

<html>
<head>
    <title>User Input Form</title>
</head>

<body>
<%
String ownerName = (String)session.getAttribute("owner");
if (ownerName != null){
    String name = (String)session.getAttribute("name");
    out.println("<h3>Welcome, " + ownerName + ".</h3>");
    out.println("Click the link See some information about <a href=\"" +
response.encodeRedirectUrl("dogAction.jsp?id=" + ownerName) + " \">" +
name + "</a>.<p>");
    out.println("If you are not " + ownerName + ", click the sign out link
to sign out.<p>");
    out.println("<h3><a href=\"" +
response.encodeRedirectUrl("dogForm.jsp?signout=true") + "\">Sign
Out</a></h3>");
}else{
%>
    <h3>Please Enter your user Id</h3>
    <form action="<%=response.encodeRedirectUrl("dogAction.jsp") %>"
method="post">
    <table border="1">
        <tr>
            <th bgcolor="#c0c0c0">Id:</td>
            <td><input type="text" name="id" size="10" value=""></td>
        </tr>
        <tr>
            <th bgcolor="#c0c0c0" colspan="2"><input type="Submit"
name="Submit" value="Submit"></th>
        </tr>
    </table>
    </form>
    Use one of the following names to login to the form:<br>
    Mario, Priya, Sean, Dvora, or Babs.
<%} %>
</body>
</html>
```

Farther down the page, the code checks the value of the session attribute whose name is owner. If the attribute has a value, the page displays a link to the dogAction.jsp page, passing the owner's name as a parameter. If the owner attribute is null, the page displays a form requesting the dog owner's name.

Since no session-specific information has been added the first time users arrive at the page, they should see a form like the one in Figure 16-1.

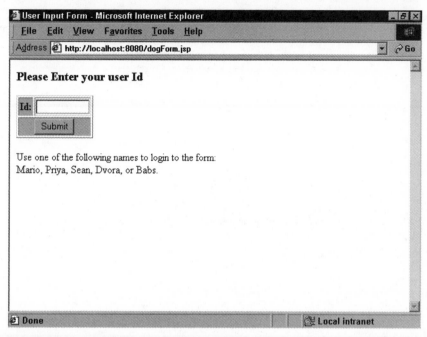

Figure 16-1 *The dogForm.jsp page collects a user's name and submits to the dogAction.jsp page.*

**10 Min.
To Go**

The dogAction.jsp page first loads the list of users and their dogs by instantiating an instance of the DogTable class. Next, it checks to see whether the user name that was submitted in the dogForm.jsp page is contained in the DogTable class. If it is, it populates three session attributes, name, breed, and food, with the values contained in the Dog object. It uses the getDogName(), getDogBreed(), and getFoodBrand() methods to populate the session attributes.

Listing 16-4 *The dogAction.jsp processes the form submission and populates the session with appropriate values.*

---

dogAction.jsp

```
<%
DogTable dt = new DogTable();
boolean userFound = false;

String user = request.getParameter("id");
if (user != null) {

   //Get the dog info
   Dog dog = (Dog)dt.get(user);
   if (dog != null){
      session.setAttribute("owner", user);
      session.setAttribute("name", dog.getDogName());
```

Continued

Listing 16-4   *Continued*

```
            session.setAttribute("breed", dog.getDogBreed());
            session.setAttribute("food", dog.getFoodBrand());
            userFound = true;
        }
    }
%>
<html>
<head>
    <title>Dog Information</title>
</head>
<body>

<%
if (userFound){
%>
<h3>Here's some information about your pet:</h3>
<table border="1">
    <tr>
        <th bgcolor="#c0c0c0">Owner Name</th>
        <td><%=session.getAttribute("owner") %></td>
    </tr>
    <tr>
        <th bgcolor="#c0c0c0">Dog Name</th>
        <td><%=session.getAttribute("name") %></td>
    </tr>
    <tr>
        <th bgcolor="#c0c0c0">Dog Breed</th>
        <td><%=session.getAttribute("breed") %></td>
    </tr>
    <tr>
        <th bgcolor="#c0c0c0">Preferred Dog Food</th>
        <td><%=session.getAttribute("food") %></td>
    </tr>
</table>
<%
}else{
    out.println("<h3>Your user id was not found!</h3>");
    out.println("Use one of the following names to login to the form
next time:<br>");
    out.println("Mario, Priya, Sean, Dvora, or Babs.");
}
%>
<p>
<a href="<%=response.encodeRedirectUrl("dogForm.jsp") %>">Back to
form</a>
</p>
</body>
</html>
```

If the user has been successfully located in the DogTable hashtable, the page displays
the values of the session objects that have been set. If the user is not found, an error message is displayed. Figure 16-2 shows the browser after a successful login.

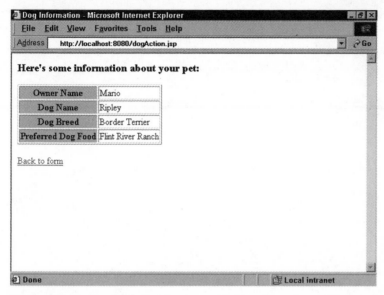

Figure 16-2 *The dogAction.jsp page displays the values of the session attributes.*

Working with Sessions and Cookies

Sessions actually employ *memory resident* cookies, cookies that are alive for the life of the session and then die, to store information. If cookies are disabled on a site that relies on sessions, the site will not function properly. To avoid the problems associated with browsers that disable cookies, use the encodeRedirectUrl(String URL) method of the response object. By invoking this method on each instance of a URL in your site, the server will append session information to the end of the site's URL for proper session tracking. Notice that each of the URLs used in the dogForm.jsp and dogAction.jsp pages employs the encodeRedirectURL method to add the session information to URLs on browsers that have cookies disabled. To test the effect, disable cookies on your browser and run the example.

Done!

REVIEW

- The Session Tracking API makes use of cookies or URL rewriting to provide a simple, elegant approach to tracking users.
- The setAttribute() session method allows storage of key-value pairs.
- The getAttribute() session method retrieves the value of a session attribute.
- The encodeRedirectURL() method insures the proper functioning of a session, even when a browser has disabled cookies.

QUIZ YOURSELF

1. What is the object that makes sessions possible?
2. Which method is used to retrieve a value from the session?
3. What is the return value of the getAttribute() session method?
4. If a browser has disabled cookies, will sessions work?

PART

III

Saturday Afternoon

1. Which method of the implicit request object returns an array of cookies available to a given JSP page?

2. Which method of the cookie class returns a boolean value specifying whether a cookie is to be transmitted over SSL (Secure Sockets Layer)?

3. Which method of the cookie class sets the domain to which the cookie applies?

4. If you have a cookie, how do you indicate that it should expire after one minute?

5. What is an accessor method?

6. What syntax is used to create an instance of a Bean called `JSPBean` and assign it to a variable called `myBean`?

7. What does the `<jsp:setProperty>` element do?

8. You have used `<jsp:usebean>` to declare a Bean called `mybean`. What `<jsp:setProperty>` syntax would you use to set `mybean`'s dbname property to the value of the request parameter named "database"?

9. How do you cause all of a Bean's properties to be automatically set to the values of the matching properties in the request?

10. What is the widest possible scope for a Bean?

11. Where do you place code that is to be executed only when a new Bean is instantiated?

12. How can JavaScript be used in a JSP application to reduce traffic on the server?

13. Do you use JSP or JavaScript to write the method that is called on a form's onSubmit event?

14. What is a mutator method?

15. How does the session tracking API manage sessions if cookies are turned off on a user's browser?

16. Which method is used to add an object to a session?

17. What does the method session.getId() return?

18. What is the return type of the session.getAttribute() method?

19. For cookies, what does the setDomain() method accomplish?

20. The getCookies() method is associated with which implicit object?

PART

IV

Saturday
Evening

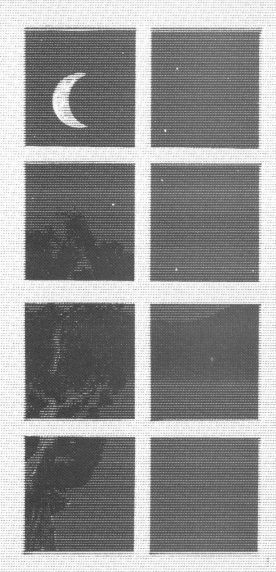

SESSION

Building a Shopping Cart

Session Checklist

✔ Code the necessary Java classes

✔ Extract data from a class

✔ Implement the shopping cart

30 Min. To Go

One of the most practical applications of your JSP knowledge is the development of shopping cart functionality. In the previous session, we learned how to leverage sessions to keep track of users as they navigate from page to page within your site. Keeping track of the items a user keeps in his or her cart is critical to any e-commerce site because it affects the site's bottom line — lose the items in the cart, and you will lose the revenue that should be coming in.

In this session, you will build a shopping cart that allows users to add items to, update quantities in, and delete items from the shopping cart. The cart makes use of sessions to track a user's cart, as well as a series of classes that contain most of the functionality.

Coding the Necessary Java Classes

To begin, you will need to code three Java classes. To deploy the classes, store them in your <tomcat-install>\webapps\ROOT\Web-inf\classes directory. Store the JSP pages shown in Listings 17-4 and 17-5 in the <tomcat-install>\webapps\ROOT directory.

Listing 17-1 shows `FruitMap.java`, the class that will hold inventory information.

Listing 17-1   *FruitMap.java contains inventory data*

FruitMap.java
```
public class FruitMap extends java.util.HashMap{
    public FruitMap() {
        this.put("apples","2.99");
```

Listing 17-1 *Continued*

```
    this.put("oranges","2.59");
    this.put("plums","3.99");
    this.put("pomegranites","5.99");
    this.put("figs","2.99");
    this.put("mangoes","4.99");
    this.put("limes","2.99");
  }
}
```

We first saw the FruitMap class in Session 14. Here it's been modified so that upon instantiation of the class, the inventory (fruits and their corresponding prices) is automatically added. In a real-world scenario, the fruit inventory information would come from a database. However, since we will not cover JDBC and connecting to a database until Session 20, we will use a HashMap to contain the data.

Listing 17-2 shows the CartItem class. The CartItem class corresponds to each item that will be added to the shopping cart.

Listing 17-2 *CartItem.java represents items that will be placed in the cart.*

CartItem.java

```java
public class CartItem {
    private String name;
    private double price;
    private int quantity;
    private double totalPrice;

    public CartItem(){}

    public CartItem(String name, double price, int quantity) {
        setName(name);
        setPrice(price);
        setQuantity(quantity);
        setTotalPrice(price, quantity);
    }

    public String getName(){
        return this.name;
    }

    public void setName(String name){
        this.name = name;
    }

    public double getPrice(){
        return this.price;
    }
```

```java
  public void setPrice(double price){
     this.price = price;
  }

  public int getQuantity(){
     return this.quantity;
  }

  public void setQuantity(int quantity){
     this.quantity = quantity;
  }

  public double getTotalPrice(){
     return this.totalPrice;
  }

  public void setTotalPrice(double price, int quantity){
     this.totalPrice = price * quantity;
  }
}
```

Notice that the CartItem class is a Bean: it has a zero args constructor and it uses getters and setters to set and return the values of its properties. Each CartItem has four properties: name, price (per unit), quantity, and totalPrice.

 Refer to Session 11 for more about JavaBeans.

Listing 17-3 shows the code for the Cart object that will hold a series of CartItems.

Listing 17-3   *Cart.java represents the shopping cart.*

Cart.java
```java
import java.util.*;

public class Cart {
  private Hashtable ht;

  public Cart() {
      ht = new Hashtable();
  }

  public void addItemToCart(CartItem item){
      String name = item.getName();
      int quantity = item.getQuantity();
      double price = item.getPrice();
      double totalPrice = item.getTotalPrice();
```

Continued

Listing 17-3

Continued

```
        CartItem oldItem = (CartItem)ht.get(name);
        if (oldItem != null){
            int q = oldItem.getQuantity();
          int newQuantity = q + quantity;
          item.setQuantity(newQuantity);
          item.setTotalPrice(price, newQuantity);
        }
        ht.put(name, item);
    }

    public void setNewItemQuantity(CartItem item){
        String name = item.getName();
        int quantity = item.getQuantity();
        if (quantity != 0 ) {
            ht.put(name, item);
        } else {
            ht.remove(name);
        }
    }

    public CartItem getCartItem(String name){
        CartItem item = (CartItem)ht.get(name);
        return item;
    }

    public boolean itemExists(CartItem item){
        String name = item.getName();
        item = getCartItem(name);
        if (item == null){
            return false;
        }else{
            return true;
        }
    }

    public Hashtable getCartList(){
        return this.ht;
    }

}
```

The cart class has a Hashtable object that will hold all of the items in the cart. Each row of the hashtable will have two items: the key will be the name of the CartItem, such as apples, and the value will be the CartItem object, which will hold the item's name, quantity, price, and totalPrice properties. The methods of the Cart class are listed in Table 17-1, along with their described functionality.

Table 17-1   *Cart Functions*

Method	Functionality
`addItemToCart(CartItem item)`	Adds a `CartItem` to the cart's hashtable
`setNewItemQuantity(CartItem item)`	Sets a new quantity for an item that already exists in the cart
`getCartItem(String name)`	Returns a `CartItem` from the cart with the specified name
`itemExists(CartItem item)`	Returns true if the specified item exists in the cart; returns false if the item is not in the cart
`getCartList()`	Returns the hashtable of `CartItems`

We will call these methods directly from the two JSP pages that make up the interface for the shopping cart.

Extracting Data from a Class

**20 Min.
To Go**

Listing 17-4 shows `fruitSale.jsp`. On this page, we extract the inventory from the `FruitMap` class and display it to the screen.

Listing 17-4   *fruitSale.jsp displays fruit inventory and allows a user to add an item to his cart.*

fruitSale.jsp
```
<%@ page import="java.util.*,java.text.DecimalFormat" %>
<%FruitMap fruitList = new FruitMap(); %>
<html>
<head>
   <title>Fruit Price Calculation</title>
      <SCRIPT language="JavaScript">
         function setAddedFruit(fruit) {
            document.fruitForm.selectedFruit.value=fruit;
         }
      </SCRIPT>
</head>

<body>
<h1>Order Fruit</h1>
<form method="POST" name="fruitForm" action="cart.jsp">
<input type="hidden" name="selectedFruit" value="">
<table border="1">
```

Continued

Listing 17-4   *Continued*

```
<tr>
    <th bgcolor="#c0c0c0">Fruit</th>
    <th bgcolor="#c0c0c0">Price</th>
    <th bgcolor="#c0c0c0">Add to Cart</th>
</tr>
<%
    //Set the formatting vars
    DecimalFormat df = new DecimalFormat ( "$#,##0.00" );

    Iterator fruitNames = fruitList.keySet().iterator();
    while (fruitNames.hasNext()) {
        String newFruit=(String) fruitNames.next();
        out.println("<tr><td>");
        out.println(newFruit + "</td><td>");
      Double price = new Double ( (String)fruitList.get(newFruit));
        out.println(df.format( price ) + " per pound</td><th>");
        out.print("<input type=\"submit\" name=\"Submit\" value=\"Add to
Cart\" onClick=\"setAddedFruit('" + newFruit +"')\" >");
        out.println("</td></tr>");
    }
%>
</table>
</form>
</body>
</html>
```

The `fruitSale.jsp` page creates an instance of the `FruitMap` class and loads the inventory into the `fruitList` variable. Then, using the `Iterator` object, we loop through the `fruitList` and display the fruits and their associated prices to the screen. This technique should look familiar to you, as it was employed in the `fruitPrice.jsp` page in Session 14. We're also using a similar JavaScript method as we used in Session 14, `setAddedFruit(fruit)`, which sets the value of the `selectedFruit` element before the page is submitted to the `cart.jsp` page.

Notice that we are including the `java.text.DecimalFormat` class in this page. The `DecimalFormat` class allows us to format a number in a precise way. In `fruitSale.jsp`, we format our price variable to include a dollar sign ($) and to limit the number of decimals to two places.

Figure 17-1 shows the `fruitSale.jsp` page in a browser.

**10 Min.
To Go**

Implementing the Shopping Cart

Listing 17-5, `cart.jsp`, is the implementation of the shopping cart.

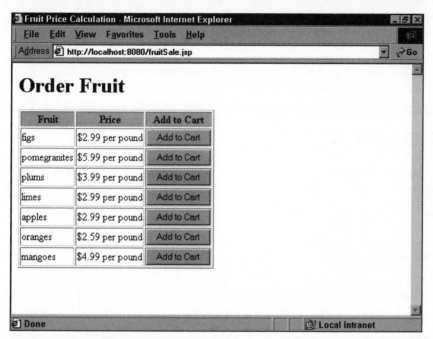

Figure 17-1   *The fruitSale.jsp page allows a user to add an item to a shopping cart.*

Listing 17-5   *cart.jsp is the shopping cart.*

---

cart.jsp

```
<%@ page import="java.util.*,java.text.DecimalFormat" %>
<html>
<head>
    <title>Cart</title>
    <SCRIPT language="JavaScript">
        function submitForm() {
            document.cartForm.submit();
        }

        function setNewQuantity(quantity) {
            document.cartForm.fruit.value=quantity;
        }

        function setFruit(fruit) {
            document.cartForm.fruit.value=fruit;
        }


    </SCRIPT>
</head>
```

Continued

Listing 17-5

Continued

```
<body>

<%
//Set up the page variables
FruitMap fruitList = new FruitMap();
CartItem item = new CartItem();
String submit = request.getParameter("Submit").trim();
String fruit = "";
Double price;
double p, totalPrice;
int quantity, existingQuantity;
Integer iQuantity, iExistingQuantity;
DecimalFormat df = new DecimalFormat ( "$#,##0.00" );

//Get an instance of the Cart;
//Create a session cart if it doesn't exist
Cart cart = (Cart)session.getValue("cart");
if (cart == null) {
   cart = new Cart();
   session.setAttribute("cart", cart);
}

//If they've added fruit to the cart, set the variables
//with the values of the submitted form
if (submit.equals("Add to Cart")){
   //Set the parameters for the new CartItem being added to the cart
   fruit = request.getParameter("selectedFruit");
   price = new Double((String)fruitList.get(fruit));
   p = price.doubleValue();
   quantity = 1;
   item = new CartItem(fruit, p, quantity);
   cart.addItemToCart(item);
} else {
   if(submit.equals("Recalculate Quantities")){
      for (Enumeration e = request.getParameterNames() ;
e.hasMoreElements() ;) {
         fruit = (String)e.nextElement();
         item = cart.getCartItem(fruit);
         if (item != null) {
            iQuantity = new Integer(request.getParameter(fruit));
            quantity = iQuantity.intValue();
            p = item.getPrice();
            if (item != null) {
               item.setQuantity(quantity);
               double newPrice = item.getPrice();
               item.setTotalPrice(p, quantity);
               cart.setNewItemQuantity(item);
            }
         }
      }
   }
```

```
      }
   }
%>
<a href="fruitSale.jsp">Add more fruit.</a><br>
<form method="post" name="cartForm">
<table border="1">
   <tr>
      <th bgcolor="#c0c0c0">Fruit</th>
      <th bgcolor="#c0c0c0">Price per Pound</th>
      <th bgcolor="#c0c0c0">Quantity</th>
      <th bgcolor="#c0c0c0">Total Price</th>
   </tr>

<%
/**Get the Cart HashTable which has all of the
user's CartItems Iterate through the list and
print the values to the screen in a formatted table **/
Hashtable cartList = cart.getCartList();
Iterator i = cartList.keySet().iterator();
while (i.hasNext()) {
   fruit = (String) i.next();
   item = (CartItem) cartList.get(fruit);
   p = item.getPrice();
   quantity = item.getQuantity();
   totalPrice = item.getTotalPrice();
   out.println("<tr><td>");
   out.println(fruit + "</td><td>");
   out.println(df.format ( p ) + "</td><th>");
   out.println("<input type=\"text\" size=\"1\" name=\"" + fruit + "\"
value=\"" + quantity + "\" ></th><td>");
   out.println(df.format ( totalPrice )+ "</td></tr>");
}
%>
<tr>
   <th colspan="4"><input type="Submit" name="Submit" value="Recalculate
Quantities"></th>
</tr>
</table>
</form>
</body>
</html>
```

In the cart.jsp page, we create an instance of the Cart object defined in the Cart.java class file. We store an instance of the cart in a session variable called cart. On subsequent visits to the page, a cart instance will be created only if there is not already an instance of the cart stored in the session.

The page has two implementations, based on which form has been submitted. If the user is adding a fruit from the fruitSale.jsp page, the code calls the addItemToCart (CartiItem item) method to add a fruit to the cart: if the fruit is not already in the cart, a new row is added to the Cart hashtable; if the fruit exists, then its quantity is incremented by one. The second implementation is called when the user has chosen to recalculate quantities on the items already in the cart.

If the user is recalculating quantities, then the quantities of each of the fruits are submitted to the cart.jsp page after the user clicks the Recalculate Quantities button. The code loops through each row in the cart and sets the new quantity for the fruits with the setNewItemQuantity(item) method. If the user has set the quantity to zero, the item is removed from the cart.

Figure 17-2 shows the fruitSale.jsp page in a browser.

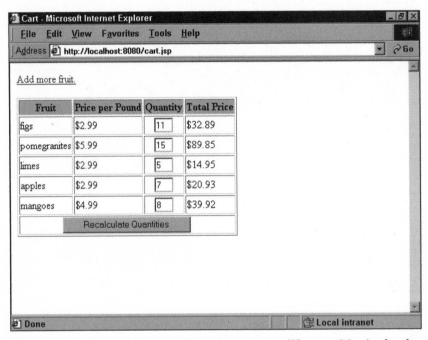

Figure 17-2 *The cart.jsp page allows a user to modify quantities in the shopping cart.*

Done!

REVIEW

- Use the session to track a user through a Web application. The session is instrumental in making a shopping cart possible.

- You can leverage custom-made Java classes by creating an instance of the object in your JSP pages.

- The Iterator object is useful for looping through a Hashtable object and printing the contents of the hashtable to the browser screen.

- The DecimalFormat class allows us to format numbers.

QUIZ YOURSELF

1. Why is it important that a shopping cart function correctly?

2. How do we make certain that we create only one instance of a Cart per user session?

3. What code must be present in a JSP page to enable the use of the DecimalFormat object? The Iterator object?

4. Which method is used to add the newly created Cart object to the session?

Includes and Forwards

Session Checklist

✔ Understand server-side includes

✔ Use includes in site forms

✔ Understand forwards

**30 Min.
To Go**

Including pages within your JSP scripts is an integral part of developing a fully functional site. When coding your pages, you want to keep any duplicate programming to a minimum. In addition, you want to keep all software modules to be used in common among your pages in one place. For example, if you want to include your company's logo on each page of your site, coding that inclusion in HTML on each page is a waste of time. If your company's logo changed, you would have to fix every page in your site to reflect your new image. Server-side includes enable you to avoid the problem having to update an entire site one page at a time. This session provides you with an overview of includes and forwards, two standard procedures used in coding JSP pages.

Understanding Server-Side Includes

A *server-side include* enables you to include either HTML pages or JSP pages within your JSP pages. Using a server-side include eliminates the need to duplicate a single display or function across a series of pages. To illustrate the point: if you've been surfing the Web for a while, you've noticed that sites tend to adopt a certain look and feel for each of their pages. Typically, a site has a style guide or a way of presenting itself visually to consumers. Site considerations include a palette of acceptable colors, fonts, and a logo, which appears on each page. Typically, the parts of the page that are always similar are contained in a single file, which is included in every other page on the site.

There are two types of server-side includes to consider within JSP, and each accomplishes a different task. The first is the *include directive,* in which the file specified is included in the calling JSP page at translation time. This type of include is used for dynamic content, such as JSP code. The second type of include, the `jsp:include` *element,* is used to include information at page request time, such as headers and footers or pages without JSP code.

@include Directive

The syntax for issuing an include directive is listed as follows, where `includeFile.jsp` is the file to be included:

```
<%@ include file="includeFile.jsp" %>
```

The include directive may appear in your pages anywhere you wish to include another page that has JSP code. The first time a JSP page that contains an include directive is accessed, the page is translated into a servlet. The resultant servlet contains all of the code that was present in the original JSP page, as well as all of the code that was present in the included file. It is important to note that even if you update the included files, they are not re-included until the JSP page that calls them is updated. Therefore, if the code within the included JSP page is updated, you must update the parent JSP page before the update can take effect.

jsp:include Element

The syntax for issuing a request-time include is listed as follows, where `includeFile.html` is the file to be included:

```
<jsp:include page="includeFile.html" flush="true" />
```

In order for the `jsp:include` element to function properly, you must remember to set the value of the `flush` attribute to true. The most common use of the `jsp:include` element is to include common page elements, such as headers and footers. Because the files are included at request time (when a user explicitly makes a request), if the content changes in the included file, those changes will automatically show up when the page is rendered. In addition to headers and footers, the `jsp:include` element can include a file that is the output of a news feed, showing the most up-to-date news every time the page comes up.

The `jsp:include` element can also be used to include dynamically generated content from another JSP page. However, the results are not the same as those derived from typing the JSP code directly into the including JSP page. As an example, when you use the `jsp:include` tag to include another JSP page, what is included is the output from the included JSP page, or whatever content is passed to `out.write()`. You can think of this technique in the following way: It is as though the included JSP page has been executed in another browser and you copied the resulting HTML source into the including JSP page. Anything other than output HTML, such as cookies or header information, will be ignored by the including page.

Using Includes in Site Forms

To minimize the work associated with updating and maintaining your site, think about creating components of related functionality within a JSP page. When creating your site's components, think in terms of functionality and content. For example, when you want to create certain functions that occur in various places, create one JSP page that can handle these functions, and include the JSP page with the include directive whenever necessary. For content, or those sections of your site that do not require the implementation of any set of functions, use the jsp:include element. You can update these elements without updating the parent page, so these elements are ideal for content.

A good candidate for an @include directive is a site's registration page. It is often necessary to collect information from your users for various reasons: to have them register for your site or, once they've registered, to log in to the site in order to have access to a fuller set of features. In addition, if your site is an e-commerce site, you will need to collect billing information from your users. Rather than create three forms to accomplish these distinct but related tasks, encapsulate your logic into one JSP page and pass a parameter to determine which form components are displayed.

Listing 18-1 is a page that enables a user to select a form to fill out: a login form, a registration form, or a billing form. The fruitHome.jsp page includes a header page, topNav.html (see Listing 18-2), and a footer page, footer.html (see Listing 18-3). In order for the examples to work, all of the files must be located within the same directory. To include files that are not in the same directory as the calling file, you can use a forward slash (/) to indicate the relative path of the file in relation to the site root.

Listing 18-1 *The fruitHome.jsp page has links to three different forms.*

---

fruitHome.jsp

```
<html>
<head>
  <title>IDGB Fruit-Of-The-Month-club</title>
</head>

<body>


<jsp:include page="topNav.html" flush="true"/>


<!--begin main content-->
<table width="100%" >
<a href="register.jsp?formMode=login">Login</a><br>
<a href="register.jsp?formMode=register">Register</a><br>
<a href="register.jsp?formMode=billing">Enter Billing Information</a><br>
</table>
<!--end main content-->

<jsp:include page="footer.html" flush="true" />


</body>
</html>
```

Listing 18-2 *The topNav.html page has navigation elements that appear on the top of the page.*

topNav.html

```
<!--begin top navigation-->
<table width="100%" border="1">
    <tr>
        <td colspan="5" align="center" bgcolor="Red">
            <p> </p>
            <h1>Fruit-Of-The-Month-Club</h1>
            <p> </p>
        </td>
    </tr>
    <tr>
        <td width="20%" align="center"><a href="#">Home</a></td>
        <td width="20%" align="center"><a href="#">Go Shopping</a></td>
        <td width="20%" align="center"><a href="#">About Us</a></td>
        <td width="20%" align="center"><a href="#">Customer Service</a></td>
        <td width="20%" align="center"><a href="#">My Cart</a></td>
    </tr>
</table>
<!--end top navigation-->
```

Listing 18-3 *The footer.html page has copyright information.*

footer.html

```
<!--begin footer-->
    <div align="center">Copyright &copy; Fruit-of-the-Month Club</div>
<!--end footer-->
```

**20 Min.
To Go**

Conditional Logic in form.jsp

Each of the three links in the fruitHome.jsp page calls the same page, form.jsp, but the implementation of the page varies based on the value of formMode.

The three implementations of the page are illustrated in Figures 18-1 through 18-3.

Figure 18-1 *The login form accepts a user name and password.*

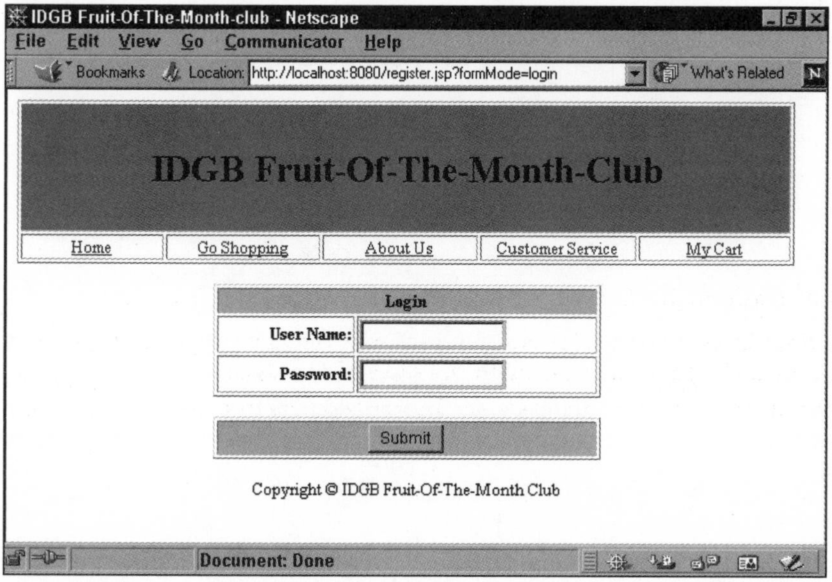

Figure 18-2 *The registration form accepts demographic information.*

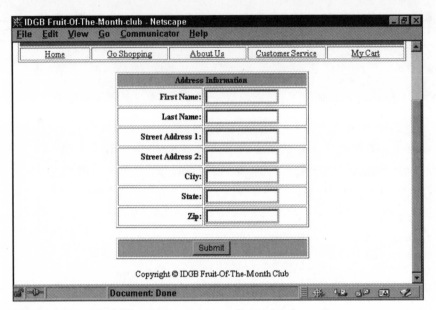

Figure 18-3   *The billing form accepts credit card information.*

The register.jsp page in Listing 18-4 includes the form.jsp page in Listing 18-5.

Listing 18-4   *The register.jsp includes the form.jsp page.*

---

register.jsp

```html
<html>
<head>
  <title>IDGB Fruit-Of-The-Month-club</title>
</head>

<body>


<jsp:include page="topNav.html" flush="true" />


<!--begin main content-->
<jsp:include page="form.jsp" flush="true" />
<!--end main content-->

<jsp:include page="footer.html" flush="true" />


</body>
</html>
```

Listing 18-5 *The form.jsp page has three different implementations, depending on what the user is trying to do.*

form.jsp

```
<% String formMode = request.getParameter("formMode"); %>

<div align="center">
<form method="post">

<% if (formMode.equals("login")) { %>
    <p>
    <!--Login form-->
    <table border="1" bordercolor="Silver" width="300">
        <tr>
            <th colspan="2" bgcolor="Silver">Login</th>
        </tr>
        <tr>
            <th align="right">User Name:</th>
            <td><input type="text" size="15" name="uid"></td>
        </tr>
        <tr>
            <th align="right">Password:</th>
            <td><input type="text" size="15" name="password"></td>
        </tr>
    </table>
<% } %>

<% if (formMode.equals("register")) { %>
    <p>
    <!--User information form-->
    <table border="1" bordercolor="Silver" width="300">
        <tr>
            <th colspan="2" bgcolor="Silver">Address Information</th>
        </tr>
        <tr>
            <th align="right">First Name:</th>
            <td><input type="text" size="15" name="firstName"></td>
        </tr>
        <tr>
            <th align="right">Last Name:</th>
            <td><input type="text" size="15" name="lastName"></td>
        </tr>
        <tr>
            <th align="right">Street Address 1:</th>
            <td><input type="text" size="15" name="address1"></td>
        </tr>
        <tr>
            <th align="right">Street Address 2:</th>
```

Continued

Listing 18-5 *Continued*

```
            <td><input type="text" size="15" name="address2"></td>
        </tr>
        <tr>
            <th align="right">City:</th>
            <td><input type="text" size="15" name="city"></td>
        </tr>
        <tr>
            <th align="right">State:</th>
            <td><input type="text" size="15" name="state"></td>
        </tr>
        <tr>
            <th align="right">Zip:</th>
            <td><input type="text" size="15" name="zip"></td>
        </tr>
    </table>
<% } %>

<% if (formMode.equals("billing")) { %>
<p>
<!--Billing form-->
<table border="1" bordercolor="Silver" width="300">
    <tr>
        <th colspan="2" bgcolor="Silver">Billing Information</th>
    </tr>
    <tr>
        <th align="right">Credit Card type:</th>
        <td>
            <select name="cc" >
                <option value="amex">Amex
                <option value="visa">Visa
                <option value="master">Master Card
            </select>
        </td>
    </tr>
    <tr>
        <th align="right">Credit Card Number:</th>
        <td><input type="text" size="15" name="lastName"></td>
    </tr>
    <tr>
        <th align="right">Expiration Date: (MM/YYYY)</th>
        <td><input type="text" size="15" name="uid"></td>
    </tr>
</table>

<% } %>

<p>
<table border="1" bordercolor="Silver" width="300">
    <tr>
```

```
        <th colspan="2" bgcolor="Silver"><input type="submit" name="submit"
value="Submit"></th>
    </tr>
</table>
</form>
</div>
```

The form.jsp page contains three related forms. It is a good idea to place related functionality within a site in a given page, such as form.jsp, so that there is only one place to update that information when it inevitably changes.

Understanding Forwards

**10 Min.
To Go**

A forward is different from a redirect. In redirects, the server sends a message to the browser instructing the browser to ask for a different page, effectively creating a completely new request. A forward happens entirely on the server side and uses the same client request.

jsp:forward

The jsp:forward element forwards users to a new page within your site. Its syntax is as follows, where forwardPage.jsp is the page to which the request is forwarded:

```
<jsp:forward page="forwardPage.jsp" />
```

Any parameters available to the page that is forwarding the request will also be available to the forwarded page. To send extra parameters to the new page, use the jsp:param element as a child of jsp:forward. The jsp:param element has two attributes, name and value, corresponding to the name and value of the parameters that are being passed:

```
<jsp:forward page="forwardPage.jsp" >
  <jsp:param name="name1" value="value1" />
  <jsp:param name="name2" value="value2" />
</jsp:forward>
```

Once the request is forwarded to the new page, the remaining code on the page that issued the forward will not be executed. The forwarding page sends the request to the forwarded page, along with all of the parameters that were originally passed to the forwarding page.

When processing online forms, it is convenient to place the HTML form and the code that processes that form on the same page: the resultant page contains the code for the form in one place and makes updating both the form layout and the form process easy. However, once the form is processed, you will want to send your users to a new Web resource without their having to do anything. The jsp:forward element handles the forwarding for you.

When using page forwards, make sure that the page is buffered. Before the forward, whatever content has been written to the page buffer is cleared. If you override the default page directive by specifying buffer="none" and content has been written to the buffer, you will get an error.

The `jsp:forward` element enables you to set up form wizards that move your users seamlessly from form to form. Each form within the wizard submits to itself, performs the necessary processing, and then forwards the user to the next page in the wizard by using the `jsp:forward` element.

Using a wizard to collect information from your users is wise when you want to break up information being collected into chunks, rather than force your users to submit an endless form. To illustrate the point, consider the process of filling out a user-satisfaction form or registering for a subscription service. These processes are often lengthy, and form wizards break them up into manageable chunks. Listings 18-6 through 18-8 use a series of forms in a wizard format to collect a user's geographic information and to display it on the screen.

Listing 18-6   *form1.jsp is the first form in the wizard.*

form1.jsp

```
<html>
<head>
    <title>Enter Your State</title>
</head>

<body>

<%
String state = request.getParameter("state");
if (state != null) {
%>
    <jsp:forward page="form2.jsp" />
<% } %>

<form method="post">
<div align="center" ><table border="1" bordercolor="Silver" width="300">
    <tr>
        <th colspan="2" bgcolor="Silver">What State do you live in?</th>
    </tr>
    <tr>
        <th align="right">State:</th>
            <td><input type="text" size="15" name="state"></td>
    </tr>
    <tr>
        <th colspan="2" bgcolor="Silver"><input type="submit" name="submit"
value="Submit"></th>
    </tr>
</table>
</div>
</form>

</body>
</html>
```

Because you want to submit the form only if the user has filled it out, test whether the form element is null. If the form element "state" is not null, you know the user has entered a value, and you pass the value of state to `form2.jsp`.

Listing 18-7   *form2.jsp is the second page in the wizard.*

---

form2.jsp

```
<html>
<head>
    <title>Enter Your City</title>
</head>

<body>

<%
String city = request.getParameter("city");
String state = request.getParameter("state");
if (city != null) {
%>
    <jsp:forward page="form3.jsp" />
<% } %>

<form method="post">
<input type="hidden" name="state" value="<%=state%>">
<div align="center" ><table border="1" bordercolor="Silver" width="300">
    <tr>
        <th colspan="2" bgcolor="Silver">What City do you live in?</th>
    </tr>
    <tr>
        <th align="right">City:</th>
        <td><input type="text" size="15" name="city"></td>
    </tr>
    <tr>
        <th colspan="2" bgcolor="Silver"><input type="submit" name="submit"
value="Submit"></th>
    </tr>
</table>
</div>
</form>

</body>
</html>
```

To keep track of the value of state entered in the previous form, set a hidden variable named state with the value submitted in form1.jsp. All name and value pairs set by using the jsp:param element are available via the getParameter() method of the request object. The last page of the wizard is form3.jsp in Listing 18-8.

Listing 18-8   *form3.jsp is the last page of the wizard, where results are displayed.*

---

form3.jsp

```
<html>
<head>
    <title>You Live In...</title>
</head>

<body>
<b>You live in <%=request.getParameter("city")%>,
<%=request.getParameter("state")%>.</b>


</body>
</html>
```

Done!

REVIEW

- Includes are a good way to make components of functionality and content in your site.

- By placing related functions or content in one place, you make updating and maintaining your site manageable.

- Whenever you find yourself repeating several lines of code, consider creating a page to be included; however, pay attention to the contents of the page. If it contains JSP code, use the include directive. If it contains only HTML, use the `jsp:include` element.

- The `jsp:forward` element enables you to forward user requests to other resources within your site and is ideal for creating effective form wizards.

QUIZ YOURSELF

---

1. What are the key differences between the include directive and the `jsp:include` element?

2. When using `jsp:param` to pass information to a page accessed via the `jsp:forward` element, how do you access the value of the `jsp:param` element?

3. What is the purpose of hidden form elements in form wizards?

4. What does it mean to make components of your site? Why is it a good idea to do so?

HTTP Requests and Responses

Session Checklist

✔ Understand the request object

✔ Explore the anatomy of an HTTP response

**30 Min.
To Go**

In this session, we will review what information is sent to the server when a browser initiates an HTTP request, and what information is sent to the browser from the resultant HTTP response. As you already know, the request and response objects are implicit objects available to all of your JSP pages.

Understanding HTTP Requests

When the browser requests information from a server, it passes to the server additional information that is peripheral to the request. This information is accessible to your JSP pages and servlets via the methods described in this session. The implicit request object is an instantiation of the HttpServletRequest interface of the javax.servlet.http package. Using the available methods enables you to access to the customary HTTP request header variables.

Table 19-1 provides an abbreviated list of the getter methods associated with the request object. For a complete list of the request object's methods, refer to the javadoc documentation for the class.

Table 19-1 *Request Object Methods*

Method	Description
getAuthType()	Returns the type of authentication scheme used to protect the servlet: BASIC, SSL, or null if no authentication scheme is used

Continued

Table 19-1   *Continued*

Method	Description
getContextPath()	Returns the portion of the request URI that indicates the context of the request
getCookies()	Returns an array of all the cookies on the client available to the servlet
getDateHeader(String name)	Returns the value of the name of the header specified as a date. Use this method only to return header values that are meant to be a date, such as "Expires."
getHeader(String name)	Returns the value of the specified request header. This method can be used to access any of the HTTP headers otherwise accessed via the "get" methods listed in this table.
getHeaders(String name)	Returns an enumeration of the values of the name of the headers specified. This method is useful for headers with multiple values. To get at the values, it is necessary to iterate through the returned Enumeration object.
getHeaderNames()	Returns an enumeration representing all of the names of the headers in a given servlet request
getIntHeader(String name)	Returns the value of the specified header as an int. Use this method only to retrieve headers whose value is an integer.
getMethod()	Returns the method used in the request: GET, POST, or PUT.
getPathInfo()	Returns extra path information after the servlet path, but before the query string
getPathTranslated()	Same as getPathInfo, but translates the value to a real path
getQueryString()	Returns the query string of the servlet request
getRemoteUser()	If an authentication scheme was associated with the servlet, this method returns the user's login credential.
getRequestURI()	Returns the URL from the protocol name until the start of the query string
GetServletPath()	Returns the part of the URL that calls the servlet and excludes host, protocol, and querystring data

In general, the getHeader(String name) method is useful for accessing the value of a request header when you know the header's name. The code in Listing 19-1 loops through the values in the enumeration returned from using getHeaderNames() to print the names and values for the available headers. Because the request headers will vary depending on the client software making the request, your results will look different for different browsers and operating systems. Remember to import the java.util package in order to access the Enumeration object.

Listing 19-1 *The getHeaderNames() methods returns the names of all request header variables.*

Request.jsp

```
<%@ page import="java.util.*"%>

<html>
<head>
  <title>Request Headers</title>
</head>

<body>
<h1>Request Headers</h1>
<%
String element = "";
String msg = "";
for (Enumeration e = request.getHeaderNames() ; e.hasMoreElements() ;) {
  element = (String)(e.nextElement());
  msg = msg + "<b>" + element + "</b> = " + request.getHeader(element) +
"<br>";
}
%>

<%=msg%>

</body>
</html>
```

You can experiment with accessing the various request headers by creating a page that simply calls each of the get methods and displays the results to the screen. There are many reasons why you might want to be able to access the request headers in order to control program flow, some of which are addressed in the following examples.

Using the Referer Header Variable

In Listing 19-2, we retrieve and display the value of the referring page by accessing the Referer header variable. (You may have noticed that Referer is misspelled, but that is the correct spelling of the variable.) This has limited usefulness in this particular example; it's unlikely you will impress users by figuring out where they came from. It becomes more useful, however, when creating a log of how your users found your site. By keeping track of the sites that refer users to your site, you can figure out where your online marketing efforts are paying off.

Listing 19-2   *The Referer header variable on a given page contains the URL of the page that contained a link to the new page.*

---

referer.html

```
<html>
<head>
  <title>Referring Example</title>
</head>

<body>
<a href="refered.jsp">Click me.</a>
</body>
</html>
```

referred.jsp

```
<html>
<head>
  <title>Referred Page</title>
</head>

<body>
You clicked a link on <b><%=request.getHeader("Referer")%></b> to get to
this page!
</body>
</html>
```

**20 Min.
To Go**

Exploring the Anatomy of an HTTP Response

The HTTP *response* contains the body of a page sent from the Web server to the browser, along with assorted response headers. Just as the client sends request headers along with the request it makes to the browser, the server response sends response headers back to the client. These headers contain information about the response, and they can be useful in customizing the response.

Table 19-2 describes some of the most commonly used methods associated with the `response` object. For a complete list of the `HttpServletResponse` methods, refer to the javadoc documentation for the class. All of the methods listed in Table 19-2 are accessible via the implicit `response` object in your JSP pages.

Table 19-2 *Response Object Methods*

Method	Description
addCookie(Cookie cookie)	Sets a cookie on the client machine
addDateHeader(String name, long value)	Adds a response header with a date value
addHeader(String name, String value)	Adds a header to the response, with the name and value specified in the parameters
addIntHeader(String name, int value)	Adds a response header with a date value
containsHeader(String name)	Returns a Boolean value stating whether the header specified has been set yet
encodeRedirectURL(String URL)	Encodes the URL specified, for the purposes of redirection
sendError(int sc)	Sends the error status code specified
sendRedirect(String URL)	Redirects the client to the resource specified
setDateHeader(String name, long value)	Sets the response header specified at the date value specified
setHeader(String name, String value)	Sets the response header specified with the value specified
setIntHeader(String name, int value)	Sets the response header specified at the int value specified
setStatus(int statusCode)	Sets the status code for the response

Anatomy of a Server Response

When the server sends a response back to the requesting client, the first line of the response includes three pieces of information: the version of the HTTP protocol being used, the status code of the response, and a status code description. Then, the server sends the response headers and the body of the document requested.

An example of a successful response is as follows:

```
HTTP/1.0 200 OK
Content-Type: text/html
Cache-Control: public

<html>
<body>
```

```
Hello World
</body>
</html>
```

The 200 status code, OK, in the first line of the response, is the status code returned for successful server responses. The two response headers listed here, Content-Type and Cache-Control, are two of the more common response headers. Table 19-3 provides a more complete list of response headers.

Table 19-3   *Complex Response Headers*

Header Name	Description
Age	Provides the age of the response content being returned
Allow	Specifies the methods to which the response can respond
Cache-Control	Specifies directives for caching content
Content-Type	Indicates the type of media the response contains. (Also referred to as MIME type.) For HTML, the content type is "text/html"
Content-Language	Indicates the language of the response content
Expires	Sets an expiration date to designate response content as "fresh" or "stale"
Last-Modified	Indicates the date when the response content was last modified
Location	Contains the location of server redirects

Status Codes

There are five classes of status codes, and each class starts with a different number (see Table 19-4). Each status code is a three-digit number, and each three-digit status code has a corresponding constant, understandable by the servlet response.

Table 19-4   *Status Code Classes*

Status Code	Description
100–199	Informational. The request was successful and the response is processing.
200–299	Success. The request was received, understood, and accepted.
300–399	Redirection. The servlet must set the value of the "Location" response header to redirect the browser to an alternative resource.
400–499	Client error. The request contains bad syntax or cannot be interpreted.
500–599	Server error. The server failed to fulfill an apparently valid request.

The javadoc documentation for the HttpServletResponse class lists each of the status codes and their meanings.

Using Response Headers

10 Min. To Go

One of the most common ways in which response headers are used is to perform *server-side redirects,* which cause the browser to issue a new request to a different resource. The 300-class error codes accomplish redirects by setting the Location header of the response, as in the example below:

```
response.setStatus(response.SC_MOVED_PERMANENTLY);
response.setHeader("Location", "http://www.yahoo.com");
```

Alternatively, you can accomplish a redirect with the following line of code:

```
response.sendRedirect("http://www.yahoo.com");
```

In Session 18, we looked at JSP forwards, which are distinct from redirects. With forwards, the request and response objects are transferred to the new page, which has access to all of the parameters that were available to the first page. This isn't the case with redirects. A redirect sends a message back to the browser telling the client to make a new request to a given resource, creating an entirely new request. All information in the original request is lost and unavailable to the new resource.

Triggering Errors with the Response Object

Your Web server is programmed to respond to certain errors. For example, when a client requests a resource that does not exist, it triggers a 404 error. To see a 404 error in action, request a Web page or folder that does not exist on your server.

There are two methods at your disposal to send a status code to the Web server: setStatus(int statusCode) and sendError(int statusCode, String errorMessage). For successful responses, you do not need to explicitly set the status of the response; the Web server will do that for you. The setStatus() method gives you the opportunity to override the status. The sendError() method sends to the client machine an error message along with the status code specified. These are not methods that you will have to call frequently, though it is useful to be aware of them.

Done!

REVIEW

- Request headers can be useful to tell servlet code where the user came from; if the user has been authenticated; or where — in the context of the Web application — the user is.
- The getHeader() method is used to retrieve request header values.
- The implicit response object also delivers the response headers to the client making the request.
- Response headers specify the age, expiration, and media type of the response.

- The setStatus() and sendError() response methods allow you to send a specific status code, indicating an error or other type of message, to the browser.
- The sendRedirect() method will redirect a user to another Web resource.

QUIZ YOURSELF

1. Which request method would you use to access request headers with multiple values?

2. In what situation would you use the getIntHeader() or getDateHeader() methods instead of the getHeader() method?

3. What does the first line of a server response contain? What is the status code for a successful response?

4. What is the status code for the most common type of error on the Web whose message is "Not Found"?

5. What is the difference between the setStatus() and sendError() response methods?

SESSION

20

Introduction to JDBC

Session Checklist

✔ Set up the Fruit.mdb database

✔ Connect your database in JSP pages

**30 Min.
To Go**

Most of the examples we've looked at thus far have been relatively simple. Any sophisticated Web site, however, needs a relational database to manage its various components, including user information, content, and shopping carts. Adding a Relational Database Management System (RDBMS) to your site gives you the capability to scale your information in an efficient manner. In this session, we will set up a sample Microsoft Access database, Fruit.mdb, that will be the source of information for our Website about the kinds of fruit for sale in our fictional, Web-based Fruit-of-the-Month Club. Additionally, we will introduce JDBC, the Java Database Connectivity API, which will allow you to connect to the database from your JSP pages.

To enable your JSP application to talk to your database, you will use JDBC as the "handshake" between the two. Through JDBC, you can pass SQL queries from your application to your database, and result sets from your database to your JSP application.

Setting Up the Fruit.mdb Database

For the purposes of this tutorial, we will connect to an Access database that will store information about our Fruit-of-the-Month Club. The Fruit.mdb database is included on the CD, and the database diagram is shown in Figure 20-1. If you do not have Microsoft Access software, you may use SQL Server or any other database. When connecting to a database in your JSP pages, you may connect to any database for which you have a JDBC driver. One of the beauties of JDBC is that once you connect to the database, the code you will employ to communicate with the database is always the same. The only difference will be the database driver and URL parameter specified by the driver/database combination.

The Fruit.mdb database will store data about the kinds of products customers may select from our Fruit-of-the-Month Club. The database will include information about the types of fruit our company offers, the months in which we will deliver the fruit, and how much each fruit will cost in a given month. The data for our company is set up according to Tables 20-1, 20-2, and 20-3.

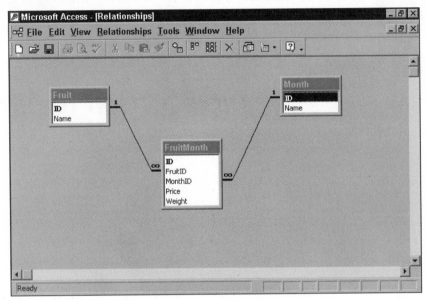

Figure 20-1 *The database diagram for Fruit.mdb*

Table 20-1 *Available Fruit*

ID(AutoNumber)	Name (Text)
1	apples
2	oranges
3	kiwis
4	bananas
5	apricots
6	plums
7	peaches
8	nectarines
9	cantaloupe
10	honeydew
11	watermelon
12	grapes

Table 20-2 *Available Months*

ID(AutoNumber)	Name (Text)
1	January
2	February
3	March
4	April
5	May
6	June
7	July
8	August
9	September
10	October
11	November
12	December

The Fruit and Month tables carry basic information about the fruits that our company offers and the months during which the fruit is for sale. In each table, the primary key, the column that ensures that each row in the table is unique, is the ID column. Each month in the Month table and each fruit in the Fruit table has its own unique ID, which will be used to identify the fruit or month name.

The FruitMonth table, shown in Table 20-3, is the table we will use to link the Fruit and Month tables. In this table, we specify (in pounds) how much of each fruit is to be sold during a specific month, and at what price (per pound).

Table 20-3 *The FruitMonth Table*

ID (AutoNumber)	FruitID (Number)	MonthId (Number)	Price (Currency)	Weight (Number)
1	1	1	$2.99	5
2	3	2	$0.99	5
3	5	3	$4.99	5
4	7	4	$4.99	5
5	8	5	$5.99	5
6	9	6	$3.99	5

The ID column of the Fruit Table is linked to the FruitID column of the FruitMonth table in a primary key/foreign key relationship. The ID column of the Month table is linked to the MonthID column of the FruitMonth table in the same way. This means that in order for a FruitID or a MonthID to be successfully entered into a row in the FruitMonth table, that ID must exist in either the Fruit or Month tables. For example, you could insert a row into the FruitMonth table that had a FruitID of 4 and a MonthID of 7, because those two IDs exist in their respective tables. You would *not* be able to insert a row into the FruitMonth table that had a FruitID of 13 and/or a MonthID of 13, because neither of those IDs exists in their respective tables.

Furthermore, the relationships between the tables have been designed to enforce *referential integrity*. Referential integrity is important for maintaining valid relationships between your tables. By enforcing referential integrity, you insure that any tables with a defined relationship do not jeopardize the integrity of the data contained therein when a row is updated or deleted. For example, notice that the FruitMonth table has a FruitID of 1 in the first row. We know that the FruitMonth's FruitID column is linked to the Fruit table's ID column with referential integrity enforced. Deleting the row from the Fruit table where the ID is 1 would put the data in the first row of the FruitMonth table in danger of being invalid. With referential integrity enforced, the database would not allow the completion of such an operation.

Connecting Your Database in JSP Pages

20 Min.
To Go

To connect to the Fruit.mdb database in our JSP pages, we will be using the JDBC 2.0 API, which is by default installed with the JDK 1.3.0. The `java.sql` package enables you to use the Java JDBC-ODBC Bridge for communication between your Java programs and your database. So, because you have already installed the JDK, you will be able to use the existing packages to complete the exercises in this session, and there is no need to download or install any additional software.

You will need to create an ODBC connection to the Fruit.mdb database. To do this, select ODBC from your Windows Control Panel. The Control Panel is accessible via the Start ⇨ Settings menu. On Windows 2000, the ODBC management icon is under Start ⇨ Settings ⇨ Control Panel ⇨ Administrative Tools. Follow the instructions below to set up the ODBC for the Fruit.mdb database

1. Select the System DSN tab and click the Add button to set up an ODBC driver for the Fruit.mdb database.

2. In the Create New Datasource dialog box, select Microsoft Access Driver, as Fruit.mdb is an Access database. (If you are running these examples on another database, then select that database from the list.)

3. In the ODBC Microsoft Access Setup dialog box shown in Figure 20-2, name the data source "Fruit," and browse to the location of the database with the Select button.

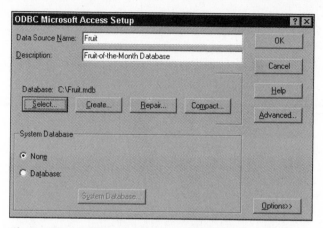

Figure 20-2   Select the Fruit.mdb database and name the DSN Fruit in the ODBC Microsoft Access Setup window.

Now that you have created an ODBC for the Fruit.mdb database, let's practice connecting to the database by creating the DbConnect.jsp page in Listing 20-1. In the dbConnect.jsp we will connect to the fruit table, execute a simple SELECT query to return the contents of the Fruit table, and print the results to the browser.

Listing 20-1   *The dbConnect.jsp page connects to the Fruit.mdb database.*

dbConnect.jsp

```
<%@ page import="java.sql.*;" %>
<html>
<head>
   <title>Database Connect Example</title>
</head>

<body>
<table border="1" cellpadding="2" cellspacing="2">
<tr>
   <th bgcolor="#c0c0c0" colspan="2">Fruit</th>
</tr>
<%
Driver drv = (Driver)
Class.forName("sun.jdbc.odbc.JdbcOdbcDriver").newInstance();
Connection conn
=java.sql.DriverManager.getConnection("jdbc:odbc:Fruit");
Statement stmt = conn.createStatement();
ResultSet rs = stmt.executeQuery("SELECT ID, Name From Fruit");
while (rs.next()) {
   int id = rs.getInt("ID");
   String name = rs.getString("Name");
   out.print("<tr><td>" + id + "</td><td>" + name + "</td></tr>");
```

Continued

Listing 20-1

Continued

```
      }
      stmt.close();
      conn.close();
      %>
      </table>

      </body>
      </html>
```

The first two lines of JSP code in the dbConnect.jsp page are the only lines of code that are driver-specific:

```
      Driver drv = (Driver)
      Class.forName("sun.jdbc.odbc.JdbcOdbcDriver").newInstance();
      Connection conn = DriverManager.getConnection("jdbc:odbc:Fruit");
```

Furthermore, since all of the driver-specific information is contained in strings, the parameters could be easily read from a properties file. This makes it very easy to change DNS or even the entire JDBC driver without changing code. The rest of the JSP code that executes a SQL statement and steps through the returned ResultSet is not specific to a certain JDBC driver or database.

Opening a connection to the database is very expensive, in terms of system resources. While so having each of your JSP pages open and close the connection isn't very efficient, it is just fine for instructional purposes. In a production system, you will want to share open connections among your different pages, probably with a connection pool maintained by your Application Server.

Stepping through the JSP code line by line, Driver drv = (Driver) Class.forName("sun.jdbc.odbc.JdbcOdbcDriver").newInstance(); loads the JDBC-ODBC Bridge driver. Once the driver has been loaded, we create a Connection object in order to establish contact with the database. The parameter passed to the getConnection() method must be in the format listed below:

```
      jdbc:subprotocol:subname
```

The jdbc tells the driver manager that it is looking for a jdbc driver. The subprotocol tells the DriverManager which particular driver it is looking for; each driver is associated with a different subprotocol name and the ODBC bridge driver is associated with ODBC. The DriverManager will look at each driver loaded into memory and see if there is a match. When it finds a match, it passes the driver subname that is the third part of the colon (:) delimited parameter. This is driver-specific connection information. For the ODBC bridge, the subname is simply DNS.

After the connection to the database has been made, we create a Statement object that is used for executing a SQL statement.

```
      Statement stmt = conn.createStatement();
```

**10 Min.
To Go**

Executing the query

We then execute our query against the database by calling the executeQuery() method of the Statement object and returning a ResultSet object that will house the results. To print the contents of the database table to the screen, we iterate through the ResultSet with a while loop and retrieve the values using the getInt() and getString() methods of the ResultSet object.

```
while (rs.next()) {
    int id = rs.getInt("ID");
    String name = rs.getString("Name");
    out.print("<tr><td>" + id + "</td><td>" + name + "</td></tr>");
}
```

Closing open connections

Finally, close the Statement and Connection objects.

```
stmt.close();
conn.close();
```

It is very important to close the open connections. Unclosed connections will cause an application to behave erratically and are difficult to track down.

When you browse to the dbConnect.jsp page, you should see a page that looks like Figure 20-3.

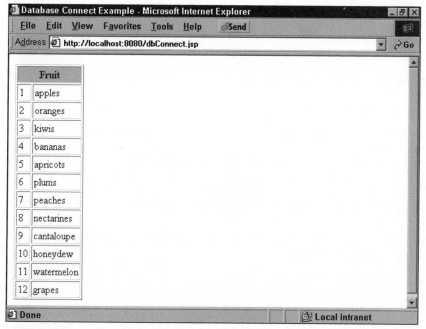

Figure 20-3 *The results of the query to the Fruit table are displayed in an HTML table.*

REVIEW

- JDBC is the Java Database Connectivity API, which allows you to connect to a database in your Java programs, including JSP.
- The Fruit.mdb database uses primary key/foreign key relationships and enforces referential integrity to maintain valid data.
- The java.sql.* package makes it possible for you to load a JDBC driver and connect to a database. This package makes it possible to connect to any ODBC datasource, but you can connect to any database for which you have a driver.

QUIZ YOURSELF

1. What is the name for the Java Database Connectivity API?
2. What is referential integrity?
3. Can you connect to databases other than Microsoft Access in your JSP pages? If so, what do you need in order to do so?
4. What is the purpose of the Statement object?

PART

IV

Saturday Evening

1. What is the purpose of the @include directive?
2. What is the difference between the @include directive and the <jsp:include> element?
3. Which attribute must be set to true in the <jsp:include> element in order for the include to function properly?
4. How are forwards different from redirects?
5. Which JSP element allows you to forward a request?
6. Which JSP element will add name=value pairs to a forwarded request?
7. Other than sessions, what is another method of keeping track of your users from page to page within a form wizard?
8. What data type is returned by the getHeaderNames() function of the implicit request object?
9. What is returned by the getQueryString() method of the implicit request object?
10. Which class and method would you use to return the URL of a given page?
11. Which class and method redirect a user to another page somewhere on the Web?
12. What is a 404 error?
13. Which class and method return the authentication scheme used to protect a JSP page?

14. If a user clicks a link on a Web page that brings him to your site, which request header variable contains the URL of that page?

15. With respect to redirects, which response header contains the URL of the new page?

16. Which range of status codes indicates a client error?

17. When retrieving data from a database, which symbol do you use to select all columns from a given table?

18. What is JDBC?

19. What is the JDBC-ODBC bridge?

20. What is the fully qualified name of the driver class for the JDBC-ODBC bridge?

☑ Friday

☑ Saturday

☑ **Sunday**

PART

V

Sunday Morning

Introduction to SQL

Session Checklist

✔ Build the SQL statements for the Fruit-of-the-Month Club administrative interface

*30 Min.
To Go*

I f you're already familiar with Structured Query Language (SQL), you can skip to Session 22 and begin making calls to the fruit.mdb database by embedding SQL in your JSP pages. In this session, we look at four types of SQL statements: SELECT, INSERT, UPDATE, and DELETE. In addition, we create the SQL statements for the administrative inter-face to our Fruit-of-the-Month Club. SQL is the language used to communicate with data-bases. Entire books have been written on SQL, and this session does not attempt to cover the topic exhaustively. Rather, this session provides you with an overview of SQL so that you will be able to do some basic database exercises with JSP. While each database uses its own version of SQL, the basic statements are standardized and called ANSI SQL.

Because each of the exercises presented in this session is meant to be executed with an Access database, the exact syntax of the statements is not identical to ANSI SQL but is in Access' SQL language, Jet SQL. Therefore, if you are trying to execute the examples against another database, such as MySQL, SQL Server, or Oracle, the syntax will be slightly different. Refer to the documentation for your database for the exact syntax rules. If you are not familiar with executing SQL statements in Access, check the Access documentation for instructions.

Building the SQL Statements for the Fruit-of-the-Month Club Administrative Interface

As the owners of a fictional Fruit-of-the-Month Club, we don't want to have to open the database to change the information it contains. Instead, we rely on a Web-based interface that JSP facilitates to accomplish basic functions such as adding fruit, specifying the month in which the fruit is for sale, and specifying the weight or price of the fruit. Each function can be accomplished through a specific call to the database. The queries are in the pages that follow.

The SELECT statement

The SELECT statement is the most basic call to the database. You use it to get information that resides in the database. For example, to select all of the rows in your Fruit table, execute the following statement:

```
SELECT * FROM Fruit
```

When executing the SELECT statement, you must specify two basic items: the column(s) you want to select and the table(s) from which you want to select those columns. To accomplish the first part, you may refer to the columns by name, or, as in the preceding example, you can use an asterisk (*) to denote all of the columns. To accomplish the second part, use a FROM clause to indicate the tables from which the data is to be retrieved. An alternative method for executing the same search as the preceding one is to code an SQL statement such as the following:

```
SELECT Id, Name FROM Fruit
```

Note that the only columns in the table are Id and Name. When you are specifying column names in the first part of a SELECT statement, make certain that you separate the values with a comma.

At times, you will want to filter the result set your SELECT statement returns to you. The WHERE clause is a way to apply a filter to your results set. For example, you might want to return all rows in the Fruit table in which the Id is less than 10 or in which the Id is equal to 10. Or you might want to return all rows in which the name of the fruit begins with the letter *a*. It's relatively easy to limit your results by using the WHERE clause, as you can see in the next three examples:

```
SELECT * FROM Fruit WHERE Id < 10
```

Executing this statement yields the result you see in the following table.

Id	Name
1	apples
2	oranges
3	kiwis
4	bananas
5	apricots
6	plums
7	peaches
8	nectarines
9	cantaloupe

```
SELECT * FROM Fruit WHERE Id = 10
```

Executing this statement yields the following results:

Id	Name
1	apples

```
SELECT * FROM Fruit WHERE Name LIKE "[a]*"
```

Executing this statement yields the following results:

Id	Name
1	apples
5	apricots

In the preceding examples, we use the greater than (>), equals (=), and LIKE operators. These operators are used in conjunction with the WHERE clause and help you limit the number of rows of data you return.

Using more complex SQL statements enables you to extract structured information from a database, even when the data resides in different tables. In our database, we store the names of fruit in the Fruit table; and we store the pricing information about the fruit in the FruitMonth table. In the Fruit table, the primary key column is the Id column. In the FruitMonth table, there is a column called FruitId. The value of FruitId corresponds to a fruit listed in the Fruit table. You use the WHERE clause to accomplish a join among your tables. A *join* is a way of linking two or more tables together on a specific column. Execute the following SQL statement to retrieve all of the rows in the FruitMonth table, which stores information about the fruits available during a given month and the weights and prices of the fruits:

```
SELECT * FROM FruitMonth
```

Executing the preceding statement yields the following table:

Id	FruitId	MonthId	Price	Weight
1	1	1	2.99	5
2	3	2	0.99	5
3	5	3	4.99	5
4	7	4	4.99	5
5	8	5	5.99	5
6	9	6	3.99	5

The meaning of the rows in this table isn't immediately apparent. The first row says that the fruit whose Id is 1 is available during the month whose Id is 1, in the quantity of five pounds at $2.99 per pound. But we are missing some crucial information: What is the name of the fruit and the name of the month? To get the complete picture, you need to utilize a join by using a WHERE clause. The WHERE clause in the following example appears in bold:

```
SELECT Fruit.Name, Month.Name, FruitMonth.Price, FruitMonth.Weight
FROM FruitMonth, Fruit, Month
WHERE Fruit.Id = FruitMonth.FruitId AND Month.Id = FruitMonth.FruitId
```

Now the meaning of the data is clear. The new result is listed in the following table:

Fruit.Name	Month.Name	Price	Weight
Apples	January	2.99	5
Kiwis	February	0.99	5
Apricots	March	4.99	5
Peaches	April	4.99	5
Cantaloupe	May	5.99	5
Watermelon	June	3.99	5

During January, five pounds of apples are available for $2.99 per pound. During February, five pounds of kiwis are available at $0.99 per pound, and so on.

Let's break down the SQL fragment by fragment so that you understand exactly what's going on. Let's start with the FROM clause:

```
FROM FruitMonth, Fruit, Month
```

The FROM clause indicates that your data is going to come from three tables: FruitMonth, Fruit, and Month. In the next fragment, we prefix the column names with the table name, so that we can make the distinction as to exactly which table holds the information:

```
SELECT Fruit.Name, Month.Name, FruitMonth.Price, FruitMonth.Weight
```

When you are retrieving data from only one table, you do not need to specify the table in the SELECT clause. However, when retrieving data from multiple tables, you must give the database a way to determine which tables hold which columns. Both tables, Fruit and Month, contain the columns Id and Name. By specifying Fruit.Nameand Month.Name, you are being clear about the tables that contain the data you want. The next fragment is the WHERE clause:

```
WHERE FruitMonth.FruitId = Fruit.Id AND FruitMonth.MonthId = Month.Id
```

Two WHERE clauses are here, separated by the operator AND. The AND operator means that both conditions in the WHERE clause must be satisfied in order for a row of data to be returned.

Let's look at the first clause, `Fruit.Id = FruitMonth.FruitId`, which means that the FruitMonth table and the Fruit table are joined on the columns specified. For example, when the FruitMonth.FruitId column has a value of one, that always refers to the row in the Fruit table in which the Id is 1. The Id column of the Fruit table is the *primary key,* and the FruitId column of the FruitMonth table is the *foreign key,* indicating that a binding relationship exists between the two tables. This interdependence is called a primary key/foreign key relationship.

But what if you want to calculate the total cost for the fruit each month? You can calculate the cost programmatically in your JSP page, but you can also get the value just as simply by embedding the math within your SQL. Look at the SQL statement and table that follow; the part of the statement in bold is where we calculate the price:

```
SELECT Fruit.Name, Month.Name, FruitMonth.Price,
FruitMonth.Weight,
(FruitMonth.Price * FruitMonth.Weight) AS TotalPrice
FROM FruitMonth, Fruit, Month
WHERE FruitMonth.FruitId = Fruit.Id
AND FruitMonth.MonthId = Month.Id
```

Fruit.Name	Month.Name	Price	Weight	TotalPrice
Apples	January	2.99	5	14.95
Kiwis	February	0.99	5	4.95
Apricots	March	4.99	5	24.95
Peaches	April	4.99	5	24.95
Cantaloupe	May	5.99	5	29.95
Watermelon	June	3.99	5	19.95

The `(FruitMonth.Price * FruitMonth.Weight) AS TotalPrice` is used to create a new column called TotalPricethat is the result of a mathematical operation applied to other columns in the database. The `AS` clause is used to name the column in this case but can also be used to rename other columns and tables.

Our final SQL clause looks like the following and yields exactly the same result as in the preceding table:

```
SELECT F.Name AS Fruit, M.Name AS Month, Price, Weight,
(Price * Weight) AS TotalPrice
FROM FruitMonth AS FM, Fruit AS F, Month AS M
WHERE FM.FruitId = F.Id AND FM.MonthId = M.Id
```

For brevity's sake, we've renamed the tables and changed the prefixes in the `SELECT` clause to reflect the change. We've also removed the prefixes for Price and Weight because they are unambiguously from the FruitMonth table.

The INSERT Statement

Use the INSERT statement to insert rows into a database table. For the administrative interface of the Fruit-of-the-Month Club, we will use an INSERT statement to accomplish two things: add new fruits to our Fruit table and add new rows to the FruitMonth table (to add new fruits for sale for a given month, for example). The first task is accomplished by using the INSERT statement as follows:

```
INSERT INTO Fruit (Name) VALUES ( "persimmons")
```

The INSERT INTO statement is followed by the name of the table and a comma-separated list of the column names within that table — in this case, Id and Name. Then, the VALUES clause contains a comma-separated list of the values to be input into the database. Note that we do not set an Id for the row because the data type of the column is AutoNumber, which means that Access will automatically generate a unique numeric id.

To insert a row into the FruitMonth table, use the SQL that follows:

```
INSERT INTO FruitMonth (FruitId, MonthId, Price, Weight) VALUES (13, 7, 4.99, 5)
```

Because all of the values being inserted are numeric, you do not put single quotation marks around them.

The UPDATE Statement

Use the UPDATE statement to update data in existing rows in your database. Use UPDATE statements with care because you can make sweeping changes to your database by applying a single, ill-conceived statement. For the Fruit-of-the-Month Club, you need to give your site administrator the ability to change the weight, the price, or the month of the fruit for sale. For example, if there were suddenly a glut of apples on the market and their price decreased from $2.99 to $0.99 per pound, you would issue the following UPDATE statement:

```
UPDATE FruitMonth
SET Price = .99
WHERE (FruitId = 1)
```

This effectively changes the price of apples. In this case, the WHERE clause localizes the change to a single database row. When creating a WHERE clause, it makes sense to think of the clause in terms of a question: Where do you want to set the price to $0.99? The answer is, where the FruitId is equal to 1. If you don't use the WHERE clause, the UPDATE statement is not localized but is applied to every row in the table. As in the SELECT statement, you can set multiple sets of criteria for the UPDATE statement by using the WHERE clause.

The DELETE statement

10 Min.
To Go

Use the DELETE statement when you want to purge the database permanently of a given row or rows. You might use a DELETE statement to delete fruits you no longer desire to sell to your customers. For example, if your operations manager threatens to quit if you don't take grapes off of the list, you can execute the following DELETE statement to rid your database of the fruit in question:

```
DELETE FROM Fruit WHERE Name = "grapes"
```

The preceding statement deletes the row of the Fruit table in which the name of the fruit is grapes.

In preparation for Session 22, where we will build a Web interface for manipulating the data in the `fruit.mdb` database, add the grapes back into the Fruit table.

Done!

REVIEW

- Structured Query Language (SQL) is the language used to communicate with databases.
- SELECT, UPDATE, INSERT, and DELETE are four basic SQL commands.
- Access databases use a flavor of ANSI SQL called Jet SQL. Each database uses a slightly different version of SQL.
- Use the WHERE clause to limit the scope of your SQL statements.

QUIZ YOURSELF

1. How do you narrow the results set returned in a SQL SELECT statement?
2. When you delete a row from a table, how can you be certain you are not affecting other tables? Are you putting the validity of your database in potential jeopardy?
3. When inserting a row into the Fruit table, how do you set up the table so that the database generates the unique Id?
4. What happens when you execute an UPDATE against a table but forget to specify a WHERE clause?

SESSION

22

Working with Databases in JSP

Session Checklist

✔ Connect to the database from your JSP page

✔ View fruits

✔ Add a fruit

✔ Delete fruits

✔ View fruit for sale

✔ Add fruit for sale

**30 Min.
To Go**

N ow that you have learned about JDBC in Session 20 and constructed the SQL necessary to support your site in Session 21, you will build the interface for the adminis-
tration side of your Fruit-of-the-Month Club. In this session, you build functionality
around the Fruit-of-the-Month administrator's interface. Initially, you embed all of the database-related code into the JSP page. In the next session, you create separate Java class files
to handle all common code, of which there is a lot.

Connecting to the Database

We will implement five basic actions, or functions, on your administrative site:

- View fruits
- Add a fruit
- Delete fruits
- View fruit for sale
- Add fruit for sale

The header and footer HTML pages, included with the jsp:include element, provide a
common look and feel, as well as links to the important function pages. Listing 22-1 shows
the adminHeader.html and adminFooter.html pages.

Listing 22-1 *The adminHeader.html and adminFooter.html pages are included in all of the pages in the administrative site.*

adminHeader.html

```
<html>
<head>
    <title>IDGB Fruit-Of-The-Month Administrator's
Interface</title>
</head>

<body>
<table width="100%" height="100%">
    <tr>
        <td bgcolor="#B3B3FF" valign="top" align="center
width="150">
            <b>Actions</b>
            <p>
            <a href="Fruit.jsp?mode=view">View Fruit</a><br>
            <a href="addFruit.jsp">Add A Fruit</a><br>
            <a href="Fruit.jsp?mode=delete">Delete Fruits</a><br>
            <a href="fruitMonth.jsp">View Fruit For Sale</a><br>
        <a href="sellFruit.jsp">Add Fruit For Sale</a><br>
        </td>
        <td valign="top">
```

adminFooter.html

```
        </td>
    </tr>
</table>

</body>
</html>
```

The header and footer pages enclose each HTML page inside a table for a uniform layout.

Viewing a Fruit

The Fruit.jsp page shows all of the fruit you have in the Fruit table of your database. This is not the same as the fruit for sale, which is contained in the FruitMonth table. The Fruit.jsp page looks like Figure 22-1, and its code appears in Listing 22-2.

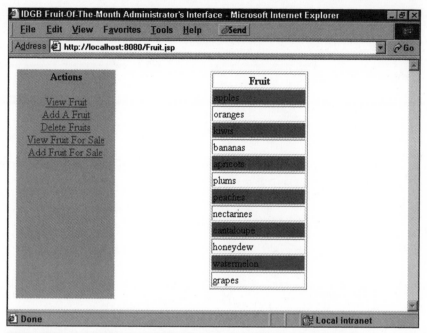

Figure 22-1   *The Fruit.jsp page displays the inventory of fruit.*

Listing 22-2   *Fruit.jsp executes a SELECT statement against the Fruit table.*

Fruit.jsp

```
<%@ page import="java.sql.*" %>
<jsp:include page="adminHeader.html" flush="true" />


<%
Driver drv = (Driver)
Class.forName("sun.jdbc.odbc.JdbcOdbcDriver").newInstance();
Connection conn = DriverManager.getConnection("jdbc:odbc:Fruit");
Statement stmt = conn.createStatement();
ResultSet rs = stmt.executeQuery("SELECT Name From Fruit");
%>

<div align="center">
<table border="1" cellspacing="2" cellspacing="2" width="150">
   <tr>
   <th>Fruit</th>
</tr>

<%
int counter = 0;
String bgColor = "";
```

Continued

Listing 22-2 *Continued*

```jsp
String mode = request.getParameter("mode");
if (mode == null) {
   mode = "view";
}

//step through the ResultSet and display the contents on the
//screen
if (rs != null) {
   while (rs.next()) {
      //alternate the background color of the rows for readability
      if ((counter % 2) == 0){
         bgColor = "#6464FF";
      } else {
         bgColor = "#FFFFFF";
      }
      String fruitName = rs.getString("Name");
      %>

      <form method="post" action="delFruit.jsp">
      <tr bgcolor="<%= bgColor %>">
         <td align="left">
            <% if (mode.equals("delete")) {%>
               <input type="checkbox" name="delFruit" value="<%=
fruitName %>">
            <% } %>
            <%= fruitName %>
         </td>
      </tr>

      <%

   counter = counter + 1;
   }

   if (mode.equals("delete")) {
   %>
      <tr>
         <td><input type="submit" name="submit" value="Delete
Checked Fruit"></td>
      </tr>
   <%
   }
}

stmt.close();
conn.close();
%>
</form>
</table>
</div>
<jsp:include page="adminFooter.html" flush="true" />
```

This code is very similar to the code in Listing 20-1 of Session 20.

To access the fruit names as you iterate through the returned ResultSet, use the getString() method.

Adding a Fruit

**20 Min.
To Go**

To add a fruit to the inventory list in the Fruit table, prompt the user with a form to add the name of the fruit. The addFruit.jsp page looks like Figure 22-2, and its code appears in Listing 22-3.

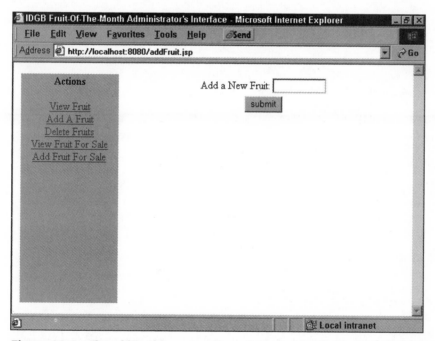

Figure 22-2   *The addFruit.jsp page allows the user to add a fruit to the inventory.*

Listing 22-3   *addFruit.jsp executes an INSERT statement against the Fruit table.*

---

addFruit.jsp

```
<%@ page import="java.sql.*" %>
<jsp:include page="adminHeader.html" flush="true" />
<%
String newFruit = request.getParameter("newFruit");
```

Continued

Listing 22-3

Continued

```
    if (newFruit != null) {
        Driver drv = (Driver)
    Class.forName("sun.jdbc.odbc.JdbcOdbcDriver").newInstance();
        Connection conn =
    DriverManager.getConnection("jdbc:odbc:Fruit");
        Statement stmt = conn.createStatement();
        String query = "INSERT INTO Fruit (Name) VALUES ('" + newFruit
    + "')";
        stmt.executeUpdate(query);
        stmt.close();
        conn.close();


    }
    %>
    <div align="center">
    <form method="post" action="addFruit.jsp">
    <table>
<%
    if (newFruit != null) {
    %>
    <tr>
        <th colspan="2"><%= newFruit %> has been added.</th>
    </tr>
        <%
    }
    %>
    <tr>
        <td>Add a New Fruit:</td>
        <td><input type="text" maxlength="30" size="10"
    name="newFruit"></td>
    </tr>
    <tr>
        <td colspan="2" align="center"><input type="submit"
    name="submit" value="submit"></td>
    </tr>
    </table>
    </form>
    </div>
    <jsp:include page="adminFooter.html" flush="true" />
```

The code first checks to see whether the form has been submitted. If a value is in the newFruit form field, you know the user has submitted the form with the intention of adding a fruit to the database. Execute the proper INSERT statement to insert the fruit into the Fruit table.

This page uses the executeUpdate() method of the Statement object to execute the INSERT statement. Unlike the executeQuery method, which returns a ResultSet object, the executeUpdate() method returns the row count of either the INSERT, UPDATE, or DELETE statement that was executed.

Deleting Fruits

To delete fruits you have added, click on the Delete Fruits link to change the `Fruit.jsp` page to delete mode. Then check the checkbox next to the desired fruit in the `Fruit.jsp` page. When in delete mode, the `Fruit.jsp` page submits to the `delFruit.jsp` page. The version of `Fruit.jsp` with checkboxes is shown in Figure 22-3.

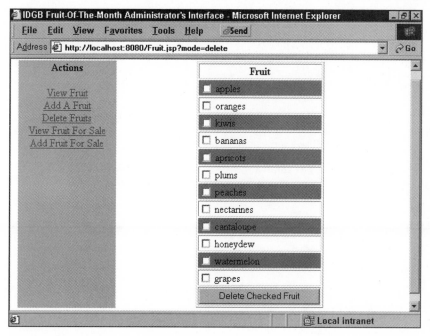

Figure 22-3   *When in delete mode, the Fruit.jsp page displays checkboxes next to the fruit names.*

The `delFruit.jsp` page shown in Listing 22-4 builds the `DELETE` statement dymanically based on the values of the `delFruit` checkbox form fields.

Listing 22-4   *delFruit.jsp executes a DELETE statement against the Fruit table.*

---

delFruit.jsp

```
<%@ page import="java.sql.*" %>
<jsp:include page="adminHeader.html" flush="true" />
<%

String query = "DELETE FROM Fruit WHERE Name IN (";
String msg = "The following fruits have been deleted:<br> ";

Driver drv = (Driver)
Class.forName("sun.jdbc.odbc.JdbcOdbcDriver").newInstance();
```

Continued

Listing 22-4   *Continued*

```
Connection conn = DriverManager.getConnection("jdbc:odbc:Fruit");
Statement stmt = conn.createStatement();
String delFruit[] = request.getParameterValues("delFruit");
int len = delFruit.length;
if (len > 0) {
    for (int i = 0; i < len; i++) {
        query = query + "'" + delFruit[i] + "',";
        msg = msg + delFruit[i] + "<br>";
    }
    query = query + "'nonsense')";
    stmt.executeUpdate(query);
    stmt.close();

}
conn.close();
%>
<div align="center">
<form method="post" action="addFruit.jsp">
<table>
<%
if (len > 0) {
    %>
<tr>
    <th colspan="2"><%= msg %></th>
</tr>
    <%
}
%>

</table>
</form>
</div>
<jsp:include page="adminFooter.html" flush="true" />
```

In this page, you execute the DELETE statement by using the executeUpdate() method. Then you display a message to the user indicating that the fruit has been deleted.

When building the DELETE statement, put each of the fruit names to be deleted in a list so that the final DELETE statement looks something like DELETE FROM Fruit WHERE Name IN ('apples', 'oranges', 'bananas', 'nonsense'). Why do you add the final element 'nonsense' to the list? As you add elements to the list that is in the WHERE clause, you append a comma (,) after each item. When you get to the last item in the list, a dangling comma is at the end, which breaks your SQL statement. The line of code query = query + "'nonsense')"; appends a final 'nonsensical' value to the list to take care of the final comma. You can use any term to complete the list; just make certain you do not use the name of a fruit you do not want to delete.

Viewing Fruit for Sale

The FruitMonth.jsp page, shown in Figure 22-4, displays the list of fruits for sale in the FruitMonth table, and Listing 22-5 displays its code.

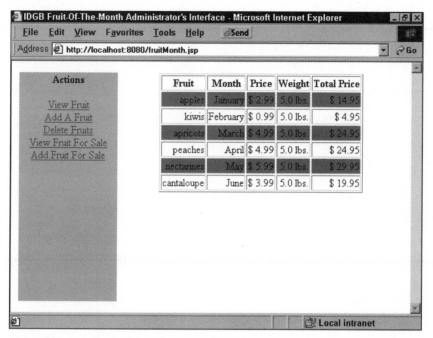

Figure 22-4 *The FruitMonth.jsp displays the fruit for sale for a given month.*

Listing 22-5 *fruitMonth.jsp executes a SELECT statement against the FruitMonth table.*

---

fruitMonth.jsp

```
<%@ page import="java.sql.*" %>
<jsp:include page="adminHeader.html" flush="true" />
<%
Driver drv = (Driver)
Class.forName("sun.jdbc.odbc.JdbcOdbcDriver").newInstance();
Connection conn = DriverManager.getConnection("jdbc:odbc:Fruit");
Statement stmt = conn.createStatement();
ResultSet rs = stmt.executeQuery("SELECT F.Name AS Fruit, M.Name
AS Month, Price, Weight, (Price * Weight) AS TotalPrice FROM
FruitMonth AS FM, Fruit AS F, Month AS M WHERE FM.FruitId = F.Id
AND FM.MonthId = M.Id ORDER BY M.Id");
%>
<div align="center">
<table border="1" cellspacing="2" cellspacing="2">
```

Continued

Listing 22-5   *Continued*

```
        <tr>
        <th>Fruit</th>
            <th>Month</th>
            <th>Price</th>
            <th>Weight</th>
            <th>Total Price</th>
        </tr>
<%
int counter = 0;
String bgColor = "";
if (rs != null) {
    while (rs.next()) {
        if ((counter % 2) == 0){
            bgColor = "#6464FF";
        } else {
            bgColor = "#FFFFFF";
        }
        String fruitName = rs.getString("Fruit");
        String monthName = rs.getString("Month");
        float price = rs.getFloat("Price");
        float weight = rs.getFloat("Weight");
        float totalPrice = rs.getFloat("TotalPrice");

        %>
        <tr bgcolor="<%= bgColor %>">
            <td align="right"><%= fruitName %></td>
            <td align="right"><%= monthName %></td>
            <td align="right">$ <%= price %></td>
            <td align="right"><%= weight %> lbs.</td>
            <td align="right">$ <%= totalPrice %></td>
        </tr>
        <%

    counter = counter + 1;
    }
}

stmt.close();
conn.close();
%>
</table>
<jsp:include page="adminFooter.html" flush="true" />
```

Does the SQL statement look familiar? It should — we created it in Session 21. For the display of the Unit Price, Weight, and Total Price, use the `getFloat()` function of the `ResultSet` object. When accessing the Price, Weight, and TotalPrice columns, use the `getFloat()` method instead of the `getString()` method to return the values as floats.

Adding Fruit for Sale

The sellFruit.jsp page enables the administrator to select a specific weight of fruit to offer for sale in a given month at a specific unit price. The interface is shown in Figure 22-5.

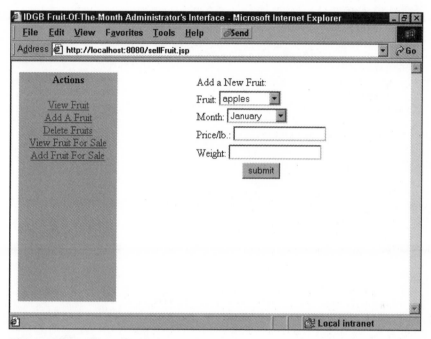

Figure 22-5   *The sellFruit.jsp page enables a user to put fruit up for sale.*

The drop-down lists are each populated dynamically, the first from the Fruit table and the second from the Month table in the database. Generate the necessary HTML by iterating through the ResultSet and appending additional options that correspond to the rows in the table. See Listing 22-6.

Listing 22-6   *sellFruit.jsp executes an INSERT statement against the FruitMonth table.*

---

sellFruit.jsp

```
<%@ page import="java.sql.*" %>
<%!
String convertResultsToSelect ( ResultSet rs, String selectName,
String idCol, String descCol ) throws SQLException
{
    StringBuffer sb = new StringBuffer ( "<select name=" +
selectName +">" );
    if (rs != null) {
        while (rs.next()) {
```

Continued

Listing 22-6

Continued

```
            sb.append ( "<option value=" );
                sb.append ( rs.getString(idCol) );
                sb.append (  ">" );
                sb.append ( rs.getString(descCol) );
                sb.append ( "</option>" );
           }
       }
     sb.append ( "</select>"    );
     return sb.toString ();
}
%>
<jsp:include page="adminHeader.html" flush="true" />
<%
String newFruit = request.getParameter("newFruit");
String msg = "";
String query = "";
Driver drv = (Driver)
Class.forName("sun.jdbc.odbc.JdbcOdbcDriver").newInstance();
Connection conn = DriverManager.getConnection("jdbc:odbc:Fruit");
Statement stmt = conn.createStatement();

String submitted = request.getParameter("submit");
if (submitted != null) {
   String fruit = request.getParameter("fruit");
   String month = request.getParameter("month");
   String price = request.getParameter("price");
   String weight = request.getParameter("weight");
   query = "INSERT INTO FruitMonth (FruitId, MonthId, Price,
Weight) VALUES (" + fruit + "," + month + "," + price + "," +
weight + ")";
   int ret = stmt.executeUpdate(query);
   msg = "Your fruit has been added for sale.";
}

//Build the Fruit Dropdown
query = "SELECT Name, Id FROM Fruit";
ResultSet rs = stmt.executeQuery(query);
String fruitSelect = convertResultsToSelect ( rs, "fruit", "ID",
"Name" );

//Build the Month DropDown
query = "SELECT Name, Id FROM Month ORDER BY Id";
rs = stmt.executeQuery(query);
String monthSelect = convertResultsToSelect ( rs, "month", "ID",
"Name" );

%>
<div align="center">
<form method="post">
<table>
```

```
<%
if (submitted != null) {
    %>
<tr>
    <th colspan="2"><%= msg %></th>
</tr>
    <%
}
%>
<tr>
    <td>Add a New Fruit:</td>
</tr>
<tr>
    <td>Fruit: <%= fruitSelect %></td>
</tr>
<tr>
    <td>Month: <%= monthSelect %></td>
</tr>
<tr>
    <td>Price/lb.: <input type="text" name="price"></td>
</tr>
<tr>
    <td>Weight: <input type="text" name="weight"></td>
</tr>
<tr>
    <td align="center"><input type="submit" name="submit"
value="submit"></td>
</tr>
</table>
</form>
</div>
<%
stmt.close();
conn.close();
%>
<jsp:include page="adminFooter.html" flush="true" />
```

Done!

REVIEW

- It is possible to embed all database-related code directly in your JSP pages.
- The executeUpdate() method for the Statement object will execute UPDATE, INSERT, and DELETE statements.
- The getString() and getFloat() methods are two methods used to access table values while iterating through a ResultSet.

QUIZ YOURSELF

1. Take a look at the addFruit.jsp page. One way to enhance its functionality is to ensure that the fruit a user is trying to add doesn't already exist in the database. How do you implement this functionality most efficiently?

2. Look at the code in Listing 22-2. Can you figure out where the connection to the database is made? Where is the SQL query executed?

3. What method do you use to iterate through the rows in a ResultSet?

4. What is the return of the executeUpdate() method?

Advanced Techniques for Working with JDBC

Session Checklist

✔ Embed database access code in a Java class

✔ Use connection pools

In your applications, it is preferable to partition your business logic away from your presentation logic. Therefore, you do not want to embed the code for connecting to and getting information from the database directly in your JSP pages. In this session, we will code a Java class that encapsulates all of the database-related code.

**30 Min.
To Go**

Embedding Database Code in a Java Class

In Session 22, you created a series of pages for the Fruit-of-the-Month Club administrative interface. Although each of the pages accomplishes different tasks, similar code elements exist in each page. For example, each page that connects to a database creates a Statement object, executes SQL, and closes the open Connection and Statement objects. Although slight variations might exist for each of these functions, we can embed the functions into a single Java class instead of coding them repeatedly in the JSP pages. Creating a class of common code in one place makes maintaining and updating code a snap.

FruitConnect.java

Our Java class is called FruitConnect.java, and the methods contained in the class are described in Table 23-1.

Table 23-1 *Functions in the FruitConnect.java class*

Function	Description
dbConnect()	Loads the JDBC driver and connects to the database
getNextItem()	Calls the next() method of the ResultSet object to move to the next row of the result set
getItemNameString (String columnName)	Returns the String data from the named column
getItemNameFloat (String columnName)	Returns the float data from the named column
selectFruits()	Populates this class's ResultSet with all of the fruits in the Fruit Table
selectMonths()	Populates this class's ResultSet with all of the months in the Month Table
selectFruitForSale()	Populates this class's ResultSet with the fruit for sale in the FruitMonth Table
insertFruit(String FruitName)	Inserts the fruit specified into the Fruit table
insertFruitForSale (String insertValues)	Inserts fruit for sale into the FruitMonth table
deleteFruit(String fruitList)	Deletes the fruits specified from the Fruit table
dbDisconnect()	Disconnects from the database and closes the statement

When creating a common class, it is important to think through the implementations of the different methods. The methods in the FruitConnect class example can be improved in certain places by consolidating reused code or by making the parameters more modular. See the review questions at the end of this session for some possibilities for making enhancements.

To run the examples in this session, first code and compile the FruitConnect.java file. Make certain to place the compiled class FruitConnect.java in the WEB-INF\classes directory underneath the ROOT directory for your files. For example, if the code that accesses the FruitConnect class resides in the <tomcat-install>\webapps\ROOT directory, your FruitConnect.class file should be in the <tomcat-install>\webapps\ROOT\WEB-INF\classes directory.

The pages in this section are identical to the pages that we coded in Session 22, except that all of the database code has been replaced by function calls to the FruitJava class. See Listing 23-1.

Listing 23-1 *The FruitConnect.java file contains all of the database access code that was previously embedded directly in the JSP pages.*

FruitConnect.java

```java
import java.sql.*;

public class FruitConnect {

    private Driver drv = null;
    private Connection conn = null;
    private ResultSet rs = null;
    private Statement stmt = null;


    public FruitConnect(){}

    public void dbConnect() throws Exception{
        drv = (Driver)
Class.forName("sun.jdbc.odbc.JdbcOdbcDriver").newInstance();
        conn = DriverManager.getConnection("jdbc:odbc:Fruit");
    }

    public boolean getNextItem() throws Exception{
        boolean ret = rs.next();
        return(ret);
    }

    public String getItemNameString(String columnName) throws Exception{
        String name = rs.getString(columnName);
        return(name);
    }

    public float getItemNameFloat(String columnName) throws Exception{
        float name = rs.getFloat(columnName);
        return(name);
    }

    public boolean selectFruits() throws Exception{
        String query = "SELECT Id, Name FROM Fruit";
        stmt = conn.createStatement();
        rs = stmt.executeQuery(query);
        boolean ret = false;
        if (rs != null)
            ret = true;
        return(ret);
    }

    public boolean selectMonths() throws Exception{
        String query = "SELECT Id, Name FROM Month";
```

Continued

Listing 23-1 *Continued*

```
        stmt = conn.createStatement();
        rs = stmt.executeQuery(query);
        boolean ret = false;
        if (rs != null)
            ret = true;
        return(ret);
    }


    public boolean selectFruitForSale() throws Exception{
        String query = "SELECT F.Name AS Fruit, M.Name AS Month, Price,
Weight, (Price * Weight) AS TotalPrice FROM FruitMonth AS FM, Fruit AS F,
Month AS M WHERE FM.FruitId = F.Id AND FM.MonthId = M.Id ORDER BY M.Id";
        stmt = conn.createStatement();
        rs = stmt.executeQuery(query);
        boolean ret = false;
        if (rs != null)
            ret = true;
        return(ret);
    }


    public int insertFruit(String name) throws Exception{
        String query = "INSERT INTO Fruit (Name) VALUES ('" + name + "')";
        stmt = conn.createStatement();
        int ret = stmt.executeUpdate(query);
        return(ret);
    }


    public int insertFruitForSale(String insertValues) throws Exception{
        String query = "INSERT INTO FruitMonth (FruitId, MonthId, Price,
Weight) VALUES (" + insertValues + ")";
        stmt = conn.createStatement();
        int ret = stmt.executeUpdate(query);
        return(ret);
    }


    public int deleteFruit(String fruitList) throws Exception{
        String query = "DELETE FROM Fruit WHERE Name IN (" + fruitList +
")";
        stmt = conn.createStatement();
        int ret = stmt.executeUpdate(query);
        return(ret);
    }

    public void dbDisconnect() throws Exception{
        stmt.close();
        conn.close();
    }


}
```

In each of the listings in this section, we instantiate the FruitConnect class with the following line of code:

```
FruitConnect fruitConnect = new FruitConnect();
```

Once the class has been instantiated, we can call each of the classes' methods within the JSP page.

**20 Min.
To Go**

View Fruit

In Listing 23-2 and the listings that follow, we instantiate the FruitConnect class with the jsp:useBean element and set the id of the class to fruitConnect. Once the class has been instantiated, we can call its methods in the JSP page.

Listing 23-2 *Fruit.jsp executes a SELECT statement against the Fruit table.*

Fruit.jsp

```
<%@ page import="java.sql.*" %>
<jsp:include page="adminHeader.html" flush="true" />

<div align="center">
<table border="1" cellspacing="2" cellspacing="2" width="150">
<tr>
  <th>Fruit</th>
</tr>

<% FruitConnect fruitConnect = new FruitConnect(); %>
<%
int counter = 0;
String bgColor = "";
String mode = request.getParameter("mode");
if ( mode == null )
mode = "view";

fruitConnect.dbConnect();
if (fruitConnect.selectFruits()) {
while (fruitConnect.getNextItem()) {
//alternate the background color of the rows for readability
  if ((counter % 2) == 0){
    bgColor = "#6464FF";
  } else {
    bgColor = "#FFFFFF";
  }
  String fruitName = fruitConnect.getItemNameString("Name");
  %>

  <form method="post" action="delFruit.jsp">
```

Continued

Listing 23-2   *Continued*

```
        <tr bgcolor="<%= bgColor %>">
          <td align="left">
            <% if (mode.equals("delete")) {%>
              <input type="checkbox" name="delFruit" value="<%=fruitName %>">
            <% } %>
            <%= fruitName %>
          </td>
      </tr>

      <%

counter = counter + 1;
}

if (mode.equals("delete")) {
%>
  <tr>
    <td><input type="submit" name="submit" value="Delete Checked
Fruit"></td>
  </tr>
<%
}
}
fruitConnect.dbDisconnect();
%>
</form>
</table>
</div>
<jsp:include page="adminFooter.html" flush="true" />
```

Add Fruit

Listing 23-3 uses the FruitConnect class's insertFruit() method, which adds a new fruit to the database. Before we used the FruitConnect class, we had to embed the SQL directly in the JSP page.

Listing 23-3   *addFruit.jsp executes an INSERT statement against the Fruit table.*

addFruit.jsp

```
<%@ page import="java.sql.*" %>
<jsp:include page="adminHeader.html" flush="true" />
<% FruitConnect fruitConnect = new FruitConnect(); %>
<%
String newFruit = request.getParameter("newFruit");
String msg = "";
if (newFruit != null) {
fruitConnect.dbConnect();
```

```
      if((fruitConnect.insertFruit(newFruit)) > 0) {
        msg = "You successfully added <b>" + newFruit + "</b>.";
      } else {
        msg = "There was an error adding <b>" + newFruit + "</b> to the
database.";
      }
    }
    %>
    <div align="center">
    <form method="post" action="addFruit.jsp">
    <table>
    <%
    if (newFruit != null) {
    %>
    <tr>
    <th colspan="2"><%=msg%></th>
    </tr>
    <%
    fruitConnect.dbDisconnect();
    }
    %>
    <tr>
    <td>Add a New Fruit:</td>
    <td><input type="text" maxlength="30" size="10"
    name="newFruit"></td>
    </tr>
    <tr>
    <td colspan="2" align="center"><input type="submit" name="submit"
    value="submit"></td>
    </tr>
    </table>
    </form>
    </div>
    <jsp:include page="adminFooter.html" flush="true" />
```

Delete Fruit

Listing 23-4 uses the deleteFruit() method of the FruitConnect class. Before the fruit is deleted, the code creates a comma-delimited list of all fruit that was checked in the fruit.jsp page.

Listing 23-4   *delFruit.jsp executes a DELETE statement against the Fruit table.*

delFruit.jsp

```
    <%@ page import="java.sql.*" %>
    <jsp:include page="adminHeader.html" flush="true" />
    <% FruitConnect fruitConnect = new FruitConnect(); %>
```

Continued

Listing 23-4   *Continued*

```
<%
String msg = "The following fruits have been deleted:<br> ";

//Build the list of fruits to delete
String delFruit[] = request.getParameterValues("delFruit");
String fruitList = "";
if (delFruit != null){
int len = delFruit.length;
fruitConnect.dbConnect();
for (int i = 0; i < len; i++) {
  fruitList = fruitList + "'" + delFruit[i] + "',";
  msg = msg + delFruit[i] + "<br>";
}
fruitList = fruitList + "'nonsense'";
if (fruitConnect.deleteFruit(fruitList) < 1) {
  msg = "There was an error deleting the fruits from the database.";
}
fruitConnect.dbDisconnect();
} else {
msg = "You must select some fruit to delete.";
}
%>
<div align="center">
<form method="post" action="addFruit.jsp">
<table>
<tr>
<th colspan="2"><%= msg %></th>
</tr>
</table>
</form>
</div>
<jsp:include page="adminFooter.html" flush="true" />
```

View Fruit for Sale

**10 Min.
To Go**

Listing 23-5 calls the selectFruitForSale() method, which returns all of the rows in the
FruitMonth table and calculates a total price for each row.

Listing 23-5   *fruitMonth.jsp executes a SELECT statement against the FruitMonth table.*

fruitMonth.jsp

```
<%@ page import="java.sql.*" %>
<jsp:include page="adminHeader.html" flush="true" />

<div align="center">
<table border="1" cellspacing="2" cellspacing="2">
<tr>
```

```
   <th>Fruit</th>
   <th>Month</th>
   <th>Price</th>
   <th>Weight</th>
   <th>Total Price</th>
</tr>
<% FruitConnect fruitConnect = new FruitConnect(); %>
<%
int counter = 0;
String bgColor = "";

fruitConnect.dbConnect();
if (fruitConnect.selectFruitForSale()) {
while (fruitConnect.getNextItem()) {
  if ((counter % 2) == 0){
    bgColor = "#6464FF";
  } else {
    bgColor = "#FFFFFF";
  }
  String fruitName =
  fruitConnect.getItemNameString("Fruit");
  String monthName =
  fruitConnect.getItemNameString("Month");
  float price = fruitConnect.getItemNameFloat("Price");
  float weight = fruitConnect.getItemNameFloat("Weight");
  float totalPrice =
  fruitConnect.getItemNameFloat("TotalPrice");

%>
<tr bgcolor="<%= bgColor %>">
  <td align="right"><%= fruitName %></td>
  <td align="right"><%= monthName %></td>
  <td align="right">$ <%= price %></td>
  <td align="right"><%= weight %> lbs.</td>
  <td align="right">$ <%= totalPrice %></td>
</tr>
<%

counter = counter + 1;
}
}
fruitConnect.dbDisconnect();
%>
</table>

<jsp:include page="adminFooter.html" flush="true" />
```

Add Fruit for Sale

Listing 23-6 retrieves the months and fruits from the database and dynamically builds drop-down select boxes.

Listing 23-6   *The sellFruit.jsp page enables a user to put fruit up for sale.*

sellFruit.jsp

```
<%@ page import="java.sql.*" %>
<jsp:include page="adminHeader.html" flush="true" />

<div align="center">
<table border="1" cellspacing="2" cellspacing="2">
<tr>
  <th>Fruit</th>
  <th>Month</th>
  <th>Price</th>
  <th>Weight</th>
  <th>Total Price</th>
</tr>
<% FruitConnect fruitConnect = new FruitConnect(); %>
<%
int counter = 0;
String bgColor = "";

fruitConnect.dbConnect();
if (fruitConnect.selectFruitForSale()) {
while (fruitConnect.getNextItem()) {
  if ((counter % 2) == 0){
    bgColor = "#6464FF";
  } else {
    bgColor = "#FFFFFF";
  }
  String fruitName =
  fruitConnect.getItemNameString("Fruit");
  String monthName =
  fruitConnect.getItemNameString("Month");
  float price = fruitConnect.getItemNameFloat("Price");
  float weight = fruitConnect.getItemNameFloat("Weight");
  float totalPrice =
  fruitConnect.getItemNameFloat("TotalPrice");

  %>
  <tr bgcolor="<%= bgColor %>">
    <td align="right"><%= fruitName %></td>
    <td align="right"><%= monthName %></td>
    <td align="right">$ <%= price %></td>
    <td align="right"><%= weight %> lbs.</td>
    <td align="right">$ <%= totalPrice %></td>
  </tr>
  <%

counter = counter + 1;
}
}
```

```
fruitConnect.dbDisconnect();
%>
</table>

<jsp:include page="adminFooter.html" flush="true" />
```

Using Connection Pools

Connecting to the database is a resource-intensive process. In each of the JSP pages in this session, we load the JDBC driver, open a database connection, and close the connection to accomplish our objectives. For the administrative interface, this isn't a problem — after all, how many people are administering the site? For the public side of the site, however, which is designed for fruit consumers, the site can easily become bogged down as it becomes a popular destination. Each time a user comes to the site to view fruits for sale, a new connection to the database is opened. As the number of concurrent users climbs, more and more connections to the database are opened, and the machine's resources on which the site is running can become drained.

The solution is to build a *connection pool,* or a series of open connections to the database, that accepts client requests. The connection pool knows which open connections are in use and which are available and able to accept additional database requests. Remember the code we use to create the initial connection to the database:

```
Connection conn = DriverManager.getConnection("jdbc:odbc:Fruit");
```

The connection pool executes that code several times to create a series of connection objects that can be called from a variety of servlets and/or JSP pages. However, instead of each JSP page creating the connection explicitly, it accesses an already open and available connection. A detailed overview of connection pooling is outside the purview of this book, but you can learn more on Sun's Java site at http://java.sun.com.

Done!

REVIEW

- You can separate your database program logic from your presentation logic by creating a Java class that contains database-related methods. Then, call the methods from your JSP pages after using the jsp:useBean element.

- Code that is called more than once in your pages should be organized as methods in order to maximize code reuse.

- A connection pool is a series of open connections to a database that can accept client requests.

Quiz Yourself

1. Note the different SELECT methods in the FruitConnect.java class: selectFruits(), selectMonths(), selectFruitForSale(). Each uses some common code. Create a function called select(String SQL) that encapsulates the code for executing a SELECT statement. Change the three SELECT methods to call the new method. Is this an improvement? Why?

2. The insertFruitForSale(String insertValues) method accepts a string that is a comma-delimited list for the VALUES () portion of an INSERT statement. The problem with this implementation is that it's not immediately apparent which pieces of information are going to be inserted into the database. Change the class file so that the function accepts four parameters: FruitId, MonthId, Price, and Weight. This changes the way the function is called in the JSP file as well, so be sure to make the appropriate change there.

3. The deleteFruit(String fruitList) function accepts one string that is a list of comma-delimited values. Change the function to accept a String array, fruitList[]. What is the advantage of this implementation?

4. What is the purpose of a connection pool?

JSP Application Architecture:
The Model-View-Controller Pattern

Session Checklist

✔ Understand the architecture of a JSP application

✔ Implement MVC

✔ Examine a sample MVC application

**30 Min.
To Go**

When you build a house, you don't just grab a pile of wood and bricks and start putting them together. Instead, you draw plans — often borrowing from houses or plans you've seen before. Creating a complex set of JSPs is similar to building a house. You need to plan your applications before you start coding.

Not only does it make sense to plan, it makes sense to build on good ideas from existing programs. Simple pages may not require much planning, but a complex system can benefit from partitioning the application into separate pieces, each with their own responsibilities. One common partitioning scheme is the Model-View-Controller (MVC) pattern. This is sometimes called Model 2.

MVC is the basis for many modern operating systems and languages that present graphical information. While MVC adds some complexity, it has proven to make it easier to maintain and extend programs, so using it with complex JSP systems makes good sense. The idea is to segregate the program into three parts: a representation of the data (the model), a display of the data (the view), and a user command handler (the controller).

In this session, we will examine the Model-View-Controller pattern in detail and look at an example of it at work.

Understanding the Architecture of a JSP

Most computer users are familiar with using a spreadsheet program. These programs are a perfect example of the MVC pattern. The spreadsheet reads a file that contains numbers and formulae. This is the model. If the user looks at the file, it probably looks like gibberish. Normally, the user views the data in a grid — the view. Finally, the user can click on the grid and enter data. That's the controller part of the MVC pattern.

What's the advantage? If the spreadsheet uses this pattern, it is easy to read the data from another source — say, a database or the Internet. You simply change the model. If you want to display the data as a graph or a chart, you use another view. You don't need to change the model at all. This partitioning makes it easier to debug your program and to add features later.

How does this relate to JSPs? Many Web applications fit this same category. Users make requests (by submitting a form, for example). The controller handles that. Your program takes that input and performs this task (which might involve accessing a database or other external resources). That's the model's job. Finally, your program produces a Web page to return to the client by using the view.

Another advantage to MVC is that you can hide the application's logic (that is, the model and the controller) from Web authors who need to modify only the JSP (the view). This segregation allows Java developers to focus on the logic while authors focus on the JSP views. Of course, complex view logic can be further concealed within JavaBeans.

 For more information on JavaBeans, see Sessions 11, 12, and 13.

Implementing MVC

**20 Min.
To Go**

There is more than one way to implement MVC using JSP. The obvious choice is to make the controller a servlet. When the user submits a form, the controller servlet will process the request. The controller forwards the request to the model for processing, receives data back, and then passes it along to the view.

The controller servlet can also perform housekeeping, such as creating and populating Beans and validating data. Most of the Java code will reside in the controller or in Beans, so that the view JSPs are mostly HTML with some JSP tags sprinkled throughout. This fosters an effective division of labor between programmers and authors.

Another advantage is that the controller can manage the workflow. In other words, if the user must traverse a series of JSPs (for example, a multipage order form), the controller can direct the user to the next step in the process. If you need to add a page or reorder the pages, there is no need to modify the individual JSPs. All the changes will reside in the controller.

Consider the following scenario:

1. A user submits a form or clicks on a link that points to the controller.
2. The controller determines what action to take by examining the referring page or using some other mechanism to uniquely identify the page.
3. The controller validates the data and passes it to the model.
4. The controller then retrieves data from the model and sends it to a JSP for display.

Just remember: the model contains the data and processing logic, while the view displays data and accepts input. The controller is like a switchboard, directing input to the proper parts of the model.

Examining an MVC Application

Consider a simple shopping cart application. How would you decompose it into a model, view, and controller?

The model, of course, is the actual shopping cart data. In a real cart, you might have a database full of items and their prices. You know how to apply shipping charges and taxes to the order. You can delete items and maybe even check to see if an item is in stock.

The view consists of the screens the users see to manipulate the cart. They push buttons to add things to and delete things from the cart. At first, it might seem as if that's the same job the model does. However, consider that the view only generates commands. It doesn't know how the model carries out the commands. So if you store your inventory in a SQL database today and decide to switch to XML tomorrow, only your model needs to know.

The controller acts as the central switchboard, accepting input from the view and making the correct calls into the controller.

For a shopping cart, the model and view parts have obvious functions. What would you want a controller to do? That will depend on your application, of course, but here's one possible list:

- Add an item
- Delete an item
- Shop (add more items)
- Check out (finish the order)

The model can be a simple JavaBean. Listing 24-1 shows a class, Item, that represents a single product. The shopping cart, then, will be a collection of these objects (in fact, we used a Vector). This object accepts a string with a product description and a price in parentheses. The constructor parses these fields apart and provides methods to access each piece. In addition, static methods allow you to get a list of all possible products (hardcoded for this example) and compute a total cost from a list of items.

Listing 24-1   *A list of these objects will make up the shopping cart's model.*

Item.java

```
import java.util.*;
import java.text.NumberFormat;

public class Item {
    private String desc;
    private String price;
    // the constructor picks out the description and price
    public Item(String init) {
int n=init.indexOf('(');
desc=init.substring(0,n);
price=init.substring(n+1);
n=price.indexOf(')');
price=price.substring(0,n);
```

Continued

Listing 24-1 *Continued*

```
    }
    public String getItem() { return desc; }
    public String getPrice() { return price; }
    public static String getTotal(Vector items) {
Item item;
float total=0.0f;
for (int i=0;i<items.size();i++) {
    item=(Item)items.elementAt(i);
    total+=Float.parseFloat(item.getPrice());
}
NumberFormat fmt=NumberFormat.getCurrencyInstance();
return fmt.format(total);
    }
    // in real life this would be a database
    public static Vector getAllItems() {
Vector v=new Vector();
v.addElement("Austrailian Frut Sampler (11.95)");
v.addElement("Strawberries and Cream Gift Set (22.50)");
v.addElement("Bannana-Rama (7.50)");
return v;
    }
    public static String getAllItemsChoice(String name) {
String s="<SELECT name='" + name +"'>";
Vector v=getAllItems();
for (int i=0;i<v.size();i++)
    s+="<option>"+(String)v.elementAt(i);
s+="</SELECT>";
return s;
    }
}
```

One goal of MVC is to isolate the JSP author from Java code as much as possible, so we added a getAllItemsChoice method to generate a drop-down box of items. You might think this is the province of the view, and in a way it is. However, this illustrates an important concept: the view is responsible for displaying data, but that doesn't mean it can't delegate that responsibility to another component. The fact that the model can generate HTML (as it does in this case) doesn't mean that the model is responsible for drawing it. It simply means that the view can use the model to do some of the HTML rendering, if it wants to do so.

Writing the Controller

The user never sees the controller — it is purely logic. However, it has to respond to user input. Therefore, most controllers are servlets. It is possible to write a controller as a JSP file (after all, a JSP turns into a servlet). However, since you don't need to directly output to the user, a servlet is a better choice.

For more information on servlets, see Session 3.

The controller in Listing 24-2 examines the form input for a `viewcmd` field (which may be hidden). Since we wanted to use a `switch` statement, only the first letter of the field is significant. In particular, an A will add an item to the cart, a D will delete an item, an S returns to shopping, while a C causes the checkout screen to appear. You could identify the action in other ways, of course. You might use an entire string (but you can use `switch` on a string) or you could examine the referring page.

The model is a `Vector` in the user's session variables. Each command sets the `url` variable, which causes the servlet to redirect to that page.

Listing 24-2 *The shopping cart controller servlet recognizes the four commands mentioned in the text.*

Controller.java

```
import java.util.*;
import java.io.*;
import javax.servlet.*;
import javax.servlet.http.*;

public class Controller extends HttpServlet {
  public void init(ServletConfig conf) throws ServletException {
    super.init(conf);
  }

  public void doPost (HttpServletRequest req,
      HttpServletResponse res)
      throws ServletException, IOException {
    HttpSession session = req.getSession(false);
    if (session == null) {
  res.sendRedirect("/error.jsp");
    return;
    }
    Vector cart =
(Vector)session.getAttribute("cart");
    String viewcmd = req.getParameter("viewcmd");
    String url="/index.jsp";
    // A = add, D= delete, C=checkout, S=shop
    switch (viewcmd.charAt(0)) {
    case 'A':
  {
  Item theItem = new Item(req.getParameter("item"));
      if (cart==null)  cart = new Vector();
  cart.addElement(theItem);
  url="/buy.jsp";
```

Continued

Listing 24-2 *Continued*

```
    break;
  }
    case 'C':
url="/total.jsp";
break;
    case 'D':
  {
      String del = req.getParameter("del");
      int deli = Integer.parseInt(del);
      cart.removeElementAt(deli);
      url="/total.jsp";
      break;
  }
    case 'S':
url="/buy.jsp";
break";
    }

    session.setAttribute("cart", cart);
    ServletContext sc = getServletContext();
    RequestDispatcher rd = sc.getRequestDispatcher(url);
    rd.forward(req, res);
    }

  }
```

The View

All that's left is to write JSP files that make use of the model and the controller to do the work. Listing 24-3 shows the file that lets you add to the cart (buy.jsp). A simple call to the model creates a SELECT tag. Notice that the form submits to the controller (controller appears in the web.xml file; see Listing 24-4). The form contains a hidden viewcmd field to tell the controller what action the user is taking.

10 Min. To Go

Listing 24-3 *The buy.jsp file lets you add items to the cart.*

buy.jsp

```
<%@ page session="true" %>
<HTML><HEAD><TITLE>Shop Til You Drop</TITLE></HEAD>
<BODY BGCOLOR=cornsilk>
<form name=shopping
      action=/mvc/controller.go
      method=post>
Choose one:
<%= Item.getAllItemsChoice("item") %>
<input type=hidden name=viewcmd value=A>
```

```
<input type=submit value="Add to Cart">
</form>
<form action=/mvc/controller.go method=post>
<input type=hidden name=viewcmd value=C>
<input type=submit value="Show Cart">
</form>
</BODY></HTML>
```

Listing 24-4   *This web.xml file defines the shopcontroller servlet.*

---

web.xml

```
<web-app>
<servlet>
   <servlet-name>/mvc/controller</servlet-name>
   <servlet-class>Controller</servlet-class>
</servlet>
<servlet-mapping>
   <servlet-name>/mvc/controller</servlet-name>
   <url-pattern>*.go</url-pattern>
</servlet-mapping>
</web-app>
```

The web.xml file is important here because it is what triggers the calling of the controller servlet. Look at the form's action element in the buy.jsp page. Its value is /mvc/controller.go. The servlet-mapping element of the web.xml file says that whenever a resource is called with a .go extension, the /mvc/controller servlet should handle it.

The other view JSP (the checkout screen) appears in Listing 24-5. Notice that this view uses a bit more knowledge of the model — it builds an HTML table with the cart's contents. It still uses the model to compute the total price, however. This is a matter of judgment as you design your system. You could write a model method that outputs the cart as an HTML table (the way SELECT was handled in buy.jsp). Sometimes which functions to handle in the view and which to process in the model is a design choice that only you can make.

Listing 24-5   *Users can view the cart and total using this JSP.*

---

total.jsp

```
<%@ page session="true" import="java.util.*"  %>
<HTML><HEAD><TITLE>Check It Out!</TITLE></HEAD>
<BODY BGCOLOR=cornsilk>
<%
  Vector cart = (Vector)session.getValue("cart");
  if (cart!=null && cart.size()!=0) {
%>
<table border=1>
<tr><td>Item</td><td>Price</td><td> </td></tr>
<% for (int i=0; i< cart.size(); i++) {
    Item item = (Item)cart.elementAt(i);
```

Continued

Listing 24-5 *Continued*

```
%>
     <tr><td><%= item.getItem() %></td>
         <td><%= item.getPrice() %></td>
<td>
<form name=deleteitem action=/mvc/controller.go method=post>
<input type=hidden name=viewcmd value=D>
<input type=hidden name=del value="<%= i %>">
<input type=submit value="Delete">
</form></td>
    </tr>
<% }  // end for %>
</table>
<BR>Total=<%= Item.getTotal(cart) %>
<% } // end if
  else { %>
Your cart is empty!
<% } %>
<form action=/mvc/controller.go method=post>
<input type=hidden name=viewcmd value=S>
<input type=submit value="Keep Shopping">
</form>
</BODY></HTML>
```

If you don't want to roll your own MVC components, you can use the Struts library (see Session 30). Struts provides tools that allow you to use MVC easily without doing all the work yourself.

Deploying the MVC Shopping Cart

Follow these steps to deply the MVC shopping cart:

1. Create a new webapp underneath the <tomcat-install>\webapps directory. Create a new directory here called mvc. Inside mvc, create a directory called WEB-INF. Inside WEB-INF, create a directory called classes.

2. Save the Item.java file in Listing 24-1 and the Controller.java file in Listing 24-2 to your <tomcat-install>\webapps\mvc\WEB-INF\classes directory. Compile the two classes.

3. Save the web.xml file in Listing 24-4 to your <tomcat-install>\webapps\mvc\ WEB-INF directory.

4. Save the buy.jsp page in Listing 24-3 and the total.jsp page in Listing 24-5 to your <tomcat-install>\webapps\mvc directory.

5. Stop and restart Tomcat.

6. Navigate to the buy.jsp page at http://localhost:8080/mvc/buy.jsp.

Done!

REVIEW

- The Model is the part of your application that deals with data storage and logic. Often, it is a JavaBean or a collection of Beans.
- The view is the display portion of the application. This is almost always a JSP.
- The controller is a servlet or JSP that accepts input from the user, possibly validates it, and processes it.

QUIZ YOURSELF

1. What is the Model? The View? The Controller?
2. What are the benefits to using MVC?
3. Can the view portion of an application delegate work to the model?
4. What are two ways for the controller to identify the requesting page?
5. Why is the controller usually a servlet?

XML Described

Session Checklist

✔ Learn XML concepts

✔ Exchange information

✔ Write well-formed documents

✔ Work with document type definitions

**30 Min.
To Go**

X ML (Extensible Markup Language) is a derivative of SGML (Standard Generalized Markup Language), both of which are constructs used to describe and structure information delivered on the Web or on other digital formats. This session does not attempt to explain the use of XML fully or to dictate its role within your Web applications. Rather, it is designed to introduce an XML novice to some of the language's features and to make some suggestions about harnessing its power.

With respect to Java, a series of XML-related APIs exists, including support for XML parsing and XML messaging. The API downloads and specifications are available at http:// java.sun.com/xml.

Learning XML Concepts

By now, you should be relatively familiar with HTML. We've used it quite a bit to render information in our browsers. Recall that servers deliver pages organized by HTML markup. The browser, which has a built-in HTML parser, renders the returned document according to the HTML specifications. The browser knows that <b></b> tags mean bold, that <i></i> tags mean italics, and so on. The universe of HTML tags has been predefined, and each tag has a specific meaning, to be implemented the same way, with some degree of variability.

While HTML is useful for data presentation, it is not so useful for describing the information being presented. For example, with HTML alone, no effective way exists to *describe* the information contained within the page. Listing 25-1 shows a series of fruit for sale. In Listing 25-1, HTML structures the information to a certain degree, but not in a way that describes the data being presented.

Listing 25-1 *The fruitDesc.html page lists fruit for sale.*

fruitDesc.html

```
<html>
<head>
<title>Fruit List</title>
</head>

<body>

<font size="+1"><b>Apples</b></font><br>
<font size="+1"><i>Granny Smith</i></font><br>
Washington<br>
11/01/2000<br>
$1.79/pound<br>
<p>
<b><font size="+1">Oranges</font></b><br>
<font size="+1"><i>Mineola</i></font><br>
Florida<br>
11/01/2000<br>
$1.59/pound<br>
<p>
<font size="+1"><b>Peaches</b></font><br>
<font size="+1"><i>Sweet Red</i></font><br>
Georgia<br>
11/01/2000<br>
$3.29/pound<br>

</body>
</html>
```

Figure 25-1 displays the results.

When you look at the HTML page, it's clear that each group of information pertains to a given fruit item: apples, oranges, or peaches. However, some information is unclear. Does the date refer to the harvest date, the purchase date, or the expiration date? Is the city the fruit's origin or destination? Furthermore, nothing in the page relates the fruit item to its descriptors (type, origin, date, and price) aside from formatting and proximity.

XML is a language used to mark up, or structure, the data being presented. Each application uses its own set of defined elements to tag data meaningfully within the page. With XML, you can define your own markup tags to give greater meaning to the content of your pages and to the relationships among distinct data items. The fruitDesc.xml document contains the same information as the fruitDesc.html document, except now the data has meaning, and the relationships are very clear, as you can see in Listing 25-2.

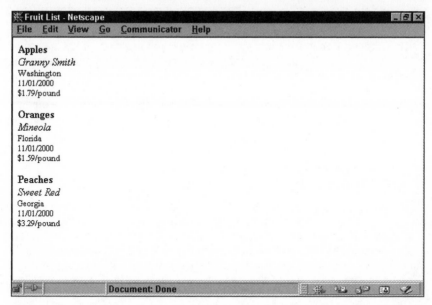

Figure 25-1 *The data in the fruitDesc.html page is formatted with HTML tags.*

Listing 25-2 *The fruitDesc.xml page uses XML to structure the data contained in the page.*

fruitDesc.xml

```
<inventory>
<fruit>
    <name>apples</name>
    <type>Granny Smith</type>
    <origin>Washington</origin>
    <harvest_date>11/01/2000</harvest_date>
    <unit_price>$1.79/pound</unit_price>
</fruit>
<fruit>
    <name>Oranges</name>
    <type>Mineola</type>
    <origin>Florida</origin>
    <harvest_date>11/01/2000</harvest_date>
    <unit_price>$1.59/pound</unit_price>
</fruit>
<fruit>
    <name>Peaches</name>
    <type>Sweet Red</type>
    <origin>Georgia</origin>
    <harvest_date>11/01/2000</harvest_date>
    <unit_price>$3.21/pound</unit_price>
</fruit>
</inventory>
```

Now you know that each location displayed is the fruit's place of origin, as opposed to its shipping destination; and the dates are the harvest dates, as opposed to the dates of freshness or expiration. In addition, with some simple queries, you can extract the names of all of the fruits for sale, the average unit prices of the fruits offered, or the most recent harvest dates; obtaining this information from the `fruitDesc.html` document is very tricky, if not impossible. But the real power of XML is that you can use the base document as the foundation for various presentations. You can create a series of presentation layers on top of the data structure layer to present the same information in various ways, depending on the user.

Exchanging Information

To understand XML's usefulness, consider it in the context of a legitimate business scenario. A fruit distribution company needs to exchange information between a single data source and a series of applications, each one designed for a different device. The same information needs to be delivered via the Web, to handheld devices, via WAP to mobile phones, and internally via a client server application written in Microsoft's Visual Basic. All four applications will display the same data, but it will be formatted differently. The same middle tier can be used to cull the data from the database or whatever backend system or systems it may be coming from. The middle tier will return XML and then you can use XSL or CCS to format the XML appropriately for the various front ends.

The information delivered to the four different systems is virtually identical: fruit inventory (see Figure 25-2). Nonetheless, this information should be presented in four different ways, tailored to the needs of each consumer. The main data source is a relational database management system (RDBMS). But database connections are costly from a resource perspective. Although connecting to a database is an option for applications that reside on the company's internal systems, an increasing need exists to share inventory information with external systems by syndicating the data.

XML adds a layer to the business diagram. The fruit information can reside in a discrete location, structured in XML, and can be parsed into a format that is readable to the different devices. This means that consumers can view information from a single XML source document, such as `fruitDesc.xml`, in a variety of formats without the application developer's having to mix the *structure* of the information with the *presentation* of the information. Furthermore, because it's much easier to define and program a series of presentation layers for a single data source than to develop multiple applications, the addition of the XML layer is pragmatic. Various methods exist for transforming XML into browser-readable code, such as by means of CSS (Cascading Style Sheets), XSL (Extensible Stylesheet Language), or other methods of server-side parsing. All of these topics are beyond the scope of this book.

Writing Well-Formed Documents

20 Min. To Go

If you can write HTML, you can write XML. The mechanics of the languages are basically the same, although XML is more rigid, forcing you to adhere to a certain method of markup to ensure that the document is well formed. A *well-formed* XML document adheres to the rules described in this section.

An element is an item denoted by an opening tag (<>) and a closing tag (</>). An example of an element in `fruitDesc.xml` is `<fruit>apple</fruit>`. The value of the element is contained between the opening and closing tags. The value can be text or other elements or both. An element without data between the opening and closing tags is called an *empty element*. You can also consolidate the empty element into one opening tag that has a forward slash (/) before the end of the opening tag: `<fruit />`. Elements that are not empty must have both an opening tag and a closing tag.

All attribute values within an element must be enclosed in single quotation marks (') or double quotation marks ("). HTML parsers do not require attribute values to be in quotation marks, but XML parsers do. HTML also is not very rigid about closing tags, particularly tags like `<br>` or `<p>`.

When nesting a series of elements, the inner elements must be closed before the outer elements are closed. The following example is incorrect because the innermost element is not closed before the inner element:

```
<bird><name>parakeet</bird></name>
```

The correct version closes the elements in the reverse order of when they are open:

```
<bird><name>parakeet</name><bird>
```

This is another example of how XML is more stringent than HTML.

Working with Document Type Definitions

The term well-formed refers to an XML document's adherence to the syntactical rules of XML. XML documents are said to be *valid* when they conform to the standards set forth by the associated document type definition (DTD). The DTD can be thought of as a rulebook for the structure of your XML. It dictates the hierarchy of the XML structure as well as the types of elements and attributes that can exist within the hierarchy. Listing 25-3 shows what the DTD for `fruitDesc.xml` would look like.

Listing 25-3   *The fruits.dtd file is the DTD for fruitDesc.xml.*

fruits.dtd

```
<!ELEMENT inventory (fruit*)>
<!ELEMENT fruit (name, type, origin, harvest_date, unit_price)>
<!ELEMENT name (#PCDATA)>
<!ELEMENT type (#PCDATA)>
<!ELEMENT origin (#PCDATA)>
<!ELEMENT harvest_date (#PCDATA)>
<!ELEMENT unit_price (#PCDATA)>
```

The `!ELEMENT` declaration declares the valid elements in your XML documents, and it takes two parameters: the name of the element and the acceptable values of the element. `#PCDATA` means that the value of the element can contain any *parsed character data* or plain text. The XML parser parses this text. Any combination of child elements and parsed character data is an acceptable element value.

Elements may contain other elements as values, either singularly or in multiples. According to the DTD, the `inventory` element can contain only the element fruit. The fruit element has five child elements:

- `name`
- `type`
- `origin`
- `harvest_date`
- `unit_price`

Use a comma-separated list, as with the `fruit` element in Listing 25-3, to designate that an element has multiple sub-elements. In addition, you can change the quantities of the sub-elements that can be underneath the parent element. Table 25-1 shows how to indicate the number of allowable child elements for a given element.

Table 25-1 *Element Symbols*

Symbol	Definition
(no symbol)	If an element has a child element without a symbol, the child element *must* exist only once under the parent element.
+	The plus sign (+) means that there must be at least one instance of the child element, but there can also be more than one.
?	The question mark means that there can be zero or one occurrence of the sub-element, but no more than one.
*	An asterisk (*) means that the child element can appear zero, one, or more times.

In the fruits.dtd, the `inventory` element *may* contain multiple fruit sub-elements, although the `fruit` element *must* contain each of its five sub-elements. Modifying the fruits.dtd even slightly affects the business rules governing the data structure. You can also implement conditional logic within your dtd's to indicate that an element can have one or another sub-element. Listing 25-4 shows a modified version of the fruits.dtd with conditional logic.

Listing 25-4 *The modified fruits.dtd file has conditional logic.*

fruits.dtd

```
<!ELEMENT inventory (fruit*)>
<!ELEMENT fruit
  (name, type, (origin | destination), (harvest_date |
purchase_date), unit_price)>
<!ELEMENT name (#PCDATA)>
<!ELEMENT type (#PCDATA)>
<!ELEMENT origin (#PCDATA)>
```

```
<!ELEMENT destination (#PCDATA)>
<!ELEMENT harvest_date (#PCDATA)>
<!ELEMENT purchase_date (#PCDATA)>
<!ELEMENT unit_price (#PCDATA)>
<!ATTLIST unit_price unit CDATA #IMPLIED>
```

The fruit element has some conditional logic embedded in the definition. The pipe character (|) signifies the *or* relationship. In Listing 25-4, the fruit element can contain either the origin or destination element *and* either the harvest_date or purchase_date element. Use parentheses to group the either/or relationships. Now look at the last line of Listing 25-4. It is an attribute declaration for the unit_price element. Attributes are defined according to the following syntax:

```
<!ATTLIST elementName attributeName attributeType required?
DefaultValue>
```

Following are three of the most common options for the attribute type:

- **CDATA** — Character data is basic text.
- **Enumerated values** — You can specify a list of possible values that are valid for the attribute.
- **ID** — The value of the attribute must be unique for each element on the page.

If you want to change the unit attribute so that a predefined list of possible values exists, the !ATTLIST declaration looks like the following line of code:

```
<!ATTLIST unit_price unit (pound | ounce | kilo) #IMPLIED >
```

There are three options for denoting whether the attribute is required to appear in the element:

- **#REQUIRED** — The attribute must always appear.
- **#IMPLIED** — The attribute may appear, but it is not required to appear.
- **#FIXED** — The attribute value is required and cannot be changed.

10 Min. To Go

Attributes versus Child Elements

There are no hard and fast rules about whether to use attributes or elements when defining your DTDs. In most cases, an item defined as an element can just as easily be an attribute, and vice versa. However, because attributes are embedded in the element, they exist in a one-to-one relationship with that element. As you have seen, sub-elements can relate to their parent in a one-to-one, many-to-one, or zero-to-one relationship. If you are certain of a one-to-one relationship among data elements, there is no real difference between structuring the information in either of the two ways:

```
<fruit name="apple" type="granny smith" origin="Washington"
unit_price="$1.79/pound"/>
```

or

```
<fruit>
   <name>apples</name>
   <type>Granny Smith</type>
   <origin>Washington</origin>
   <harvest_date>11/01/2000</harvest_date>
   <unit_price>$1.79/pound</unit_price>
</fruit>
```

In general, attributes are a better choice for storing information *about* the information contained between the opening and closing tags, such as ids, date information, or other information peripheral to what is eventually displayed in the application.

A DTD can be embedded within the document internally or externally. Listing 25-5 shows an example of an internal dtd which is contained within the XML page itself.

Listing 25-5   *An internal dtd is contained in the XML page.*

---

fruitDesc.xml (internal dtd)

```
<?xml version="1.0" standalone="yes"?>
<!DOCTYPE inventory [
<!ELEMENT fruits (fruit)>
<!ELEMENT fruit (name, type, origin, harvest_date, unit_price)>
<!ELEMENT name (#PCDATA)>
<!ELEMENT type (#PCDATA)>
<!ELEMENT origin (#PCDATA)>
<!ELEMENT harvest_date (#PCDATA)>
<!ELEMENT unit_price (#PCDATA)>
]>
<inventory>
<fruit>
   <name>apples</name>      <type>Granny Smith</type>
   <origin>Washington</origin>
   <harvest_date>11/01/2000</harvest_date>
   <unit_price>$1.79/pound</unit_price>
</fruit>
</inventory>
```

The dtd declaration is contained within the <!DOCTYPE []> declarations. More often than not, however, you want to associate an XML document with an external DTD. Listing 25-6 associates the document with a DTD located at http://localhost:8080/fruit.dtd. This example shows an XML page that references an external DTD.

Listing 25-6   *XML pages can reference an external dtd specified in the <!DOCTYPE> element.*

---

fruitDesc.xml

```
<?xml version="1.0" standalone="no"?>
<!DOCTYPE fruits SYSTEM "http://localhost:8080/fruit.dtd">
```

```
<fruits>
<fruit>
  <name>apples</name>
  <type>Granny Smith</type>
  <origin>Washington</origin>
  <harvest_date>11/01/2000</harvest_date>
  <unit_price>$1.79/pound</unit_price>
</fruit>
</fruits>
```

Notice the first line of both versions of `fruitDesc.xml`: `<?xml version="1.0" standalone="yes"?>`. This is the standard XML declaration and is typically included in all of your XML files. If the document refers to an external dtd, the value of the standalone attribute must be set to no.

Done!

REVIEW

- XML provides a standard method of structuring and organizing content.
- Well-formed XML adheres to the XML syntax standards.
- Valid XML adheres to the data structure defined in a dtd.
- A document type definition (dtd) defines the structure of an XML document.

QUIZ YOURSELF

1. Is the following HTML code considered well formed? Why or why not? If it is not well formed, what change can you perform to make it well formed?

   ```
   This is an <b>XML</b><p>example.
   ```

2. In the situation where there are more than one of the same type of element on a given page, how would you define an attribute of the element so that the value of each attribute is unique?

3. What does #PCDATA stand for?

4. What is an empty element and how does it differ syntactically from a non-empty element?

SESSION

XML and JSP

Session Checklist

✔ Learn the basics of XSLT syntax

✔ Set up the example environment

**30 Min.
To Go**

In the previous session we saw how data can be encoded in XML, and we mentioned that the same data can be rendered in different ways using an XSL stylesheet. XSL enables XML to be rendered differently for different purposes. Data in XML can be transformed into an array of HTML formats for presentation on the Web, into WAP for wireless devices, or into another XML format for an external application. In this session we'll look at the how the data transformation process works. We'll learn how to write a basic XSL stylesheet, and we'll learn how to equip our JSP engine to handle data transformation. Then we'll look at how to incorporate this process into our JSP pages.

Learning the Basics of XSLT Syntax

The *Extensible Stylesheet Language* (XSL) is used to describe how other XML documents should be displayed. *Extensible Stylesheet Language Transformations* (XSLT) is concerned with restructuring XML documents for a particular presentation of the data. XSLT is a tool that allows XML data to be transformed for a specific purpose and presented in a specific manner appropriate for that purpose. XSLT traverses an XML document and organizes the data by wrapping XML values in HTML formatting elements.

The first thing we can say about XSLT syntax is that it is well-formed XML. That should tell you that an XSLT document starts with an XML declaration, its tags are case-sensitive, and the values of its attributes are quoted. Listing 26-1 shows the fruitDesc.xml file presented in the previous session. In this session, we will use XSLT to transform the fruitDesc.xml file into an HTML document. For now, code the examples as we come to them. Later in this session, we will create a webapp specifically for this example.

Listing 26-1   *The fruitDesc.xml file structures data with XML tags.*

FruitDesc.xml

```
<?xml version="1.0" ?>
<inventory>
  <fruit>
      <name>apples</name>
      <type>Granny Smith</type>
      <origin>Washington</origin>
      <harvest_date>11/01/2000</harvest_date>
      <unit_price>$1.79/pound</unit_price>
  </fruit>
  <fruit>
      <name>Oranges</name>
      <type>Mineola</type>
      <origin>Florida</origin>
      <harvest_date>11/01/2000</harvest_date>
      <unit_price>$1.59/pound</unit_price>
  </fruit>
  <fruit>
      <name>Peaches</name>
      <type>Sweet Red</type>
      <origin>Georgia</origin>
      <harvest_date>11/01/2000</harvest_date>
      <unit_price>$3.21/pound</unit_price>
  </fruit>
</inventory>
```

While the XML document is useful for structuring the information, it is not readable by all browsers. We use XSLT to effect the transformation from XML into browser-readable HTML code.

You can think of the XSLT stylesheet as a set of rules for how the data in an XML file should be visually presented. The stylesheet is applied to the XML document by a program called a *stylesheet processor*. The processor traverses the XML document and, for each element it encounters, checks the stylesheet to see if there is a rule that describes how to display that element. If it finds a rule, it applies the rule to the appropriate element.

A Rule for the Root Element

The first element in the XML document that the processor will encounter is the root element: the <inventory> element. We can create a rule for the root element of the document, no matter what it is called. We can use this rule to generate the elements of the HTML page that are not specific to the data, such as the <HTML> tags. Listing 26-2 shows the rule that turns the root element of an XML document into HTML elements used for opening and closing a document.

Listing 26-2   *XSLT is like a rule book for displaying XML documents.*

```
<xsl:template match="/">
  <html>
      <head>
            <title>Fruit List</title>
      </head>
      <body>
            <xsl:apply-templates />
      </body>
  </html>
</xsl:template>
```

The template in Listing 26-2 says that when the root element, denoted by a forward slash (/), is encountered, the stylesheet processor should write out the <HTML> tag, the <head> tags, the <title> tags and their contents, and the <body> tag. Then, the <xsl:apply-templates> tag tells the stylesheet processor to continue processing the XML document and to apply rules where appropriate. Were you to leave this tag out of the XSLT document, the resultant HTML page would be without content. After all rules have been processed, the XSL processor will write out the </body> tag and the </html> tags to close the HTML document. The </xsl:template> tag concludes the XSLT document.

The stylesheet processor expects the XSL stylesheet to be well-formed XML, and the parsing process will fail if it finds that the XSL document is not well formed. Therefore, the HTML tags included in the stylesheet must conform to the rules of *well-formedness*. For example, if you have used a <br> tag, that <br> tag needs to be closed by a </br> tag, or it should be an empty tag, as in <br />.

Notice that each of the XSL tags has a prefix, xsl, that is separated from the name of the tag by a colon. This prefix maps the xsl tags to a particular *namespace*, a string that guarantees their uniqueness. The stylesheet processor will not recognize the XSL instructions without referencing the xsl namespace.

Defining Rules by Element Name

**20 Min.
To Go**

We defined a rule above to match the root element of the document, regardless of its name. Listing 26-3 shows an alternate method of defining a rule for a root element, this time naming the root element, <inventory>, explicitly.

Listing 26-3   *It is possible to reference the root element explicitly when making XSL rules.*

```
<xsl:template match="inventory">
  <html>
      <head>
            <title>Fruit List</title>
      </head>
      <body>
```

Continued

Listing 26-3   *Continued*

```
              <xsl:apply-templates />
         </body>
   </html>
</xsl:template>
```

This rule in Listing 26-3 describes the presentation for the `<inventory>` tag, regardless of where it is found in the document.

Some More XSL Tags

To process the document further, we need to iterate through each of the `<fruit>` tags and present the data found in their child elements wrapped in HTML. To do this, we'll need two more tags: `<xsl:for-each>` and `<xsl:value-of>`. Listing 26-4 is the XSL document that defines all of the rules for the `<fruit>` elements in the `fruitDesc.xml` document.

Listing 26-4   *The xsl:for-each and xsl:value-of tags enable us to process the remaining XML tags in the fruitDesc.xml document.*

fruitStyle.xsl

```
<?xml version="1.0" ?>
<xsl:stylesheet version="1.0"
xmlns:xsl="http://www.w3.org/1999/XSL/Transform">
<xsl:template match="inventory">
   <html>
        <head>
                <title>Fruit List</title>
        </head>
        <body>
        <xsl:for-each select="fruit">
                <font size="+1"><b><xsl:value-of select="name" />
</b></font><br/>
                <font size="+1"><i><xsl:value-of select="type" />
</i></font><br />
                <xsl:value-of select ="origin" /> <br />
                <xsl:value-of select ="harvest_date" /> <br />
                <xsl:value-of select ="unit_price" /> <br /><p />
        </xsl:for-each>
        </body>
   </html>
</xsl:template>
</xsl:stylesheet>
```

In the `fruitStyle.xsl` document, we first insert an XML declaration, followed by the `<xsl:stylesheet>` element, which declares that the document is an XSL document. We then add the `<xsl:template>` element to handle the the root element by writing out the opening HTML document tags. Then, in place of the `<xsl:apply-templates>` tag present in Listings 26-2 and 26-3, we use the `<xsl:for-each>` tag. This tag loops through the children of the root element. Inside the loop, we use the `<xsl:value-of>` tag to access the child elements of the `<fruit>` element; we set the value of the `select` attribute of the `<xsl:value-of>` element to the name of the element we are formatting. The XSL rules tell the stylesheet processor to wrap the value of the `xsl:value-of` elements in HTML. Note that the `<xsl:value-of>` tag will format the first match that it that it finds and writes only one value, even if multiple children match the `select` attribute. This is in contrast to the `<xsl:for-each>` tag, which is intended for cases where there are multiple matches.

`<xsl:value-of>` **returns only one value, no matter how many matches are found.**

Listing 26-5 shows the `transform.jsp` page, which allows us to apply the stylesheet to the XML document. The first line is the `taglib` directive, which specifies a prefix, `xsl`, to be used for our custom tags. The second line uses the `xsl:appy` custom tag to apply the `fruitStyle.xsl` stylesheet to the `fruitDesc.xml` document.

Listing 26-5 *The taglib directive allows us to use custom tag libraries.*

```
<%@taglib uri="http://jakarta.apache.org/taglibs/xsl-1.0" prefix="xsl" %>
<xsl:apply xml="/xml/fruitDesc.xml" xsl="/xml/fruitStyle.xsl"/>
```

Refer to Sessions 27–29 for more on tag libraries.

Setting Up the Example Environment

**10 Min.
To Go**

To see the example in action, you need to deploy Apache's custom XSL tag library and stylesheet processor. Follow these directions to run the example:

1. Create and deploy a new Web application for the XSL example. In your <tomcat-install>\webapps directory, create a directory and name it \xsl. Place the `transform.jsp` page in the \xsl directory. Inside the \xsl directory, create two directories and name them \WEB-INF and \xml. Inside the \WEB-INF directory, create two directories and call them \classes and \lib. Place the `fruitDesc.xml` and `fruitStyle.xsl` files you coded in this session in the \xml directory.

2. Download the most recent XSL tag library from http://jakarta.apache.org/builds/jakarta-taglibs/nightly/projects/xsl/. The download is a tag library that allows you to access XSLT operations from a JSP page using JSP custom tags. Extract the file you downloaded using Winzip. From the extracted file folder, copy the `xsl.jar` file into the <tomcat-install>\webapps\xsl\lib directory. Copy the `xsl.tld` file into the <tomcat-install>\webapps\xsl\WEB-INF directory.

3. Download the most recent version of the Apache XSLT processor, Xalan-J, from `http://xml.apache.org/xalan-j/`. Extract the file you downloaded using Winzip. From the extracted file folder's \bin directory, copy the `xalan.jar` and the `xerces.jar` files into the <tomcat-install>\webapps\xsl\WEB-INF\lib directory. Add the new path to these two files to the `CLASSPATH` variable of your system.

4. Create a `web.xml` file with the code in Listing 26-5. Save the `web.xml` file to the <tomcat-install>\webapps\xsl\WEB-INF directory.

5. Stop and restart Tomcat.

6. Navigate to the `http://localhost:8080/xsl/transform.jsp` page.

Listing 26-5 *The web.xml file tells your application where to find the tag library file.*

---

web.xml

```
<?xml version="1.0" encoding="ISO-8859-1"?>

<!DOCTYPE web-app PUBLIC "-//Sun Microsystems, Inc.//DTD Web Application
2.2//EN" "http://java.sun.com/j2ee/dtds/web-app_2.2.dtd">

<web-app>
  <taglib>
    <taglib-uri>http://jakarta.apache.org/taglibs/xsl-1.0</taglib-uri>
    <taglib-location>/WEB-INF/xsl.tld</taglib-location>
  </taglib>

</web-app>
```

Done!

REVIEW

- XSLT is an XML language for transforming XML.
- XSLT creates rules to describe how elements in the XML document should be processed.
- XSLT is processed by a program called a stylesheet processor.
- XML and XSLT achieve a separation of presentation and data.

QUIZ YOURSELF

1. What does the "T" in XSLT stand for ?
2. What is the purpose of an XSLT stylesheet?
3. What is the root element of an XSL stylesheet?
4. Which XSL tag is useful for iterating through a set of tags of the same name?
5. What do you have to do to embed line breaks in an HTML page using XSLT?

PART

5

Sunday Morning

1. Name four types of SQL statements.
2. When executing an INSERT statement, when is it unnecessary to specify the names of the columns into which you are inserting data?
3. What SQL call do you use to change data that already exists in a database table?
4. What SQL statement would you use to delete all the rows in a table called "news" where the column "printed" is "Y"?
5. What code would you execute to close a Statement object named stmt?
6. Which object is returned by the executeQuery() method of the Statement object?
7. Which object is returned by the createStatement() method of the Connection object?
8. Which method moves you to the next row of a ResultSet?
9. In M-V-C, what is the role of the Model?
10. In M-V-C, what is the role of the View?
11. In M-V-C, what is the role of the Controller?
12. What does XML stand for?
13. What makes an empty XML element empty?
14. What does the term DTD stand for?
15. What does a plus sign (+) signify, in the context of a DTD?
16. What does #PCDATA stand for?

17. What is the root element of any XSLT stylesheet?

18. What does the instruction `<xsl:apply-templates>` do?

19. What attribute is used with `<xsl:value-of>` and `<xsl:for-each>` to match the node or nodes to which the associated rule applies?

20. True or false: XSLT can be used only to transform XML into HTML.

PART

VI

Sunday Afternoon

Working with Tag Libraries

Session Checklist

✔ Understand the need for taglibs and custom tags

✔ Create a Hello custom tag

✔ Learn about the tag library descriptor

✔ Deploy custom tags

**30 Min.
To Go**

In addition to standard JSP tags, developers can create new custom *tag libraries*. Tag libraries are repositories of code where each code segment is defined as a custom tag that can be reused on different JSP pages. We have already seen and used several JSP tags, among them the `jsp:useBean`, `jsp:setProperty`, `jsp:getProperty`, `jsp:forward`, and `jsp:include` tags. While these tags have been pre-designed for use in *all* JSP pages by *all* JSP developers, tag libraries make it possible for you to write *your own* tags for doing tasks specific to *your own* application. Once you develop your custom tags, HTML developers can employ the elements on a JSP page without knowing the particular implementation details (the inner workings) of the tags themselves. Thus, because custom tags look and act precisely like HTML tags, they allow HTML developers and JSP programmers to work together seamlessly, each devoted to his own specialty.

In this session, we will learn how to create and deploy a simple tag library. The example is an application that displays a user's account balance in black if he is cash-flow-positive and red if he is in debt. We will use a custom tag to house the logic for the display instead of using HTML markup.

Understanding the Need for Custom tags and taglibs

To take advantage of custom tags, you must create a tag library and supporting Java classes that delineate the behavior of the tags defined in the tag library. In the tag library descriptor, the developer provides XML markup that defines the syntax of each tag. Then, in each JSP page that includes the custom tags, the JSP author adds a reference to the tag library document near the top of the page; this enables the use of the custom tags as if they were any other JSP element, such as the `jsp:useBean` or the `jsp:setProperty` elements.

Just like XML, tags have attributes and bodies, as in the example syntax below:

```
<namespace:tag attribute1="value1" attribute2="value2">body</tag1>
```

Special handler classes dictate the behavior of the tag in concert with the values defined in the tag's attributes and the body of the tag (if there is one). The `@taglib` directive allows developers to use tags on a given page.

To illustrate how tag library tags function, consider an HTML example of the standard first-level-heading tag, `<h1>`. Suppose you wanted to write a Java method, `formatH1( String text)`, that wrapped the text parameter in `<h1>` tags. With a Bean or a method declared in your page, you would need to pass the text to the method as a parameter, as in the example below:

```
formatH1("Welcome to the Fruit-of-the-Month Club!");
```

This method gets the job done, but it does not work in the same fashion as HTML or XML, where you would wrap the text inside opening and closing markup tags. The same example using custom tags would look like the next line of code:

```
<format:h1>Welcome to the Fruit-of-the-Month Club!</format:h1>
```

Custom tags are not used only for formatting, but the example should be instructive: tags allow you to accomplish certain tasks in a manner that is intuitive to someone familiar with markup languages.

Behind the scenes, when the JSP engine sees a tag that is associated with a tag library, it calls the handler class for that tag and passes it the information contained in the attributes and body of the tag. The JSP engine then inserts any content returned from the handler class into the document in place of the custom tags.

Creating a Hello World Custom tag

In the next example, we will deploy a simple custom tag library, a handler class, and a page that uses a tag in our library.

Coding the tag Library

By convention, tag library files have a `.tld` extension, as in `myLibrary.tld`, and are placed in the WEB-INF directory of your webapp. Tag libraries are structured with XML and are case-sensitive. Listing 27-1 shows a tag library with a single tag, named `hello`.

Listing 27-1 *This simple tag library descriptor defines a single tag.*

display.tld
```
<?xml version="1.0" encoding="ISO-8859-1" ?>
<!DOCTYPE taglib
```

```
PUBLIC "-//Sun Microsystems, Inc.//DTD JSP Tag Library 1.1//EN"
"http://java.sun.com/j2ee/dtds/web-jsptaglibrary_1_1.dtd">

<taglib>
  <tlibversion>1.0</tlibversion>
  <jspversion>1.1</jspversion>
  <shortname>display</shortname>
  <uri></uri>
  <info>A tag library for displaying information</info>

  <tag>
    <name>accountTag</name>
    <tagclass>ch27.AccountTag</tagclass>
    <info>Displays Negative Accounts in a different color</info>
    <attribute>
        <name>color</name>
        <required>false</required>
    </attribute>
  </tag>
</taglib>
```

Like all XML documents, Listing 27-1 begins with an xml declaration. The DOCTYPE element defines the Document Type Definition (DTD) for the descriptor file; you can use the DTD maintained by Sun, as the preceding example does.

Refer to Session 25 for more information on XML and DTDs.

The first group of tags relate to the library as a whole:

- **taglib** — This tag introduces the library.
- **tlibversion** — You'll use this tag to specify the version number of your library.
- **jspversion** — This tag specifies the JSP version this library assumes.
- **shortname** — The library's short name is used by some Java builder tools as the default prefix for the tags.
- **uri** — You can optionally specify a Uniform Resource Identifier (usually a URL) that points to the library's documentation.
- **info** — You can place a short description of the library in the info tag.

For each custom tag the library defines, you'll need a tag section. The tag element has the following child tags:

- **name** — This specifies the name of the custom tag.
- **tagclass** — This tag points to the Java class that supports this tag. The class that will handle the class is the AccountTag.java class presented in the next section.
- **info** — Use the info tag to provide a description of the tag.

- **bodycontent** — This tag specifies what the custom tag expects in its body. EMPTY, the value used in this case, means there is no body at all. Other possible values are JSP and tagdependent.

The display.tld **file uses tag attributes and bodies; these two concepts are are covered more fully in Session 28.**

The elements described above are sufficient for the tag library we are developing now, though more sophisticated tags will require that other elements be present in the tag library.

Coding the Handler Class

**20 Min.
To Go**

To interpret custom tags, you must code a Java class, also called a tag handler, which will perform the custom tag's logic. When the JSP page encounters the custom tag, it asks the tag handler class to determine what to do. The handler class must implement the javac.servlet.jsp.tagext.Tag interface. When coding the handler class, it should extend one of the provided base classes, such as BodyTagSupport, which has default versions of all the necessary methods.

Listing 27-2 shows the code for a handler class that extends the BodyTagSupport class to support the hello tag.

Listing 27-2   *This Java class provides the logic for the custom hello tag.*

AccountTag.java

```
package ch27;

import java.io.*;
import javax.servlet.jsp.*;
import javax.servlet.jsp.tagext.*;

public class AccountTag extends BodyTagSupport
{
    private String _color = "#EC374E";

    public void setColor ( String newColor )
    {
        _color = newColor;
    }

    public int doAfterBody() throws JspTagException
    {
        BodyContent bc = getBodyContent();
        String body = bc.getString();
```

```
                    bc.clearBody();
                    Float f;
                    boolean isNegative = false;
                    StringBuffer output = new StringBuffer();

                    try
                    {
                        try
                        {
                            f = new Float ( body );
                            if ( f.floatValue () < 0 )
                                isNegative = true;

                        }
                            catch ( Exception e )
                        {
                            // If the value can't be converted to a number,
                            // just display as is.
                        }

                        if ( isNegative )
                            output.append ( "<font color=\"" + _color + "\">" );

                        output.append ( body );

                        if ( isNegative )
                            output.append ( "</font>" );

                        getPreviousOut().print(output.toString());
                    }
                     catch (IOException e)
                    {
                     throw new JspTagException("AccountTag: " + e.getMessage());
                    }
                    return SKIP_BODY;
                }
            }
```

In the AccountTag class, the doAfterBody() method returns an int value whose job it is to tell the JSP container how to further process the tag. Since there is no body for the AccountTag in Listing 27-2, the doAfterBody() method returns the SKIP_BODY constant, a value that means that the container should skip over the tag's body. Some tags that have a body may still want to conditionally return SKIP_BODY to ignore the body.

Calling the tag Library from a JSP Page

Listing 27-3 is the JSP page that references the display.tld tag library and uses the hello tag.

Listing 27-3   *The @taglib directive allows you to reference tag libraries in your JSP pages.*

AccountTag.jsp

```jsp
<%@ taglib uri="/WEB-INF/display.tld" prefix="display" %>
<html>
    <head>
        <title>Tag Library Example</title>
    </head>
    <body>
    <table cellspacing="2" cellpadding="2" border="2">
        <tr>
        <th>Account</th>
         <th align="right">Balance</th>
         </tr>
         <tr>
            <td>Checking</td>
            <td align="right"><display:accountTag>-
10</display:accountTag></td>
        </tr>
        <tr>
            <td>Savings</td>
            <td
align="right"><display:accountTag>50</display:accountTag></td>
        </tr>
        <tr>
            <td>Brokerage</td>
            <td align="right"><display:accountTag color="#00FF00">-
200.25</display:accountTag></td>
        </tr>
        <tr>
        <td>401K</td>
        <td
align="right"><display:accountTag>35.35</display:accountTag></td>
        </tr>
    </table>
</html>
```

The @taglib directive tells the JSP page where to find the tag library. The uri attribute specifies the location of the tag library descriptor file. The prefix attribute specifies the name you will use to prefix to the tags in a particular library. This feature is similar to the jsp prefix that you are familiar with in tags such as jsp:useBean and jsp:forward. With the prefix, mutltiple tag libraries can define tags with the same name without any conflict: the prefix will distinguish the different tag libraries. In Listing 27-3, the prefix value is display. Between the HTML <body></body> tags, we've inserted our custom <display:accountTag> tag.

Deploying the Tag Library

**10 Min.
To Go**

Deploying tag libraries will vary for each server. The instructions below will deploy the tag library on our version of tag library.

1. Create a new webapp underneath the <tomcat-install>\webapps directory. Create a new directory here called taglib. Inside taglib, create a directory called WEB-INF. Inside WEB-INF, create a directory called classes. Inside classes, create a directory called ch27, which will hold the tag handler class.

2. Save the `display.tld` file in Listing 27-1 to your <tomcat-install>\webapps\ taglib\ \WEB-INF directory.

3. Create a web.xml file in the <tomcat-install>\webapps\taglib\WEB-INF directory. Code the web.xml file to look like Listing 27-4.

4. Save the `TagHandler.java` class file to your <tomcat-install>\webapps\taglib\ WEB-INF\classes\ch27 directory. Open up a command prompt window and navigate to the class's directory using `cd` commands. Compile the class using the `javac` command: `javac AccountTag.java`.

5. Save the `AccountTag.jsp` file to your <tomcat-install>\webapps\taglib directory.

6. Stop and restart the Tomcat server.

Listing 27-4   *The web.xml file points your JSP page to the appropriate tag library descriptor.*

AccountTag.jsp

```
<?xml version="1.0" encoding="ISO-8859-1"?>
<!DOCTYPE web-app PUBLIC "-//Sun Microsystems, Inc.//DTD Web Application
2.2//EN"
    "http://java.sun.com/j2ee/dtds/web-app_2_2.dtd">
<web-app>
  <taglib>
      <taglib-uri>/WEB-INF/display.tld</taglib-uri>
      <taglib-location>/WEB-INF/display.tld</taglib-location>
  </taglib>
</web-app>
```

To access the page, navigate to http://localhost:8080/taglib/AccountTag.jsp.

Done!

REVIEW

- Custom tags enable Java programmers to provide sophisticated features for JSP authors.
- Creating a `taglib` requires an XML descriptor file and a Java class for each tag.
- Using custom tags in a JSP page requires a `taglib` directive.

Quiz Yourself

1. What does the return value of `doStartTag` control?
2. What is the purpose of the tag library descriptor?
3. What are the attributes of the `taglib` directive?
4. What is the purpose of the prefix for a JSP tag library?

Tag Libraries: Attributes and Tag Bodies

Session Checklist

✔ Process body text

✔ Examine attributes in custom tags

**30 Min.
To Go**

he previous session introduced the basic elements involved in creating custom JSP tags: the tag handler class, the tag library descriptor file, and the JSP `taglib` directive. In the tag we created in Session 27, we used the body text and attributes, but we glossed over the particulars of their use. In this session we will look at these two aspects of JSP tag libraries in more detail.

Processing Body Text

The body of an element is the text found between the opening and closing elements, as in the example below:

```
<custom:showitem>apples</custom:showitem>
```

The body text is the string between the opening and closing tags, `apples`.

The next example supposes we are developing the Fruit-of-the-Month Club application using the Model-View-Controller pattern. Each form in the application will have common characteristics: each will submit to the same same servlet (listening to the `controller.go` URL); each will have a hidden field that identifies the form to the controller; and each will use the `post` method and have a standard Submit button.

This session uses the Controller servlet we coded in Session 24.

Listing 28-1 shows the tag descriptor file with a single defined tag, quickForm, which we will use to generate a prebuilt form.

Listing 28-1   *This form.tld descriptor file defines the quickform custom tag.*

form.tld

```
<?xml version="1.0" encoding="ISO-8859-1" ?>
<!DOCTYPE taglib
  PUBLIC "-//Sun Microsystems, Inc.//DTD JSP Tag Library 1.1//EN"
  "http://java.sun.com/j2ee/dtds/web-jsptaglibrary_1_1.dtd">

<taglib>
  <tlibversion>1.0</tlibversion>
  <jspversion>1.1</jspversion>
  <shortname>display</shortname>
  <uri></uri>
  <info>A tag library for displaying information</info>

  <tag>
      <name>quickForm</name>
      <tagclass>tag.QuickForm</tagclass>
      <info>This tag provides a readymade form for the fruit of the month
club, to which form elements can be added by means of the tag body </info>
      <bodycontent>JSP</bodycontent>
    </tag>

</taglib>
```

In the descriptor file, we set the name element to quickForm, the tagclass element to tags.QuickForm (the location of the QuickForm.java class in Listing 28-2), and the body-content element to JSP, which indicates that the tag accepts *any* JSP content inside its body. Listing 28-2 shows the tag handler class for a custom form tag. This tag provides all the common form elements for the form author. The author specifies only the unique portions of the form in the tag's body. However, the author still has to provide the hidden field that identifies the form to the controller.

**20 Min.
To Go**

Listing 28-2   *This custom tag will standardize application forms.*

QuickForm.java

```
package tag;

import java.io.*;
import javax.servlet.jsp.*;
```

```
import javax.servlet.jsp.tagext.*;

public class QuickForm extends TagSupport {

    public int doStartTag(){
        try{
            JspWriter out = pageContext.getOut();
            out.print("<table width=\"100%\" cellpadding=\"0\"
cellspacing=\"0\" border=\"1\" bgcolor=\"#c0c0c0\"><tr><td valign=\"top\"
align=\"left\">");
            out.print("<form action=\"controller.go\" method=\"POST\">");
        } catch(IOException ioex){
            System.out.println("Error in quickform - " + ioex);
        }
        return(EVAL_BODY_INCLUDE);
    }

    public int doEndTag() {
        try{
            JspWriter out = pageContext.getOut();
            out.print("<input type=\"submit\" value=\"Submit\">");
            out.print("</form>");
            out.print("</td></tr></table>");
        } catch(IOException ioex){
            System.out.println("Error in quickform - " + ioex);
        }
        return(EVAL_BODY_INCLUDE);
    }
}
```

In the tag handler class, the doStartTag() method prints out the start of the form, and the doEndTag() method prints out the end of the form. The doStartTag() method returns the EVAL_BODY_INCLUDE constant to indicate that the tag should evaluate the body of the tag into the existing out stream. The doEndTag method should return the EVAL_PAGE constant.

Embedding tags in JSP

Now you can quickly create forms for the Fruit-of-the-Month Club using the custom tag. You can see an example in Listing 28-3 and the resulting HTML in Listing 28-4.

Listing 28-3 *This JSP uses the custom tag to create a form.*

QuickForm.jsp
```
<%@ taglib uri="/WEB-INF/form.tld" prefix="form" %>
<html>
<body>
    <form:quickForm>
        <input type="hidden" name="formType" value="Shipping">
```

Continued

Listing 28-3 *Continued*

```
<table border="0">
  <tr>
    <td colspan="2"><h1>Shipping Address</h1></td>
  </tr>
  <tr>
    <td>Street Address:</td>
    <td><input type="text" name="address"></td>
  </tr>
  <tr>
    <td>Apartment</td>
    <td><input type="text" name="apt"></td>
  </tr>
  <tr>
    <td>City</td>
    <td><input type="text" name="city"></td>
  </tr>
  <tr>
    <td>State</td>
    <td><input type="text" name="state"></td>
  </tr>
  <tr>
     <td>Zip</td>
     <td><input type="text" name="zip"></td>
  </tr>
</table>
    </form:quickForm>
  </body>
</html>
```

Although this example uses only normal HTML in the tag's body, you could include any JSP elements, including scriptlets, expressions, or directives.

Adding Attributes to Custom Tags

10 Min.
To Go

In the form generation examples in Listings 28-1 through 28-3, the JSP author still has to know to include a hidden field that identifies the form's type. In addition, notice that the author specifies the title of the form in the first row of the form's table. In the next example, we will modify the tag descriptor file, the tag handler class, and the JSP page so that the title of the form and the value of the hidden form element are included as tag attributes.

Listing 28-4 shows the revised form.tld file, which has additional attributes. The text in bold is the attribute declarations.

Listing 28-4   *This taglib file specifies a custom tag with two attributes.*

form.tld

```
<?xml version="1.0" encoding="ISO-8859-1" ?>
<!DOCTYPE taglib
 PUBLIC "-//Sun Microsystems, Inc.//DTD JSP Tag Library 1.1//EN"
 "http://java.sun.com/j2ee/dtds/web-jsptaglibrary_1_1.dtd">

<taglib>
  <tlibversion>1.0</tlibversion>
  <jspversion>1.1</jspversion>
  <shortname>display</shortname>
  <uri></uri>
  <info>A tag library for displaying information</info>

  <tag>
  <name>quickForm</name>
  <tagclass>tag.QuickForm</tagclass>
  <info>This tag provides a readymade form for the fruit of the month
club, to which form elements can be added by means of the tag body </info>
  <bodycontent>JSP</bodycontent>
  <attribute>
      <name>type</name>
      <required>true</required>
  </attribute>
  <attribute>
      <name>title</name>
      <required>false</required>
  </attribute>
   </tag>
</taglib>
```

When the container is translating the JSP page and encounters a custom tag attribute, it calls the corresponding setter method behind the scenes. Of course, you also need to make changes in the descriptor file that describes the tag. In particular, you'll use the attribute tag. Within this tag are three subtags:

- name — You'll use this tag to specify the attribute name (for example, title).
- required — This tag determines if the attribute is optional.
- rtexprvalue — You can set this option to tell the JSP container to evaluate the value of the attribute so that you can use JSP expressions in the value.

You must specify the name and required tags. You can omit rtexprvalue if you want the default value (false). Listing 28-5 shows the taglib XML required for the quickform tag with attributes. In our QuickForm.java class, we must code methods to handle tag attributes. You could add two instance fields to the tag handler class. One field, type, would hold the form's type; the other, title, would hold the title. You'll also write setType() and setTitle() methods. Finally, the other methods — doStartTag() and doEndTag() — can use the fields to generate their output. Listing 28-5 shows the new QuickForm.java file with changes in bold.

Listing 28-5 *Changes to the tag handler class enable it to handle attributes.*

QuickForm.java

```java
package tag;

import java.io.*;
import javax.servlet.jsp.*;
import javax.servlet.jsp.tagext.*;

public class QuickForm extends TagSupport {

  public String title="No Title";
  public String type="?";

  public void setTitle(String title){
      this.title=title;
  }
  public void setType(String type){
      this.type=type;
  }

   public int doStartTag(){
      try{
         JspWriter out = pageContext.getOut();
         out.print("<table width=\"100%\" cellpadding=\"0\"
cellspacing=\"0\" border=\"1\" bgcolor=\"#c0c0c0\"><tr><td valign=\"top\"
align=\"left\">");
         out.print("<form action=\"controller.go\" method=\"POST\">");
         out.print("<h1>" + title + "</h1>");
         out.print("<input type=\"hidden\" name=\"id\" value=\"" + type +
"\">");
      } catch(IOException ioex){
         System.out.println("Error in quickform - " + ioex);
      }
      return(EVAL_BODY_INCLUDE);
   }

   public int doEndTag() {
      try{
         JspWriter out = pageContext.getOut();
         out.print("<input type=\"submit\" value=\"Submit\">");
         out.print("</form>");
         out.print("</td></tr></table>");
      } catch(IOException ioex){
         System.out.println("Error in quickform - " + ioex);
      }
      return(EVAL_BODY_INCLUDE);
   }
}
```

The new `QuickForm.jsp` page is in Listing 28-6. The new `quickForm` start tag is listed in bold.

Listing 28-6 *The new quickForm tag has two attributes.*

QuickForm.jsp
```
<%@ taglib uri="/WEB-INF/form.tld" prefix="form" %>
<html>
<body>
    <form:quickForm type="Shipping" title="Shipping Address">
        <table border="0">
            <tr>
                <td>Street Address:</td>
                <td><input type="text" name="address"></td>
            </tr>
            <tr>
                <td>Apartment</td>
                <td><input type="text" name="apt"></td>
            </tr>
            <tr>
                <td>City</td>
                <td><input type="text" name="city"></td>
            </tr>
            <tr>
                <td>State</td>
                <td><input type="text" name="state"></td>
            </tr>
            <tr>
                <td>Zip</td>
                <td><input type="text" name="zip"></td>
            </tr>
        </table>
    </form:quickForm>
</body>
</html>
```

Done!

REVIEW

- Add attributes to a custom tag to enable authors to set options.
- The class file requires an instance field for each attribute, and a method to set the attribute.
- Use the `attribute` tag in the descriptor file to specify legal attributes and their characteristics.

Quiz Yourself

1. What changes, if any, are necessary to the `taglib` directive when using custom tags that have attributes?

2. Which method performs actions after the processing of a tag's body?

3. True or false: All attributes for tags are always required.

4. Can the body of a tag contain HTML, JSP statements, or only plain text?

5. Can a custom tag abort the processing of the remainder of the JSP page?

Tag Libraries: Bodies

Session Checklist

✔ Manipulate the tag body

✔ Process the tag body

✔ Make modifications

**30 Min.
To Go**

The custom tags developed in previous sessions could insert information before and after their body text. However, they did not actually work with the body text themselves. Sometimes you want more control over the process. You can conditionally include or reject the body, and you can also read and potentially modify data in the body.

For example, you might want to create a tag that allows its body to appear in the final Web page only until a certain date. After that date, the body disappears. You also might want the tag to scan its body, perhaps substituting database text for placeholders, for instance.

Manipulating the tag Body

A common task is to either include or reject the body based on some condition. For example, you might create a custom tag that enables an author to turn off text after a certain date. Or, you might have a tag that surrounds content visible only to an administrator.

First, you must decide whether you want to apply processing rules to the body of a given tag. You can have the doStartTag() method return EVAL_BODY_INCLUDE if you want body processing, or SKIP_BODY if you want to ignore the body.

The custom tag example in Listing 29-1 shows how the Fruit-of-the-Month Club might extend a special offer to members who have been with the club for more than a year. Assume that upon logging in, the script consults a cookie or database record to determine when the member joined the club. Based on that information, the login script sets the isAYearOld variable in the Session object. For testing purposes, you could also just set the variable in the JSP page and see what happens.

For more information about cookies and sessions, see Sessions 15 and 16.

Listing 29-1 *This tag handler can conditionally accept or reject its body.*

Special.java

```java
import javax.servlet.jsp.*;
import javax.servlet.jsp.tagext.*;
import java.io.*;
import javax.servlet.*;
import javax.servlet.http.HttpSession;

public class Special extends TagSupport
{

    public int doStartTag()

    {
        ServletRequest request=pageContext.getRequest();
        HttpSession session=pageContext.getSession();
        String isAYearOld = (String) session.getAttribute("isAYearOld");
        if (isAYearOld!=null && isAYearOld.equals("TRUE"))
            return EVAL_BODY_TAG;
        else
            return SKIP_BODY;
    }

    public int doEndTag() {
        return EVAL_BODY_INCLUDE;
    }

}
```

Using the tag in a JSP page would be simple (see Listing 29-2).

Listing 29-2 *The Special.jsp page uses the special.tld tag library descriptor.*

Special.jsp

```jsp
<%@ taglib uri="WEB-INF/special.tld" prefix="spcl" %>
<!-- next line for testing only -->
<% session.setAttribute("isAYearOld","TRUE"); %>
<spcl:special><A HREF="deal.jsp">
Click for your special deal!</A>
</spcl:special>
```

Of course, you could substitute any condition you wanted for the session variable check. Listing 29-3 shows a suitable taglib descriptor file for this tag.

Listing 29-3 *This descriptor defines the special tag.*

special.tld

```
<?xml version="1.0" encoding="ISO-8859-1" ?>
<!DOCTYPE taglib PUBLIC
  "-//Sun Microsystems, Inc.//DTD JSP Tag Library 1.1//EN"
  "http://java.sun.com/j2ee/dtds/web-jsptaglibrary_1_1.dtd">

<taglib>
    <tlibversion>1.0</tlibversion>
    <jspversion>1.1</jspversion>
    <shortname>specials</shortname>
    <info>A tag to enclose specials for old customers only</info>

    <tag>
        <name>special</name>
        <tagclass>Special</tagclass>
        <info>A tag to enclose specials for old customers only
</info>
<bodycontent>JSP</bodycontent>
    </tag>

</taglib>
```

For more information about `taglib` **descriptors, see Session 28.**

Processing the tag Body

20 Min. To Go

Instead of relying on the container to process the body, a sophisticated custom tag can read and process the body itself. To do this, the tag handler class should extend `BodyTagSupport` instead of `TagSupport`. Actually, the object needs to implement only the `BodyTag` interface, but extending `BodyTagSupport` is the easiest way to do that. As you might expect, `BodyTagSupport` itself implements `BodyTag`.

The `BodyTagSupport` class provides several important methods for processing the body. Table 29-1 summarizes these methods.

Table 29-1 *BodyTagSupport Methods for Manipulating the tag's Body*

Method	Explanation
doAfterBody	The container calls this method when it finishes the tag body (i.e., when it reaches the matching end tag). This is where you do your custom processing. If you do perform custom processing, this method returns SKIP_BODY so the container will ignore the body.
getPreviousOut	This method retrieves the JSPWriter referred to by the out object of the enclosing page. You must use this method to be sure that the results of this tag handler are included by any enclosing tag handler.
getBodyContent	This method returns a BodyContent object (see Table 29-2).

The **BodyContent** object's methods appear in Table 29-2. These methods enable you to read the body's contents and write data as a result of processing the body.

Table 29-2 *The BodyContent Object's Methods*

Method	Explanation
clearBody	This method clears the current instance of content. It is guaranteed not to throw an exception, unlike the clear method of JspWriter.
getEnclosingWriter	This method gets the JspWriter of the page in which the tag appears.
getReader	This method gets a Reader that contains the contents of the body.
getString	This method gets the body of the tag as a String.
writeOut	This method writes out the contents of the body into the Writer passed in as a parameter to this method.

Making Modifications

**10 Min.
To Go**

Suppose you wanted to modify the previous example so that the discount granted to members varies. The system administrator might set the discount amount in a properties file, for example. Another part of the application could store this discount amount in the Application object (in the discount attribute). Listing 29-4 shows one possible way to write this tag. The code searches for a percent sign in the body and replaces it with the appropriate discount. Notice that the base class has changed. Also, to process the body, you want the doStartTag to return EVAL_BODY_TAG instead of EVAL_BODY_INCLUDE.

Listing 29-4 *This tag handler dynamically changes its body content.*

Special.java

```java
import javax.servlet.jsp.*;
import javax.servlet.jsp.tagext.*;
import java.io.*;
import javax.servlet.*;
import javax.servlet.http.HttpSession;

// Note changed base class to BodyTagSupport!
public class Special extends BodyTagSupport
{

public int doStartTag()

{
    ServletRequest request=pageContext.getRequest();
    HttpSession session=pageContext.getSession();
    String isAYearOld = (String)
        session.getAttribute("isAYearOld");
    if (isAYearOld!=null && isAYearOld.equals("TRUE"))
      return EVAL_BODY_TAG;
    else
      return SKIP_BODY;
}


public int doAfterBody()
{
        ServletContext app=pageContext.getServletContext();
  BodyContent body = getBodyContent();
// getBodyContent is a member of BodyTagSupport
  String theBody = body.getString();
  StringBuffer newBody = new StringBuffer();
  newBody.append(theBody.substring(0,theBody.indexOf("%")));
  // read the custom discount
  String disc=(String)app.getAttribute("discount");
  if (disc==null) disc="5"; // 5% default
  newBody.append(disc);
  newBody.append(theBody.substring(theBody.indexOf("%")));
  try
    {
    JspWriter newout = body.getEnclosingWriter();
    newout.print(newBody.toString());
    }
  catch(Exception ex){ex.printStackTrace();}
  return(SKIP_BODY);
}
}
```

This example does not require any changes to the existing `taglib` descriptor file. You can still set the `bodycontent` element to JSP. You can see an example of this tag's use in Listing 29-5 (for simplicity, this JSP page artificially sets the discount rate).

Listing 29-5   *This example JSP page uses the custom discount tag.*

SpecialDiscount.jsp

```
<%@ taglib uri="/WEB-INF/special.tld" prefix="FOTM"  %>
<% session.setAttribute("isAYearOld","TRUE"); %>
<% application.setAttribute("discount","15");%>
<!-- the above code sets the discount and status, which would really be
done by the system administrator using an external script or property file
-->


<html>

<body>
<h1>Fruit Price</h1>
<h2>Fruit:  Peaches</h2>
<h2>In Season:  Yes</h2>
<h2>Price: $2.99/lb.</h2>
<FOTM:special>
<font color="orange">As a member of the Fruit of the Month club for a year
or more,  you are entitled to a special % discount on this product!</font>
</FOTM:special>
<form>
<input type="submit" value="Order this fruit!">
</form>
</body>

</html>
```

Another common use of body modification is to create a looping tag. For example, suppose you wrote a custom tag to retrieve multiple rows from a database. The body of the tag could describe how to format each row. Then the custom tag could replace that format line with many lines, one for each returned row.

Listing 29-6 shows a simple tag that illustrates this idea. The tag reads an integer number from its body and generates a list of integers, one per line, from 1 to the number you select. The tag attempts to do some error checking on the number so it can provide a meaningful error message.

Listing 29-6   *This looping tag generates a list of integers.*

CountTag.java

```
import javax.servlet.jsp.*;
import javax.servlet.jsp.tagext.*;
import java.io.*;
```

```java
import javax.servlet.*;
import javax.servlet.http.HttpSession;


public class CountTag extends BodyTagSupport
{

public int doStartTag()

{
    return EVAL_BODY_TAG;
}


public int doAfterBody()
{
  BodyContent body = getBodyContent();
// getBodyContent is a member of BodyTagSupport
  String theBody = body.getString();
  StringBuffer newBody = new StringBuffer();
  boolean good=true; //legal number?
  int n=-1;
  try {
      n = Integer.parseInt(theBody);
  }
  catch (Exception e) {
      good=false;
  }
  if (n<=0||n>10000) good=false;
  if (good) {
      for (int i=1;i<=n;i++) {
          newBody.append(Integer.toString(i));
          newBody.append("<BR>");
      }
  }
  else
      newBody.append("Data input error in count tag");
  try
      {
          JspWriter newout = body.getEnclosingWriter();
          newout.print(newBody.toString());
      }
  catch(Exception ex){ex.printStackTrace();}
  return(SKIP_BODY);
}
}
```

The taglib file (in Listing 29-7) is almost identical — only the class names and descriptions are different.

Listing 29-7   *This descriptor defines the looping tag.*

count.tld
```
<?xml version="1.0" encoding="ISO-8859-1" ?>
<!DOCTYPE taglib PUBLIC
  "-//Sun Microsystems, Inc.//DTD JSP Tag Library 1.1//EN"
  "http://java.sun.com/j2ee/dtds/web-jsptaglibrary_1_1.dtd">

<taglib>
    <tlibversion>1.0</tlibversion>
    <jspversion>1.1</jspversion>
    <shortname>count</shortname>
    <info>A looping tag</info>

    <tag>
        <name>count</name>
        <tagclass>CountTag</tagclass>
        <info>A looping tag</info>
  <bodycontent>JSP</bodycontent>
    </tag>

</taglib>
```

Finally, you can find an example JSP page in Listing 29-8. Try putting incorrect data in the body and see what happens.

Listing 29-8   *This JSP uses the looping tag.*

Count.jsp
```
<%@ taglib uri="WEB-INF/count.tld" prefix="ct" %>
<H1>Drum roll please....</H1>
<ct:count>10</ct:count>
```

Done!

REVIEW

- Your custom tags can process their bodies.
- Custom tags can conditionally accept or reject their bodies.
- A custom tag may use data from the body to generate multiple lines of output.

QUIZ YOURSELF

1. What method returns a value that enables you to accept or discard the body contents of the tag?

2. What class should the tag handler extend if you want to manipulate the body of the tag?

3. What special information is required in the `taglib` descriptor file for tags that process their body?

4. A tag handler can read the tag body using what object?

5. What method do you use to obtain a `JspWriter` that allows you to write alternate body output from a tag handler?

SESSION

30

The Apache Struts Framework

Session Checklist

✔ Install Struts

✔ Configure the Struts controller

✔ Run the application

30 Min. To Go

I n Session 24, you learned about the Model-View-Controller application framework, also known as MVC. The MVC is a framework in which business logic is truly separated from presentation logic; this separation is the Holy Grail of software development. The Struts framework is an open-source, free MVC framework available from Apache. An application that uses Struts effectively will have achieved the separation between business logic and presentation logic that has been advocated at length throughout this book. This session is an advanced session; before doing the examples, make certain that you understand the MVC architecture and how to code and implement tag libraries. These two concepts form the foundation of the Struts framework.

Installing Struts

In this session, we will implement an example login application that leverages the Struts framework. First, we will install and set up Struts. Then we will create the JSP pages and Java classes that make up the application.

Before installing Struts, create a webapp that will contain the code as well as the necessary Struts files. To create a new Struts webapp, create a new directory called struts in your <tomcat-install>\webapps directory. Inside the new Struts directory, create a new directory and name it WEB-INF. Inside the WEB-INF directory, create two additional directories, classes and lib.

The distributed version of Struts at the time of this writing is 1.0 beta 1; refer to the Struts home page at http://jakarta.apache.org/struts to download the most recent version. To install Struts, follow these instructions:

1. Download the Struts zip file and extract its contents to your hard drive.

2. Copy the struts.jar file from the <struts-install>\lib directory to the <tomcat-install>\webapps\struts\WEB-INF\lib directory.

3. Copy all files with a .tld extension from the <struts-install>\lib directory to the <tomcat-install>\webapps\struts\WEB-INF directory. These files are the struts tag library descriptor files.

4. Inside the <tomcat-install>\webapps\struts\WEB-INF directory, create a web.xml file that contains the XML shown in Listing 30-1. The web.xml file tells your application where to find the Struts tag library descriptor files, and when to call the Struts action servlet

Listing 30-1   *The web.xml file holds webapp configuration information.*

web.xml

```
<?xml version="1.0" encoding="ISO-8859-1"?>
<!DOCTYPE web-app PUBLIC "-//Sun Microsystems, Inc.//DTD Web Application
2.2//EN"
    "http://java.sun.com/j2ee/dtds/web-app_2_2.dtd">
<web-app>
   <servlet>
      <servlet-name>action</servlet-name>
      <servlet-class>org.apache.struts.action.ActionServlet</servlet-
class>
      <init-param>
         <param-name>application</param-name>
         <param-
value>org.apache.struts.example.ApplicationResources</param-value>
      </init-param>
      <init-param>
         <param-name>config</param-name>
         <param-value>/WEB-INF/struts-config.xml</param-value>
      </init-param>
      <init-param>
         <param-name>debug</param-name>
         <param-value>3</param-value>
      </init-param>
      <init-param>
         <param-name>detail</param-name>
         <param-value>3</param-value>
      </init-param>
      <init-param>
         <param-name>validate</param-name>
         <param-value>true</param-value>
      </init-param>
      <load-on-startup>2</load-on-startup>
   </servlet>
   <!-- Action Servlet Mapping -->
   <servlet-mapping>
```

```
          <servlet-name>action</servlet-name>
          <url-pattern>*.do</url-pattern>
     </servlet-mapping>
     <!-- Struts Tag Library Descriptors -->
     <taglib>
          <taglib-uri>/WEB-INF/struts-bean.tld</taglib-uri>
          <taglib-location>/WEB-INF/struts-bean.tld</taglib-location>
     </taglib>
     <taglib>
          <taglib-uri>/WEB-INF/struts-html.tld</taglib-uri>
          <taglib-location>/WEB-INF/struts-html.tld</taglib-location>
     </taglib>
     <taglib>
          <taglib-uri>/WEB-INF/struts-logic.tld</taglib-uri>
          <taglib-location>/WEB-INF/struts-logic.tld</taglib-location>
     </taglib>
</web-app>
```

Coding the View

The example we will be coding collects a user name and password and grants permission to view a welcome page. In a real-world example, you would authenticate the user against a database, but for the purposes of this example, we will just implement logic that forces the user to log in four times. On the fourth try, the user is redirected to the welcome page.

The login.jsp page in Listing 30-2 uses the @taglib directive to include two Struts tag libraries. We use the struts-html tag library to construct our form. The struts-bean tag library outputs a time stamp and helps us to track the number of a given user's login attempts. The code in bold is the Struts-specific code.

Listing 30-2   *The login.jsp page uses pre-built Struts tag libraries.*

---

login.jsp

```
<%@ taglib uri="/WEB-INF/struts-html.tld" prefix="form" %>
<%@ taglib uri="/WEB-INF/struts-bean.tld" prefix="bean" %>

<HTML>
<HEAD>
  <TITLE>User Login</TITLE>
  <META http-equiv="Content-Type" content="text/html; charset=iso-8859-1">
</HEAD>

<BODY bgcolor="#FFFFFF">

<form:errors />

  <form:form action="login.do" name="loginForm"
type="chstruts.forms.LoginForm" scope="request">
  <form:hidden property="tryCount"/>
```

Continued

Listing 30-2

Continued

```
<TABLE width="445" border="0" cellspacing="0" cellpadding="0">
  <TR bgcolor="#3333FF">
    <TD colspan="3"><FONT color="#FFFFFF">User Login</FONT></TD>
  </TR>
  <TR>
    <TD width="50"> </TD>
    <TD width="117" align="right">UserName:</TD>
    <TD width="278">
      <form:text property="userName" size="16"/>
    </TD>
  </TR>
  <TR>
    <TD width="50"> </TD>
    <TD width="117" align="right">Password: </TD>
    <TD width="278">
      <form:password property="password" size="16"/>
    </TD>
  </TR>
  <TR>
    <TD width="50"> </TD>
    <TD width="117"> </TD>
    <TD width="278">
     <form:submit property="action" value="login" />
    </TD>
  </TR>
  <TR>
    <TD colspan="3"> </TD>
  </TR>
  <TR bgcolor="#3333FF">
      <TD colspan="2" align="left"><FONT color="#FFFFFF"><bean:write
name="loginForm" property="timeStamp"/></FONT></TD>
   <TD align="right"><FONT color="#FFFFFF">Try Number: <bean:write
name="loginForm" property="tryCount"/></FONT></TD>
   </TR>
  </TABLE>
  </form:form>
</BODY>
</HTML>
```

Notice that all of the form elements are constructed with custom tags. One of the key benefits of the Struts framework is the availability of several custom tag libraries.

We are going to keep track of five properties on the login.jsp page:

- tryCount — The number of login attempts
- userName — The user's user name
- password — The user's password
- action — Used to tell the controller what the user wants to do
- timeStamp — The time the form was accessed

You will see the preceding properties listed again when coding the model component of the example application. Listing 30-3 is a simple welcome page that users see once they've attempted three logins.

Listing 30-3 *The welcome.jsp page is a simple welcome page.*

---

welcome.jsp
```
<HTML>
<HEAD>
  <TITLE>Welcome to Struts</TITLE>
</HEAD>

<BODY bgcolor="#FFFFFF">
  <h1>Welcome to Struts</h1>
</BODY>
</HTML>
```

In your Struts webapp, create a new directory under <tomcat-install>\webapps\struts called chstruts. Store the login.jsp and welcome.jsp pages in this directory.

Coding the Application Model

20 Min. To Go

In the application model, there are typically two types of classes: Form and Action. The Form class extends the Struts ActionForm class; the Action class extends the Struts Action class.

Note

The javadoc for Struts is included in the Struts installation zip file. To install the Struts javadoc, copy the struts-documentation.war **file from the** **<struts-install>\webapps directory to your <tomcat-install>\webapps direc-tory. Stop and restart Tomcat. The documentation will be unpacked to <tom-cat-install>\webapps\struts-documentation, and you can navigate to it at** http://localhost:8080/struts-documentation/api/index.html.

The LoginForm class in Listing 30-4 holds the properties that are going to show up in our JSP page. This class contains getter and setter methods to get and set the properties in the application. The LoginAction class is where the business logic for the application resides.

Listing 30-4 *The LoginForm class gets and sets the properties to be used in the login.jsp page.*

LoginForm.java
```
package chstruts.forms;

import org.apache.struts.action.ActionForm;

public class LoginForm extends ActionForm
{
```

Continued

Listing 30-4 *Continued*

```
    private String password;
    private String userName;
    private String timeStamp;
    private String action;
    private int     tryCount;

    public String getPassword(){ return password; }
    public void setPassword(String password){ this.password = password; }

    public String getUserName(){ return userName; }
    public void setUserName(String userName){ this.userName = userName; }

    public String getTimeStamp(){ return timeStamp; }
    public void setTimeStamp(String timeStamp){ this.timeStamp =
timeStamp; }

    public int getTryCount(){ return tryCount; }
    public void setTryCount(int tryCount){ this.tryCount = tryCount; }

    public String getAction(){ return action; }
    public void setAction(String action){ this.action = action; }
}
```

In the `LoginForm.java` file in Listing 30-4, you should recognize the five properties that are set and returned with getter and setter methods. These five properties were present in the `login.jsp` page in Listing 30-2 and have dynamic values that will vary from user to user. No logic is being performed in this class; that is the purpose of the `LoginAction.java` class in Listing 30-5.

Listing 30-5 *The LoginAction.java class holds the application logic for processing the login.jsp form inputs.*

LoginAction.java

```
    package chstruts.actions;

    // application imports
    import chstruts.forms.LoginForm;

    // struts imports
    import org.apache.struts.action.Action;
    import org.apache.struts.action.ActionErrors;
    import org.apache.struts.action.ActionForward;
    import org.apache.struts.action.ActionMapping;
    import org.apache.struts.action.ActionForm;

    // servlet imports
    import javax.servlet.ServletException;
    import javax.servlet.http.HttpServletRequest;
```

```java
import javax.servlet.http.HttpServletResponse;
import javax.servlet.http.HttpSession;

// java imports
import java.io.IOException;
import java.text.SimpleDateFormat;
import java.util.Date;

public class LoginAction extends Action
{

    SimpleDateFormat _sdf = new SimpleDateFormat ( "MM/dd/yy HH:mm:ss" );

    public ActionForward perform( ActionMapping mapping,
                                  ActionForm form,
                                  HttpServletRequest request,
                                  HttpServletResponse response) throws
IOException, ServletException
    {
        String thisMethod = "perform() ";
        debug ( thisMethod, "in" );
        debug ( thisMethod, "form = " + form );

        LoginForm          loginForm    = (LoginForm) form;
        String             action       = loginForm.getAction();
        String             af           = null;

        try
        {
            debug ( thisMethod, "action=" + action );

            if ( action == null )
            {
                af = handleQuery ( loginForm );
            }
            else if ( action.equals ( "login" ) )
            {
                af = handlePage ( loginForm );
            }

            debug ( thisMethod, "done" );
            return mapping.findForward ( af );
        }
        catch (Exception e)
        {
            servlet.log("Action Exception", e);
            return (mapping.findForward("login"));
        }
    }

    private String handleQuery ( LoginForm form )
```

Continued

Listing 30-5

Continued

```
    {
        String thisMethod = "handleQuery() ";
        debug ( thisMethod, "in" );

        // This is a simple example, just stick today's date formatted in
the form.
        // If it were a more complex example we would probably be hitting
a database
        // and populating the form fields from that.

        form.setTimeStamp ( _sdf.format ( new Date() ) );

        String actionForward = "login_ready";
        debug ( thisMethod, "done" );

        return ( actionForward );
    }

    private String handlePage ( LoginForm form )
    {
        String thisMethod = "handlePage() ";
        debug ( thisMethod, "in" );

        String actionForward;
        String uid      = form.getUserName ();
        String pwd      = form.getPassword ();
        int    tryCount = form.getTryCount ();

        debug ( thisMethod, "uid = " + uid + " pwd = " + pwd + " tryCount
= " + tryCount );

        // Code here to lookup this uid pwd combo
        if ( tryCount < 3 )
        {
            form.setTryCount ( tryCount + 1 );
            actionForward = "login_failure";
        }
        else
        {
            actionForward = "login_complete";
        }

        // Have to update the timestamp
        form.setTimeStamp ( _sdf.format ( new Date() ) );

        debug ( thisMethod, "done returning: " + actionForward );

        return ( actionForward );
    }
```

```
    private void debug ( String method, String msg )
    {
        System.out.println ( "LoginAction." + method + ":" + msg );
    }
}
```

You should familiarize yourself with three methods in this class:

- perform() — This method processes the HTTP request and returns an HTTP response. The perform() method is inherited from the parent Action class. We don't really put any logic in the perform() method. It just looks at the action parameter and decides which method needs to be called to perform the appropriate action. If our page were more complex, we would probably have more handle methods, possibly handleDelete(), handleInsert(), and so on.

- handleQuery() — This method is called only when the login.jsp page first loads. It sets the value of the time stamp. This method sets the value of the actionForward variable to login_ready. The actionForward variable comes into play when configuring the controller in Listing 30-6.

- handlePage() — This method is called each time the user submits the form. It checks the value of the tryCount variable. If the user has attempted to log in fewer than three times, it sets the actionForward variable to login_failure; if the user has attempted to log in three or more times, it sets the actionForward variable to login_complete. Additionally, this method sets the value of the time stamp that is displayed on the login.jsp page.

Notice that the two classes in Listing 30-4 and Listing 30-5 are in packages. To compile the classes, follow these steps:

1. The LoginForm.java file should be saved to the <tomcat-install>\webapps\ struts\WEB-INF\classes\chstruts\forms directory. The LoginAction.java file should be saved to the <tomcat-install>\webapps\struts\WEB-INF\classes\ chstruts\actions directory.

2. Compile the two classes. To compile, first set the class path temporarily to point to the struts.jar file; next, compile the LoginForm.java file; finally, compile the LoginAction.java file. *The order of these steps is important.* To complete the steps, open up a command prompt and navigate to the <tomcat-install>\webapps\ struts\WEB-INF\classes directory using cd commands. Type in the following commands in order (the first command assumes that your Tomcat installation is under the C:\ drive):

```
Set classpath=%classpath%;C:\jakarta-tomcat\webapps\struts\
WEB-INF\lib\struts.jar
```

```
javac chstruts\forms\LoginForm.java
```

```
javac chstruts\actions\LoginAction.java
```

Configuring the Struts Controller

The Struts framework has a built-in controller component. When a browser issues a request to the Web server, the controller intercepts the request and forwards it to the model application component, which processes the request.

The struts-config.xml file is the configuration file for the Struts controller. Code the file in Listing 30-6 and place it in the <tomcat-install>\webapps\struts\WEB-INF directory.

Listing 30-6   *The struts-config.xml file holds webapp configuration information.*

struts-config.jsp

```
<?xml version="1.0" encoding="ISO-8859-1"?>
<!DOCTYPE struts-config PUBLIC "-//Apache Software Foundation//DTD Struts
Configuration 1.0//EN"
            "http://jakarta.apache.org/struts/dtds/struts-config_1_0.dtd">
<struts-config>

<!-- ==== Form Bean Definitions ==== -->
  <form-beans>
        <!-- Login Bean-->
        <form-bean name="loginForm" type="chstruts.forms.LoginForm"/>
  </form-beans>

<!-- ==== Action Mapping Definitions ==== -->
  <action-mappings>
        <!-- Show Login Page Page -->
        <action path="/login" type="chstruts.actions.LoginAction"
name="loginForm" scope="request" validate="false">
            <forward name="login_ready" path="/chstruts/login.jsp"
redirect="false"/>
            <forward name="login_complete" path="/chstruts/welcome.jsp"
redirect="true"/>
            <forward name="login_failure" path="/chstruts/login.jsp"
redirect="false"/>
        </action>
  </action-mappings>
</struts-config>
```

The form-bean element is where you tell the controller the name of the Form class. The name attribute is set to the name of the Form class, and the type is the fully qualified class name of the class. In this case, our LoginForm class resides in the chstruts.forms package.

The action mappings tell the controller how to handle requests. Notice the name attribute of the forward elements. The different values, login_ready, login_complete, and login_failure, correspond to the values of the actionForward variable defined in the LoginAction class. Based on the value, the controller forwards the request to the page listed as the value of the path attribute.

Running the Application

To run the application, stop and restart the Tomcat server, and navigate to `http://localhost:8080/struts/login.do`. The .do extension of the login file tells the controller to intercept the request. The screen should look like the one shown in Figure 30-1.

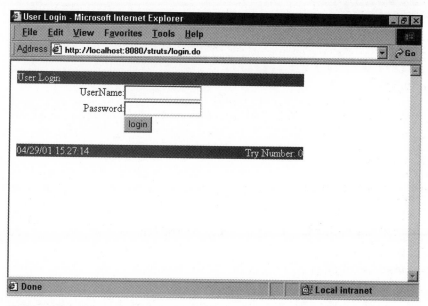

Figure 30-1 *The login page is part of a Struts framework application.*

Done!

REVIEW

- Struts is an open-source, free Model-View-Controller application framework available from Apache. The home page for Struts is `http://jakarta.apache.org/struts`.
- Struts has several custom tag libraries, including one for outputting standard HTML.
- The model in the Struts application is made up of two classes: `Form` and `Action`. The `Form` class contains getters and setters for properties; the `Action` class contains the application's processing logic.
- The `struts-config.xml` file configures the Struts controller.

QUIZ YOURSELF

1. True or false: Struts is an MVC framework.
2. Which tag library contains tags for outputting HTML?
3. In the Struts `Action` class, which method processes HTTP requests?
4. Which class will your `Form` class typically extend?

PART

Sunday Afternoon

1. What is a tag library?
2. True or false: Each JSP page must have its own tag library. Tag libraries cannot be shared among different pages.
3. What is the extension of a tag library descriptor file?
4. In the tag library descriptor file, what must the value of the tagclass element be set to?
5. What is the purpose of the tag handler class?
6. What is the function of the doStartTag() method of a tag handler class?
7. What is the purpose of the prefix attribute of the taglib directive?
8. True or false: Custom tags cannot contain attributes.
9. What value should the <bodycontent> tag be set to if the tag does not have a body?
10. What does the SKIP_BODY constant mean?
11. What does the EVAL_BODY_INCLUDE constant mean?
12. What are the three child elements of the <attribute> element in the tag library descriptor?
13. True or false: When coding a tag handler, it is not possible to embed logic to conditionally handle a tag's body.
14. What is the purpose of the doAfterBody() method?
15. What is the purpose of the getPreviousOut() method?
16. Which object represents the body of a custom tag?

17. What is the purpose of the `writeOut()` method of the `BodyContent` class?

18. What is the purpose of the `getEnclosingWriter()` method of the `BodyContent` class?

19. What is the purpose of the `clearBody()` method of the `BodyContent` class?

20. Struts is an example of what type of framework?

Answers to Part Reviews

Following are the answers to the part review questions at the end of each part in this book. Think of these reviews as mini-tests that are designed to help you prepare for the final — the Skills Assessment Test on the CD.

Friday Evening Review Answers

1. Hypertext Transfer Protocol
2. Hypertext Markup Language
3. Client/server architecture
4. N-tier architecture
5. Request and response
6. CLASSPATH
7. Port 80
8. War file
9. Declarations
10. String
11. A JSP page has HTML and Java code embedded in it; a servlet is a Java class with a specific structure.
12. Applets are Java programs executed in a browser; servlets are Java programs run on the server.
13. Strong type safety, security, portability, object-orientation
14. The request object
15. False. Declarations can also be used to declare methods.
16. The @ symbol denotes a directive.
17. A scriptlet is Java code in a JSP page surrounded by <% %> tags.
18. The out object
19. To import Java packages, use the import attribute of the @page directive.
20. The service() method

Saturday Morning Review Answers

1. The `getParameter()` method
2. Querystring
3. The form submits to itself.
4. Each radio button must have the same value for the name attribute.
5. Reset
6. The request object
7. The `getParameterValues()` method
8. The `contentType` attribute
9. The `info` attribute
10. The type is application/msword.
11. The `java.lang.Throwable` class
12. Translation-time errors occur when the JSP page is compiled into a servlet; runtime errors occur when the compiled servlet receives a request.
13. False. Java blocks can be opened in one scriptlet and closed in another.
14. The `errorPage` and `isErrorPage` attributes
15. The default value is `java`.
16. True. Setting the session attribute of the @page directive to false will mean that the page cannot access the session object.
17. The `Name`, `ID`, `Class`, and `Style` attributes
18. The return is a String array.
19. The `getMessage()` method
20. The `printStackTrace()` method

Saturday Afternoon Review Answers

1. `getCookies()`
2. `getSecure()`
3. `setDomain()`
4. 60 seconds
5. A method that retrieves the value of an object's property
6. `<jsp:useBean class="JSPBean" id="myBean"/>`
7. It sets a property on the Bean specified by the name attribute.
8. Set the `param` attribute of the `setProperty` element to the name of the request parameter.
9. Set the `property` attribute of the `<jsp:setProperty>` tag to *.
10. The widest scope is application scope.
11. Place the code in the body of the `<jsp:useBean>` element.

12. JavaScript can accomplish form validation at the browser, before the form data is submitted to the server.

13. JavaScript

14. A method that retrieves the value of an object's property

15. The session information is appended to the URL.

16. The `setAttribute()` method

17. It returns the unique identifier associated with the session.

18. Object

19. The `setDomain()` method sets the domain to which the cookie applies.

20. The request object

Saturday Evening Review Answers

1. The `@include` directive includes a file at translation time.

2. The `@include` directive includes a file at translation time; the `<jsp:include>` element includes a file at runtime.

3. The `flush` attribute

4. A forward uses the same client request; a redirect triggers the browser to make a brand-new request for the new resource.

5. The `<jsp:forward>` element

6. The `<jsp:param>` element

7. Use hidden form fields to store state information.

8. The Enumeration object

9. The `querystring`, or all the characters after the main part of the URL, is returned

10. The `getRequestURI()` method

11. The `sendRedirect()` method

12. The requested resource was not found on the server.

13. `getAuthType()`

14. Referer

15. Location

16. 300–399

17. asterisk (*)

18. The Java DataBase Connectivity API

19. It allows Java programs to connect to ODBC drivers.

20. `sun.jdbc.odbc.JdbcOdbcDriver`

Sunday Morning Review Answers

1. SELECT, INSERT, UPDATE, and DELETE
2. When you are inserting a piece of data into each column
3. The UPDATE statement
4. The ResultSet object
5. stmt.close()
6. The ResultSet object
7. The Statement object
8. The next() method
9. Extensible Markup Language
10. The model stores the application logic.
11. The view presents the information.
12. Extensible Markup Language
13. An empty element doesn't contain a body (text between the opening and closing tags).
14. Document Type Definition
15. The element may appear once or more than once in the XML document.
16. Parsed Character Data
17. xsl:stylesheet
18. It tells the XSL processor to process the children of the current node and to continue to apply rules where appropriate.
19. The select attribute
20. False. XSL can be used to parse XML into any kind of markup.

Sunday Afternoon Review Answers

1. A tag library is a repository of custom tags that can be used in JSP pages.
2. False. A single tag library may be used for an entire application.
3. The extension is .tld.
4. The fully qualified class name of the tag handler class.
5. The tag handler class interprets the custom tags.
6. The doStartTag() method processes the start of a given tag library element.
7. The prefix attribute specifies the name you will use to prefix to the tags in a particular library.
8. False
9. It should be set to empty.
10. It means to not evaluate a tag's body.
11. It means to evaluate the body into the existing out stream.

12. The attributes are `name`, `required`, and `rtexprvalue`.

13. False. You can embed conditional logic for handling tag bodies in the tag handler class.

14. This method gets called after the tag's body has been processed.

15. This method retrieves the JSP writer referred to by the `out` object of the tag's page.

16. The `BodyContent` object

17. This method writes out the contents of the body into the `Writer` passed in as a parameter to this method.

18. This method gets the `JSPWriter` of the page in which the tag appears.

19. This method clears the current instance of body content.

20. The M-V-C framework

What's on the CD-ROM?

This book's CD-ROM includes the source code from all the examples in this book and the *JSP Weekend Crash Course* assesment test. The following sections briefly explain each component of the CD-ROM.

Source Code Listings

The sample source code for the book is included on the CD-ROM. There is a folder for each session in the book that contains an HTML or JSP code listing. Each folder contains the HTML or JSP file listing. To deploy the files in most of the sessions, you will need to place them in your <tomcat-install>\webapps\ROOT directory, or into a new folder underneath the webapps directory. In some sessions, however, you will need to pay close attention to the location of your files in order for the examples to work.

Access Database

The Fruit.mdb Access 2000 database corresponds to the database used for the examples in Sessions 20–23. You can use the database on the CD, you can create your own version in Access, or you can use another database with the same scheme.

Assessment Test

The CD-ROM contains 60 multiple-choice questions with answers. These questions serve two purposes. You can use them to assess how much JSP knowledge you already have and thereby determine what sessions you can skip. You can also go through them after reading this book in its entirety to assess how much you have learned. The questions are organized by session and follow the order of topics discussed in this book. The session to which each question corresponds is noted next to each question.

Tomcat 3.2.1

Tomcat is a servlet container and JavaServer Pages implementation. Once you've installed Tomcat on your computer, you will be able to deploy each of the examples contained in this book. Tomcat also supports tag libraries, covered in Sessions 27 through 29. For detailed information about installing Tomcat, refer to Session 2, "Installing and Configuring the JSP Development Environment."

Links Page

The CD also contains a links page for the following URLs:

URL	Description
http://jakarta.apache.org/tomcat	Tomcat is the reference implementation for the Java Servlet 2.2 and JavaServer Pages 1.1 Technologies.
http://java.sun.com/j2se/	In order to run, Tomcat requires that the JDK version 1.1 or later be installed.
http://jakarta.apache.org/taglibs/doc/xsl-doc/intro.html	A pre-built XSL tag library is available from Apache.
http://xml.apache.org/dist/xalan-j/	The xalan-j download, in concert with the Apache XSL tag library, enables XSL processing in a JSP page.
http://jakarta.apache.org/struts	The Struts Framework enables you to develop applications according to the Model-View-Controller paradigm.
http://java.sun.com/products/jsp/	Sun is a good source of information for JavaServer Pages Technology Homepage.
http://java.sun.com/products/jdbc/	JDBC Technology allows you to connect to databases from your JSP pages.
http://java.sun.com/products/jsp/industry.html	There are many add-on engines on the market which will run JSPs.
http://www.allaire.com/Products/HomeSite/	HomeSite is a popular programming editor for coding JSP pages.

Index

Continued

Continued

Continued

Continued

U

V

W

X

Get Up to Speed
in a Weekend!

Flash™ 5 Weekend Crash Course™
by Shamms Mortier
408 pages
ISBN 0-7645-3546-3

Red Hat® Linux® 7 Weekend Crash Course™
by Naba Barkakati
432 pages
Red Hat Linux 7 on 3 CDs
ISBN 0-7645-4741-0

Visual Basic® 6 Weekend Crash Course™
by Richard Mansfield
408 pages
ISBN 0-7645-4679-1

Dreamweaver® 4 Weekend Crash Course™
by Wendy Peck
408 pages
ISBN 0-7645-3575-7

Also available:

Access® 2000 Programming Weekend Crash Course™
by Cary N. Prague, Jennifer Reardon, Lawrence S. Kasevich, Diana Reid, and Phuc Phan *600 pages* ISBN 0-7645-4688-0

Active Server Pages 3 Weekend Crash Course™
by Eric Smith *450 pages* ISBN 0-7645-4756-9

C++ Weekend Crash Course™
by Stephen R. Davis *552 pages* ISBN 0-7645-4689-9

C# Weekend Crash Course™ (Available July 2001)
by Stephen R. Davis *432 pages* ISBN 0-7645-4789-5

HTML 4.01 Weekend Crash Course™
by Greg Perry *480 pages* ISBN 0-7645-4746-1

Java™ 2 Weekend Crash Course™
by Julio Sanchez and Maria Canton *432 pages* ISBN 0-7645-4768-2

JavaScript Weekend Crash Course™
by Steven Disbrow *408 pages* ISBN 0-7645-4804-2

JSP Weekend Crash Course™
by Andrew Utter And Geremy Kawaller *408 pages* ISBN 0-7645-4796-8

Linux® Weekend Crash Course™
by Terry Collins and Naba Barkakati *450 pages* ISBN 0-7645-3593-5

Each book comes with a CD-ROM and features 30 fast, focused lessons that will have you up and running in only 15 hours.

**Available wherever books are sold,
or go to:
www.hungryminds.com**

Hungry Minds™

Hungry Minds, Inc.
End-User License Agreement

READ THIS. You should carefully read these terms and conditions before opening the software packet(s) included with this book ("Book"). This is a license agreement ("Agreement") between you and Hungry Minds, Inc. ("HMI"). By opening the accompanying software packet(s), you acknowledge that you have read and accept the following terms and conditions. If you do not agree and do not want to be bound by such terms and conditions, promptly return the Book and the unopened software packet(s) to the place you obtained them for a full refund.

1. **License Grant.** HMI grants to you (either an individual or entity) a nonexclusive license to use one copy of the enclosed software program(s) (collectively, the "Software") solely for your own personal or business purposes on a single computer (whether a standard computer or a workstation component of a multi-user network). The Software is in use on a computer when it is loaded into temporary memory (RAM) or installed into permanent memory (hard disk, CD-ROM, or other storage device). HMI reserves all rights not expressly granted herein.

2. **Ownership.** HMI is the owner of all right, title, and interest, including copyright, in and to the compilation of the Software recorded on the disk(s) or CD-ROM ("Software Media"). Copyright to the individual programs recorded on the Software Media is owned by the author or other authorized copyright owner of each program. Ownership of the Software and all proprietary rights relating thereto remain with HMI and its licensers.

3. **Restrictions On Use and Transfer.**

   (a) You may only (i) make one copy of the Software for backup or archival purposes, or (ii) transfer the Software to a single hard disk, provided that you keep the original for backup or archival purposes. You may not (i) rent or lease the Software, (ii) copy or reproduce the Software through a LAN or other network system or through any computer subscriber system or bulletin-board system, or (iii) modify, adapt, or create derivative works based on the Software.

   (b) You may not reverse engineer, decompile, or disassemble the Software. You may transfer the Software and user documentation on a permanent basis, provided that the transferee agrees to accept the terms and conditions of this Agreement and you retain no copies. If the Software is an update or has been updated, any transfer must include the most recent update and all prior versions.

4. **Restrictions on Use of Individual Programs.** You must follow the individual requirements and restrictions detailed for each individual program in Appendix B of this Book. These limitations are also contained in the individual license agreements recorded on the Software Media. These limitations may include a requirement that after using the program for a specified period of time, the user must pay a registration fee or discontinue use. By opening the Software packet(s), you will be agreeing to abide by the licenses and restrictions for these individual programs that are detailed in Appendix B and on the Software Media. None of the material on this Software Media or listed in this Book may ever be redistributed, in original or modified form, for commercial purposes.

5. **Limited Warranty.**

    (a) HMI warrants that the Software and Software Media are free from defects in materials and workmanship under normal use for a period of sixty (60) days from the date of purchase of this Book. If HMI receives notification within the warranty period of defects in materials or workmanship, HMI will replace the defective Software Media.

    (b) **HMI AND THE AUTHOR OF THE BOOK DISCLAIM ALL OTHER WARRANTIES, EXPRESS OR IMPLIED, INCLUDING WITHOUT LIMITATION IMPLIED WARRANTIES OF MERCHANTABILITY AND FITNESS FOR A PARTICULAR PURPOSE, WITH RESPECT TO THE SOFTWARE, THE PROGRAMS, THE SOURCE CODE CONTAINED THEREIN, AND/OR THE TECHNIQUES DESCRIBED IN THIS BOOK. HMI DOES NOT WARRANT THAT THE FUNCTIONS CONTAINED IN THE SOFTWARE WILL MEET YOUR REQUIREMENTS OR THAT THE OPERATION OF THE SOFTWARE WILL BE ERROR FREE.**

    (c) This limited warranty gives you specific legal rights, and you may have other rights that vary from jurisdiction to jurisdiction.

6. **Remedies.**

    (a) HMI's entire liability and your exclusive remedy for defects in materials and workmanship shall be limited to replacement of the Software Media, which may be returned to HMI with a copy of your receipt at the following address: Software Media Fulfillment Department, Attn.: *JSP™ Weekend Crash Course™*, Hungry Minds, Inc., 10475 Crosspoint Blvd., Indianapolis, IN 46256, or call 1-800-762-2974. Please allow four to six weeks for delivery. This Limited Warranty is void if failure of the Software Media has resulted from accident, abuse, or misapplication. Any replacement Software Media will be warranted for the remainder of the original warranty period or thirty (30) days, whichever is longer.

(b) In no event shall HMI or the author be liable for any damages what-soever (including without limitation damages for loss of business profits, business interruption, loss of business information, or any other pecuniary loss) arising from the use of or inability to use the Book or the Software, even if HMI has been advised of the possibil-ity of such damages.

(c) Because some jurisdictions do not allow the exclusion or limitation of liability for consequential or incidental damages, the above limi-tation or exclusion may not apply to you.

7. **U.S. Government Restricted Rights.** Use, duplication, or disclosure of the Software for or on behalf of the United States of America, its agencies and/or instrumentalities (the "U.S. Government") is subject to restric-tions as stated in paragraph (c)(1)(ii) of the Rights in Technical Data and Computer Software clause of DFARS 252.227-7013, or subparagraphs (c) (1) and (2) of the Commercial Computer Software - Restricted Rights clause at FAR 52.227-19, and in similar clauses in the NASA FAR supple-ment, as applicable.

8. **General.** This Agreement constitutes the entire understanding of the par-ties and revokes and supersedes all prior agreements, oral or written, between them and may not be modified or amended except in a writing signed by both parties hereto that specifically refers to this Agreement. This Agreement shall take precedence over any other documents that may be in conflict herewith. If any one or more provisions contained in this Agreement are held by any court or tribunal to be invalid, illegal, or oth-erwise unenforceable, each and every other provision shall remain in full force and effect.

CD-ROM Installation Instructions

The directory named Self-Assessment Test contains the installation program Setup_st.exe. With the book's CD-ROM in the drive, open the Self-Assessment Test directory and double-click on the program icon for Setup_st to install the self-assessment software and run the tests. The self-assessment software requires that the CD-ROM remain in the drive while the tests are running.

To access the code samples, use Windows Explorer or My Computer to navigate through the directory structure. Note that if you copy the files to your hard drive, you will need to right-click on them, select Properties from the pop-up menu, and uncheck the "read only" attribute.

For more information about the CD-ROM, see Appendix B.